ETHICAL ARGUMENTS FOR ANALYSIS

ETHICAL ARGUMENTS FOR ANALYSIS

Robert Baum and James Randell
Rensselaer Polytechnic Institute

HOLT, RINEHART AND WINSTON, INC.
New York   Chicago   San Francisco   Atlanta
Dallas   Montreal   Toronto   London   Sydney

Cover cartoon courtesy Publishers-Hall Syndicate.

Preface

There are numerous uses to which the arguments contained in this volume can be put—not only in ethics courses, but also in courses in logic, introduction to philosophy, and perhaps even social and political philosophy. It has been designed as a *supplementary* text which can be used with a wide range of traditional texts and anthologies. To encourage experimentation and originality in its use, and to keep it compatible with as many different techniques as possible, the editorial comment has been kept brief and general, and the layout has been kept loose and informal. We hope that every teacher of philosophy may be able to use this book to *add* to courses that he is already teaching, and that by so doing he will be able to increase student interest in and benefit from his courses without decreasing the rigor and intellectual sophistication which has traditionally been distinctive of philosophy courses. We present the following list of uses of this book simply as report of what we and others have found to be effective and valuable in a number of courses. We would appreciate hearing from others of any additional uses.

1. If students are encouraged to simply browse through the book at the beginning of a course, they often are more highly motivated for attacking the more abstract theoretical material in the standard texts. We have also found that many students really aren't sure what an argument, and more specifically a moral argument, is when they enter a course, and thus these examples will serve to orient the students and provide a framework in which they can approach the theoretical material.

2. In ethics courses, individual examples can be used to illustrate the application of various normative and meta-ethical theories to the discussion of specific moral problems. We believe that almost every kind of moral theory is represented in the arguments. Unfortunately, because of the lack of a single set of categories for classifying moral theories, and because of the diversity of names and techniques of classification used in the various texts and by different instructors, we must leave the identification of appropriate examples to the individual instructor. Some of the examples are actually internally inconsistent and appeal to more than one theory in the course of a single argument. Also, because of the vagueness and ambiguities built into everyday discourse, another person, in applying what we refer to in the

Introduction as the "principle of charity," might read more or less into a specific example than we would, and thus, for example, he might classify as deontological an argument that we would list as utilitarian, or vice versa.

3. The class (be it in ethics, logic, or introduction to philosophy) as a group can carefully examine each argument in a given section, to see the number of ways in which an apparently straightforward problem can be attacked.

4. Each student can be asked to select a specific example to work on for the duration of the course, and then to present an in-depth evaluation of it either orally to the class or as a term paper to the instructor.

5. Students can be asked to identify the theories used in specific examples as homework assignments, quizzes, or in-class exercises.

This book represents a "first" in philosophy texts, and neither the editors nor the publishers could have anticipated the time and effort that ultimately proved to be necessary to see it through to publication. It is impossible to name the literally hundreds of individuals who assisted in the various phases of this project—locating specific items, securing reprint permissions, reading and making suggestions concerning the editorial comments and the selection of arguments, and so on. To all the copyright-holders, librarians, members of the editorial staff of Holt, Rinehart and Winston, students, and colleagues who have contributed in one or more ways, we can only say thank you and reiterate that without their assistance this book would not exist today. Three individuals must be named in recognition of their special contributions: Gail Baum, whose skills as a professional librarian were exploited to the fullest in the locating of arguments; John Schumacher, whose criticisms of early drafts of the introduction led to numerous improvements; and Christine Korin, who patiently and efficiently assisted in many ways with the acquiring of permissions and the preparation of the manuscript.

September 1972   *R. B.*
                                                                          J. R.

Contents

ETHICAL ARGUMENTS FOR ANALYSIS

SECTION I
Introduction

Abortion is morally wrong because it violates the sixth commandment.

A fetus is not a human being and thus abortion is not immoral.

Abortion is simply a form of genocide and therefore is wrong.

The fetus is merely a part of a woman's body, and a woman has the right to do anything she wishes with her body, including having parts of it surgically removed.

Abortion should be legalized in order to benefit society as a whole.

A dead fetus is better than an unwanted child.

Abortion is not a moral issue at all—it is a legal or political question.

These are only a few of the statements included among the arguments about abortion collected in this volume. And these arguments are only representative of the wide variety of such statements to which everyone is exposed daily in magazines and newspapers, on television and radio, and in ordinary conversation. This apparent superfluity of moral judgments and arguments is probably one of the basic causes of the kind of despair expressed by the comic–strip character on the cover of this volume—the attitude that it is useless, or not worth the time or effort, even to think about what one ought to do and why one ought to do it. But we must be careful not to confuse a difficult task with a fruitless or impossible one.

We are convinced that deliberation about moral problems, dilemmas, and the like can and should be considered a special case of reasoning. As such, it can be good or bad, valid or invalid, crass or sophisticated, informed or uninformed, fruitless or productive. Given a choice among these alternatives, the rational option is for the good, the valid, the sophisticated, the informed, the productive. We believe that everyone, in fact, has such a choice, and we hope that this volume will contribute to the emergence of good, valid, sophisticated, informed, and productive moral reasoning.

Like most reasoning about important matters, ethical reasoning is not always easy. It is helpful to distinguish two types of ethical inquiry: normative ethics and meta-ethics. The first six statements at the beginning of this introduction are examples of normative arguments or judgments. The seventh statement is meta-ethical. The subject matter of meta-ethics consists of the normative ethical assertions and terms themselves: "Are ethical terms definable?" "What is the meaning of 'right?'" "Can ethical assertions be true or false?" "Are ethical disputes amenable to rational decision?" In hopes of preventing confusion, we shall use the terms "moral" and "ethical" to refer to *normative* ethics in the remainder of this book.

Some meta-ethicists hold that the canons of rational argumentation are inappropriate to (normative) ethical discourse. We believe that such a view is not entirely correct, and that the arguments reproduced in this volume provide ample evidence that there are many people who do participate in

1

rational discussions of moral issues, and who apparently believe that their arguments are significant enough to have them published and subjected to evaluation by the general public. However, even if it is true that (normative) moral reasoning is impossible, the proponents of this theory must provide a reasoned defense of their meta-ethical position, as well as an account of how so many people could have been so mistaken as to have expended such a great amount of energy arguing about something which cannot be argued about. Another meta-ethical theory maintains that moral judgments are directly intuited rather than logically derived, but the advocate of such a view is also obligated to give arguments in support of his general meta-ethical theory and must also be able to reply cogently to the arguments in favor of competing theories.

It is not always easy to know when we are dealing with a moral argument. We expect that some readers would appreciate something a little more specific (or perhaps more general) than the few examples already given as an aid to identifying *normative* arguments. Unfortunately we cannot provide much further assistance on this matter here. A (normative) moral argument can be characterized (somewhat trivially) as an argument which is (or can be) offered to support or criticize a particular moral judgment. Moral judgments in turn can frequently be identified as such by the appearance of certain terms or phrases in them, such as "right," "wrong," "good," "bad," "ought," "duty," "responsibility," and similar words which are considered evaluative or ethical. But the mere appearance of such words is not sufficient to guarantee that the sentence in which they appear expresses a moral judgment, for most of these terms can be used in nonmoral statements also—for example, "This is a good apple," "He got lost because he made a wrong turn at the corner" etc. On the other hand, the mere absence of a "moral" word in a sentence does not guarantee that it does not express a moral judgment, for in the proper context simple statements such as "He broke his promise" can be interpreted as moral judgments.

In addition to looking for possible "indicator words," it is sometimes useful also to take into consideration other aspects of the statement in question. For example, most of the time moral judgments are made concerning the actions of human beings which have some effect on other human beings. But again we must warn that this is neither a necessary nor a sufficient condition for a moral judgment. Some people would claim that moral judgments can be made about actions which affect *only* the agent, and some would argue that actions affecting dogs, cats, rats, and other animals are subject to moral evaluation. Others claim that the actions of a group (e.g., a state or corporation) are not open to moral evaluation but only to political analysis, while some argue that all political judgments are ultimately reducible to ethical ones. However, even though we cannot provide any set of hard-and-fast rules for identifying moral arguments and statements, we feel confident that the average person will be able to recognize easily many of those contained in the selections in this volume, and we hope that he will be able to improve his skills by carefully considering those cases which are not obvious.

Moral arguments are usually offered in support or criticism of specific (normative) moral judgments. Meta-ethical as well as normative arguments may come into play in a debate over a particular normative judgment. To be interested in the truth or acceptability of a moral statement is in part to be interested in determining what moral argument proves or disproves it, lends credence to it, or casts doubt on it. Even someone who wants to act immorally should be interested in moral arguments, for he would have no other way to determine which actions are immoral. It is worth emphasizing here that the point of carefully examining the ethical arguments in this volume should not be to teach one how to defend one's own ethical prejudices (if such they be) in defiance of all reasonable counterarguments, nor to teach one how to befuddle any adversary in an ethical argument. Rather, the goal in considering an ethical argument should be the truth, or, if truth be unattainable, well-founded belief. Given this account of the point of trying to improve one's moral reasoning, anyone who supposes that the careful moral reasoner is merely an intellectual hair-splitter is simply mistaken.

This volume contains many different moral arguments. With some the reader will doubtless concur; from others he will dissent. Moreover, some readers will concur with arguments from which other readers will dissent. Given such a diversity of moral arguments and attitudes toward them one naturally wonders whether there is any way to acquire a reasoned position on a moral issue. We suggest an affirmative answer to this question. Rather than present a theoretical defense of this assertion, we shall use the limited space available here to provide the reader with some guidelines to assist him in clearly expounding and cogently defending or attacking a given moral argument, that is, to enable him to take a reasoned position on that argument.

Good reasoning, in ethics or in any discipline, is not mechanical but creative. One learns to reason well by reasoning—by criticizing and evaluating others' arguments and by constructing one's own arguments. The purpose of this volume is to provide the raw material, actual arguments on which the student can develop his reasoning skills in moral argumentation and learn to apply them to his own life and moral concerns. In evaluating any moral argument, we should be concerned with determining not only whether the argument's conclusion is true, but also whether that argument establishes its truth. If it does not, and we still believe the conclusion, our belief is reasoned only to the extent that we can construct another argument which does establish the conclusion.

Whether a given argument does *in fact* establish its conclusion depends on three things: 1) whether the truth of its premises logically guarantees the truth of its conclusion; 2) whether its premises are true; and 3) whether its premises could be known to be true without already knowing the truth of its conclusion. Arguments which satisfy condition one are *valid*; in a valid argument, *if* the premises are true, *then* the conclusion must be true. A classic example of a valid argument is the following:

> All men are mortal.
> Socrates is a man.
> ___
> Therefore, Socrates is mortal.

But the fact that all the premises and the conclusion of a particular argument are true says nothing about the validity of that argument. The premises and conclusion of the following argument appear to be true, but the conclusion obviously does not follow from the premises, and it is thus invalid.

> Lyndon Baines Johnson was president of the United States in 1964 A.D. 1964 A.D. was a leap year.
> ___
> Therefore murder is morally wrong.

It is also possible for a valid argument to have a false conclusion, if at least one premise is false, as in this example.

> The unjustified taking of human lives is morally right.
> Hitler's program to exterminate the Jews was an unjustified taking of human lives.
> ___
> Therefore Hitler's program to exterminate the Jews was morally right.

If the first two conditions are satisfied, that is, if the argument is valid *and* all of the premises are true, then the argument is sound. The first example above is sound, the second is unsound because it is not valid (even though both premises are true), and the third argument is unsound because at least one premise is false (even though the argument is valid).

To have a reasoned position on an argument is to have determined that all three conditions are satisfied. If the third condition is not satisfied, the argument can be both valid and sound, but it is also worthless for purposes of argumentation. Such an argument is circular—it begs the question. It is often quite difficult to recognize a circular argument in everyday discourse, for it can be easily hidden in vague and ambiguous wordings and in elaborate digressions from the main line of argumentation. However, once the vagueness and ambiguity are removed and the basic argument is separated from the digressions, the circularity usually becomes readily apparent insofar as the conclusion is explicitly stated in the premises, as in the following all-too-common example.

> Whatever the Bible says is true.
> The Bible says that whatever the Bible says is true.
> ___
> Therefore whatever the Bible says is true.

Although a knowledge of formal logic may be helpful for testing the validity of an argument, it is not essential, since anyone who can read this book already has a tacit knowledge of logic that merely needs cultivation and exercise. People who have never studied logic carry on arguments all the time and some do so with conspicuous success. However, readers who have not studied logic must keep in mind that in a valid deductive argument the conclusion must already be contained in the premises, so that *if* the premises are true, *then* the conclusion must also be true. To determine the validity of an argument it is not necessary to determine whether the premises are, in fact, true. In testing an argument for validity, it is sometimes helpful to see whether you can imagine all the premises to be true and at the same time conceive the conclusion to be false. If you can, the argument is invalid. But the failure to think of an invalidating instance does *not* mean there is not one to be found. Hence this informal procedure is at best a rough-and-ready guide to an argument's validity. A more certain guide can be acquired by studying formal logic.

Rather than talk about arguments in the abstract we shall focus our attention on some concrete examples, the first being an argument offered by Lyndon Johnson, who, when asked why he sent troops to Vietnam, replied that it was his moral duty because it was in the United States' interest. We cannot tell whether this argument—indeed whether any argument—is valid unless we can identify the conclusion and premises. We can often, but not invariably, identify premises and conclusions by the presence of certain words. Premises often follow "since" or "because"; conclusions frequently begin with "thus," "therefore," or "it follows that." If we simply cannot tell what the premises and conclusions of a particular argument are, then we have discovered something important about the argument—it is so vague or ambiguous that we cannot tell what, precisely, the premises and conclusions are, and consequently the argument can neither gain our assent nor merit our further attention. The premise and conclusion of President Johnson's argument are easily recognizable, and we can now rewrite it in the following form:

Sending troops to Vietnam was in the United States' interest.

Therefore the president had a moral obligation to send troops to Vietnam.

The argument is invalid as written, because the premise *could* be true when the conclusion is false, if for example, national interest were irrelevant to moral obligation. Readers might regard this last remark as mere sophistry, judging that the rewriting of the argument still does not convey Lyndon Johnson's intent. Any ethical argument worthy of our attention deserves our sympathetic attention. In examining an argument we should give its proponent the benefit of every doubt; we should not allow our zeal in fault-finding to prevent us from learning something from an argument. Such an attitude towards the arguments we evaluate exemplifies adherence to what we will call the "principle of charity." It bids us to seek to put an argument in its best light.

Not only should we give the most favorable interpretation of vague and ambiguous terms, but we should not always expect to find all the premises explicitly stated, particularly in arguments from everyday sources. A common feature of oral and written communication is that the author or speaker leaves important things unsaid and expects his audience to supply them. For example, if we were to tell you that a whale is not a fish because it is a mammal, we would be justified in expecting you to understand that we believe no mammals are fishes. Thus we should not be surprised that the original, literal formulation of someone's argument will often be inadequate. There will often be "suppressed" premises which are not explicitly stated, but which are needed to make an argument valid. Also, people sometimes state their premises and leave it to the reader or hearer to draw out the implicit conclusion. The principle of charity requires that we supply such missing statements for any argument we are evaluating.

Approaching President Johnson's argument in this spirit, we find that the following is a more reasonable reconstruction.

A1. Sending troops to Vietnam was in the interest of the United States.
A2. The president is obligated to do whatever is in the interest of the United States.

A3. Therefore the president was obligated to send troops to Vietnam. Let us assume that this reconstruction sympathetically and explicitly states the intended logical structure. In this form it is indeed valid, because it is impossible for this argument to have true premises and a false conclusion.

We can now proceed to inquire "Are the premises true, and how are we to know?" The premises of any moral argument fall into two classes: the moral and the nonmoral (not the moral and the immoral). As indicated earlier, whether moral sentences can be distinguished from nonmoral sentences is an unresolved problem in theoretical ethics. For our purposes it is sufficient for us to discern in the context of particular arguments which premises are most obviously moral and which are not. Many people think that moral sentences are especially difficult to test for truth or falsity. Indeed, some even think that the words "true" and "false" are as inappropriate to ethical sentences as they are to imperatives. We have too little space to do justice to this meta-ethical position. We shall only note in passing that we use the terms "true" and "false" in what follows simply for convenience. We could have chosen other terms, but we judged "true" and "false" less confusing and more natural to those not familiar with current controversies in meta-ethics.

Assuming we can in principle determine the truth or falsity of both moral and nonmoral premises, let us try to do so for the premises of Lyndon Johnson's argument. Is A1 a nonmoral premise? Whether the notion of "interest" is a moral one is another issue discussed in meta-ethics. Some would regard "interest" as a moral notion, being roughly equivalent to "good." Others believe that "being in a person's interest" means "promoting that individual's happiness or pleasure," and whether something does any of these things is normally considered a matter of nonmoral fact. Since this latter view is more common, let us interpret premise A1 as nonmoral.

To determine the truth or falsity of the first premise, we must be clear about what it means. It is both vague and ambiguous. To what group or entity does "the United States" refer? To all living citizens? To all present and future citizens? To the present administration? Until we know this we cannot even hazard a guess about what is or is not in the United States' interest. Applying the principle of charity, let us assume that "the United States" refers to all present and *future* citizens. This suggests that we must now interpret "interest" as "long-run interest." Unfortunately, "long-run interest" is still vague in that we do not know what should count as being in the United States' interest. Is it in the long-run interest of all present and future citizens of this country to increase the gross national product and decrease unemployment while harming the balance of trade? Or are such considerations irrelevant to the national interest? Insofar as no hint at answers to these questions is provided in the argument, the premise remains hopelessly vague. This means that even if we knew *all* the facts, we would still not know whether A1 is true. If we could determine what is and what is not in the United States' interest, then we could go on to determine if A1 is true. But even if we were to do this, we would want to know to how long a duration "long-run interest" refers. If it refers to an indefinitely long span of time, it would appear to be virtually unknowable, and thus the argument becomes useless for the demonstration of the truth of its conclusion. Even if the time period were restricted to several years, it would be almost impossible to determine what would be in the interest of over 200 million people.

The necessary brevity of this introduction, and the resulting terseness of many of our comments, may give some readers the impression that the evaluation of moral arguments is a coldly impersonal, mechanical process. However, no impression could be more mistaken or further from the truth. Certainly the testing of an argument for validity requires use mainly of one's reasoning powers, but in the more complex cases it also requires a considerable amount of creativity and inventiveness. The removal of ambiguity and vagueness demands not only a good knowledge of the grammar and vocabulary of the language, but also a nonformalizable "feel" for the language. It is in the process of ascertaining the truth or falsity of particular premises, however, that we are called upon to use *all* of our human faculties, including our imagination, our emotions, and our feelings. With regard to premise A1, determining what is in the best interest of each of the citizens of the United States would seem to require much more than a purely rational analysis of the economists' statistics concerning the G.N.P., the international balance of payments, and the unemployment rate. In addition to applying one's analytical powers to these abstract quasi-objective facts, one must also try to place himself in the position of each and every one of the 200 million people involved (which certainly requires exceptional imaginative powers), and must try to feel what these people feel in various situations—as when their sons, husbands, brothers, and fathers are killed or maimed in battle in a country halfway around the world. Questions must also be answered concerning basic value judgments, such as whether the loss of one human life can be justified by even a one billion dollar increase in the G.N.P. This has not even scratched the surface of the issues involved, but we hope that it will give the reader some idea of the very human, and very nonmechanical, nature of moral reasoning.

We shall not attempt here to ascertain to what extent Lyndon Johnson and his advisors took these human factors into account in drawing the conclusion that the first premise is true. Rather, we shall assume for the sake of argument that it is true, and now proceed to the second premise. The burden of proof for each premise of an argument falls upon the argument's advocate. Thus Lyndon Johnson needs to show why the United States' interest and its interest alone is relevant in this argument. Since it seems to be arbitrary to pick out one particular nation as the only one whose interests count in the determining of obligations, there is good reason to doubt that A2 is true. President Johnson himself was apparently aware of the weakness of this premise, for in other places he gave different justifications for the war, including claims that it was for the benefit of the citizens of South Vietnam, that it was in the best interests of "the free world," and that it would ultimately bring peace and prosperity to all mankind.

This premise is also susceptible to another objection. Imagine that we understand precisely what "interest" means in the context of the argument. Further imagine that in that sense it is in the interest of the United States to kill all United States' citizens whose incomes are less than $5,000 per year. In such circumstances A2 implies that the United States would have a moral obligation to kill such persons. But if we know anything about what we ought to do, we surely know that an act such as this, other things being equal, would be wrong. So A2 implies that an act which we know is *not* obligatory *is* obligatory. We have thus discovered what is known as a *counterexample* to A2. This mode of argumentation frequently occurs in "real life" ethical arguments as well as in debates among ethical theorists. Readers who have qualms about this way of arguing are urged to pursue the matter further by studying ethical theory—by no means are all ethical theorists satisfied with this technique.

Our analysis has thus shown that Lyndon Johnson's argument, even when interpreted in the most sympathetic manner, is not adequate to establish the conclusion that it was morally right to send troops to Vietnam. This is *not* to say that we have established that its conclusion is false. We can do this only by constructing an argument which proves that its contradictory ("It was morally wrong to send troops to Vietnam") is true. It is important to note that our analysis applies equally to the argument that "The Vietnam war is, in truth, morally wrong because it serves no American interest." (This is the wording of an argument by Alexander Bickel in the October 17, 1970, issue of *The New Republic*.) The premises are no less vague or ambiguous in this formulation, and their truth is no more easily established. However, even though our efforts thus far have led to negative results, we are not back where we started. We have learned, among other things, the weaknesses of this kind of argument, and we can now set out to determine whether it can be strengthened. Or, if we are convinced that it has some irreparable flaws, we can start afresh in the search for an argument which *does* adequately establish either the rightness or wrongness of the sending of troops to Vietnam. In doing this we will know not to pursue the vague, ambiguous, and arbitrary lines of thought of the argument just analyzed. It is this (perhaps small) gain that makes our effort worthwhile.

On the basis of our experience in evaluating even this one argument, we are now able to construct a partial list of some of the important points which should be considered in the evaluation of *any* moral argument. In analyzing moral arguments it is necessary to:

1. Identify the premises and conclusion(s). (It should be noted that in many everyday arguments, and in some of the examples in this volume, several distinct conclusions, and thus an equal number of arguments, can be found in a single paragraph.)

2. Supply suppressed premises if needed to make the argument valid. (Sometimes, as will be seen in the next example, it is even necessary to supply additional *arguments* in support of certain premises of the argument being analyzed.)

3. Identify all instances of vagueness and ambiguity and attempt to correct the faulty statements.

4. Determine the argument's validity, using the techniques of formal logic if possible.

5. Identify the nonmoral premises and determine whether they are true or false.

6. Identify the moral premises, and determine what moral theories, normative and/or meta-ethical, are being appealed to.

7. Determine whether the moral theory (or theories) is (are) true or acceptable.

8. Determine whether the argument is circular, that is, whether the conclusion is explicitly stated in the premises. If it is circular, then nothing has really been proved after all.

9. Identify and evaluate possible counter-arguments.

10. Make sure that in every step of the evaluation that the principle of charity has been fairly applied.

In addition to recognizing that this list is not exhaustive, we must realize that these rules need not be applied one at a time in the given sequence. We must often carry out several of the procedures simultaneously, and sometimes repeat a given step at different points in our analyses of arguments. We must also appeal to our common sense and our "feel" for the language, procedures which cannot be reduced to sets of formal rules. For example, even though formal logic requires that arguments contain only declarative sentences, this volume contains poems, cartoons, jokes, pictures, questions, and so forth which can be translated into or interpreted as moral arguments. But there is no formal procedure which anyone can give for carrying out such translations or interpretations.

With the explicit statement of these guidelines in mind, let us briefly examine an argument frequently put forward by critics of the Vietnam war.

The United States soldiers in Vietnam are acting wrongly because they are breaking the sixth commandment.

Making the reasoning of this argument explicit, we get:

B1. United States soldiers in Vietnam kill people.
B2. "Do not kill" is a valid moral rule.
B3. Anyone who breaks a valid moral rule does something wrong.
B4. United States soldiers in Vietnam break the valid moral rule "Do not kill."

B5. Therefore United States soldiers in Vietnam act wrongly.

This argument is relatively free from serious ambiguity or vagueness. Furthermore all its premises are either clearly true or very plausible at first glance. The crucial part of this argument appears to be the second premise. B2 is neither implausible nor patently question-begging, but it is not defended. That is, argument B gives us no reason to believe B2, though in fact many people do believe it. Should we let the matter rest here? No. For one thing, the original argument adequately indicates the kind of argument that might be given for B2:

If God decrees a moral rule, then that moral rule is valid.
God decreed the moral rule "Do not kill."

Therefore "Do not kill" is a valid moral rule.

Thus our interest in B2 quickly focuses upon this last argument. We will assume that this argument is the only one urged on behalf of B2, so we can let our evaluation of B2, and hence of argument B, rest with our decision about the plausibility of this argument. This argument has been subjected to very close analysis by numerous philosophers, and it is possible here only to sketch a few of the problems unveiled by these analyses. What reason do we have for believing that God did, in fact, issue such a moral rule? Are we entitled to believe, for example, that Satan did not issue it? These questions aside, does the fact that God issued this rule make it a valid one, or did God issue it because it is valid? If the latter, the fact that God issued it is not essential for establishing that it is a valid moral rule. If the former, why does the fact that God issued the statement "Do not kill" make it a valid moral rule? Might he rescind the order and make "Kill!" a valid moral rule? These questions are enough to illustrate the point that even the most obvious—*apparently* obvious, that is—premises can have perplexing ramifications. The proponent of this argument for B2 is responsible for cogent answers to these questions, or else he must provide a sound alternative argument. Some people can and do answer these questions, but many do not. The good reasoner is one who can anticipate such questions and provide answers for them. Rather than pursue argument B any further let us simply note that it is one of those arguments which one accepts or rejects according as one accepts or rejects its underlying ethical theory. And accepting or rejecting an ethical theory often involves accepting or rejecting, in turn, many additional arguments.

So we see that the serious moral reasoner never really finishes his moral deliberations. This does not mean he always thinks and never acts. A moment's reflection tells him this would be unwise. Not finishing moral deliberation, then, simply means being open to learning—from new experiences, new arguments, or whatever else there is from which to learn. Openness to learning is not the suspension of belief, but rather the willingness to exchange inadequate beliefs for better ones. And it is by acting on moral beliefs so acquired that one becomes a truly responsible, autonomous moral agent.

Hopefully, at this point the reader will be somewhat reassured concerning the feasibility of rationally evaluating moral arguments, and will also recognize that despair is no alternative to moral commitment. In fact, there is *no* alternative to moral commitment on the part of any individual who possesses any reasoning powers. Human agents are often committed to definite moral positions, whether they want to be or not. The pregnant woman must decide whether to have an abortion or not; the draftee must decide whether to allow himself to be inducted into the army or to resist; the student must decide whether or not to cheat on an ethics examination, or whether or not to pay someone else to write a term paper. In each case, a decision *will* be made. The only question is whether or not the decision will be made by the agent on the basis of an intelligently considered evaluation of the alternatives or whether it will be made without thinking. This is the moral question posed by the cartoon on the cover of this book—"Is it better to make ethical decisions on the basis of thoughtful deliberation or without thinking?" We believe that the former alternative, although certainly not the easiest choice, is the right one. Our examples have shown that there is no guarantee that moral deliberation will always result in a decision that will never be reversed. Most of the time we do not have as much time as we would like for evaluating a situation—a woman has only a few months to make a decision concerning abortion, just as the student has only a few minutes in the exam room—but we still believe that our decision is better if we have used every available opportunity to subject it to rational consideration. This is one of the main reasons for studying arguments such as those reproduced on the following pages: if and when we find ourselves confronting similar or analogous situations in our own future experience, we will already have a certain amount of background to facilitate our evaluation of whatever the problem may be. Some readers may be tempted to assert that the war is almost over, that the Calley case has been settled, that abortion has been legalized in some states, and that therefore most of the arguments in this volume are no longer worth studying and evaluating. The numerous references to the Nuremburg trials in discussions of the Calley case provide an all too vivid reminder that history can and does repeat itself. If we have learned anything from the past, it is that we can learn from the past and that this learning can positively affect our future and the future of mankind.

Finally, we must make several comments on the criteria used for selecting and arranging the arguments in this volume. As indicated by the analyses outlined in this introduction, a large number of different factors come into play in a single moral argument. It follows from this that there is no one simple or "right" way of selecting and organizing the examples. The criteria used for the selection of arguments were many, and we would be the first to admit that there are probably additional factors which were not consciously considered. One of our most important goals was to include arguments from as wide a variety of sources as possible, and thus one can find examples from all parts of the United States as well as from several foreign countries, from left-wing and right-wing political groups, from large and small-circulation publications, from a variety of religious sects, etc. The general topics (such as abortion) were also selected on a variety of grounds, some because they involve very commonly discussed moral problems and others because they are not very often discussed, some because they are of intrinsic interest to students, and others because we believe that they *should* be considered, even though at first glance they may not appear too interesting. Specific arguments on each topic were selected in part on the basis of the specific kind of moral argument being used, but other factors also entered into the making of these decisions.

For several reasons, not the least of which is the lack of any more rational criterion, we have chosen to group the arguments according to the problems they are addressing, rather than with regard to any particular formal feature such as degree of difficulty. We feel that one is only deceiving oneself if one attempts to classify the arguments as "simple" or "complex," "easy" or "difficult." An argument which *seems* to be simple with regard to its normative content may, upon closer analysis (adhering to the principle of charity), appear quite complex. It may also be complex with regard to its logical structure, it may require sophisticated linguistic analysis to clarify the meanings of basic terms, and/or it may involve thorny nonmoral questions. The length of an argument is a particularly unreliable criterion for determining complexity or difficulty, since some of the briefest arguments are among the hardest to evaluate. If one accepts the statement that an argument should not be rejected without offering a better one in its place, another complicating factor is added. We warn here that the analyses of *none* of the arguments will be easy; it is likely that the evaluation of a particular argument as more or less difficult will differ from person to person. We hope that the practice gained from analyzing these examples will make the analysis of future problems easier, but we also recognize that the complexity of the world will prevent any moral problem from being too easy.

SECTION II

On Cheating,
Stealing, Lying, etc.

To most people statements such as "Murder is wrong" and "Dishonesty is wrong" often appear to be obviously, if not gratuitously, true. One seldom if ever comes across a serious debate about the truth of such statements. This is because terms such as "murder" and "dishonesty" carry a connotation of wrongness as part of their generally accepted meaning. "Murder" is not defined as merely "the taking of a life," but as "the taking of a human life *unjustifiably*." Similarly, "dishonesty" is defined in the dictionary as the "lack of adherence to a code of moral values." Thus there seems to be little doubt that dishonest acts are wrong. But our knowledge of the wrongness of dishonest acts is of little value if we cannot determine which specific cases truly involve dishonesty and which do not. The arguments in this section provide examples of situations in which different people find themselves involved in everyday life, the honesty or dishonesty of which seems to be open to debate.

There are several strategies for arguing about the moral value of a particular act, such as Jones taking Smith's car without his permission. One could grant that "Stealing is wrong" is a true moral principle, but deny that this is a case of stealing. One would then have to argue that stealing essentially involves characteristics not found in the present case. One could also deny that stealing is wrong, while admitting that this is a case of stealing. This strategy can be pursued in one of several ways. One could assert that only acts that produce bad consequences are bad, and then show that the present case of stealing does not produce bad consequences. More generally, one could argue that a particular ethical theory truly picks out right and wrong acts, and then point out that according to that theory this case of stealing is not wrong.

Another strategy would involve admitting that one has, generally speaking, an obligation not to steal. However, it could be pointed out that one also has an obligation not to break one's promises. Then it could be shown that this case happens to be one in which these two obligations conflict, and that the obligation of keeping one's word is the more important of the two obligations. Still another strategy involves asserting that any "normal" human agent should simply be able to *see* that this act is right. Each of these strategies is exemplified by an item in this section.

A word of caution: One point we felt it important to exemplify in the present volume is that arguments that at first glance seem appealing and instructive can, upon analysis, turn out to be mere empty rhetoric. Thus some arguments in this volume were selected with this point in mind. There may be no such arguments in this section, but then again there may. The careful reasoner should be able to find such arguments wherever they occur. Thus all you can assume about the items reprinted in this section is that they are meant to exemplify some point about moral reasoning. The important thing to be kept in mind is that in this book, as in life, which arguments you endorse are your own responsibility. You can take this responsibility lightly or seriously, but you cannot renounce it.

If he hollers, let him go

Employes Who Snitch

by TIMOTHY H. INGRAM

No one likes a fink—yet our initial revulsion at snitching and our concept of employe loyalty may need serious revision. Clearly the employer has the right to expect a reasonable amount of loyalty from his employes, and to demand confidentiality in everyday business, in contract negotiations, trade secrets, client and personnel lists, and the like. But there are areas of concern to the public—as, for example, uncovering frauds, thefts, and serious improprieties—which require that the informer not be muzzled by employer censorship.

Moreover, the corporate hard-hats holding a "Your company, love it or leave it" attitude are depriving themselves of a useful mechanism for reform, capable of correcting an institution's seemingly unlimited capacity for organized error. Snitchers, in fact, are often a firm's *most* loyal members, for it takes a greater degree of attachment to stay with a firm and to protest than it does to "opt out," by remaining silent or moving on.

Stealing Cars Is a Growth Industry

By PETER HELLMAN

EVEN the thieves are able to justify their work. A veteran, very professional thief who lives in New Jersey reasons, "What I do is good for everybody. First of all, I create work. I hire men to deliver the cars, work on the numbers, paint them, give them paper, maybe drive them out of state, find customers. That's good for the economy. Then I'm helping working people to get what they could never afford otherwise. A fellow wants a Cadillac but he can't afford it; his wife wants it but she knows he can't afford it. So I get this fellow a nice car at a price he can afford; maybe I save him as much as $2,000. Now he's happy. But so is the guy who lost his car. He gets a nice new Cadillac from the insurance company—without the dents and scratches we had to take out. The Cadillac company—they're happy too because they sell another Cadillac.

"The only people who don't do so good is the insurance company. But they're so big that nobody cares *personally*. They got a budget for this sort of thing anyway. So here I am, a guy without an education, sending both my kids to college, giving my family a good home, making other people happy. Come on now—who am I really hurting?"

Above, from the *New York Times* magazine, June 20, 1971.
Below, from *Family Weekly*, September 19, 1971.
Left, from *The Progressive*, January 1971.

Ask Them Yourself

Want to ask a famous person a question? Send the question on a postcard, to "Ask," Family Weekly, 641 Lexington Ave., New York, N. Y. 10022. We'll pay $5 for published questions. Sorry, we can't answer others.

FOR BOB VOGEL, Baltimore Colts
What is your reaction when people say pro athletes should set an example for youngsters?—Mrs. R. L. Little, Durham, N.C.

● Why should I have to set an example for other people's kids? That's not my job. I think each one of us should take stock of where we stand and assess our relationship with our own children. It doesn't make any difference what kind of example an athlete sets if, when the kid gets home, his own father is a hypocrite and a liar and a cheater.

15

A Little Larceny Can Do a Lot For Employee Morale

by Lawrence R. Zeitlin

The dishonest worker is enriching his own job in a manner that is very satisfactory (for him). This enrichment is costing management, on the average, $1.50 per worker per day. At this rate, management gets a bargain.

Toolbox. The important word is *control*. Properly utilized, controlled employee theft can be used as another implement in management's motivational toolbox. As in the case of most motivational tools, costs and conditions of utilization must be carefully studied. (Ethically, of course, it would be more desirable for management to motivate employees by means other than inviting them into lives of petty crime. It is traditionally considered better to have workers directing their energies toward furthering the course of the business rather than toward satisfying their individual larcenous desires.)

Before deciding to minimize or eliminate employee theft, management should ask itself these four practical questions:

1. How much is employee theft actually costing us?

2. What increase in employee dissatisfaction could we expect if we controlled theft?

3. What increase in employee turnover could we expect?

4. What would it cost to build employee motivation up to a desirable level by conventional means of job enrichment or through higher salaries?

Cost. Setting aside ethical and emotional considerations, management may decide that the monetary cost of enforcing honesty is too great.

I do not advocate abandonment of the traditional responsibilities of management, but I suggest that management adopt a more realistic and certainly less hypocritical attitude to business "honesty" and publicly recognize that there is benefit to be obtained by utilizing employee theft as a motivational tool.

☐ Zeitlin justifies peoples' stealing because they are bored. This is fallacious thinking for several reasons. First: it's like saying, "I'm bored so I'm going to cut off your arm. Shall I cut it off here, or here?" Second: it encourages people to destroy the necessary interdependence among all of us; whereas, we need more and more to encourage and foster dependable healthy relationships. Third: he is advising these persons to hurt themselves by becoming more callous, less sensitive, amoral (if he doesn't concede that stealing is actually immoral) like the very "machinery" they're bucking. Fourth: he underestimates industrial psychologists (I hope). Surely he and they can use their ingenuity to think of constructive alternatives (i.e. profit-sharing, alternating jobs) to help meet the needs he says cause the stealing. . . .

Ellen Smith

Normal, Ill.

Above left, reprinted from *Psychology Today*, June 1971. Copyright © Communications/Research/Machines, Inc.
Above, courtesy of Ellen Smith (Mrs. Ralph L.), Normal, Ill.

Multiplied Theft

The widespread availability of photocopying machines provides another means of stealing—as if there weren't already enough ways to break the eighth commandment. The problem involves the laws of copyright, established to protect the rights of individuals to monetary income for their labors. Writers, composers, and illustrators, for example, support themselves and their families not by creative work itself but by *selling* the product of their creativity. Moreover, their income is usually a few cents on each sale; it's the large number of copies sold that enables them to make a living.

But the culprits—those who would never think of stealing another's tangible property, or who would never think of taking copyrighted material and typesetting it, printing it, and selling it for themselves—misuse the photocopying machine. They will buy, for example, one copy of an anthem for the choir to sing, and then photocopy enough copies for every choir member to have his own. No conscientious person should engage in such an obviously illegal action.

But there's one other culprit: the highly unrealistic state of copyright law in view of modern developments in photocopying and information storage and retrieval systems. According to copyright law it is a violation either to make one photocopy of one page of a thousand-page tome or to make a hundred copies of an entire piece of music. Until the writers, publishers, consumers, lawmakers, and other interested parties come up with a rational, equitable, enforceable set of laws to bring copyright and technology into reasonable alignment, individuals and groups should avoid photocopying multiple copies or single copies of significant portions of a work without permission. We will be glad, however, to give you permission to reproduce without payment as many copies of this particular editorial as you wish! □

Above, copyright 1971 by *Christianity Today*; reprinted by permission.

Above right, courtesy of Ann Landers and Publishers-Hall Syndicate.

Right, © 1960 Jules Feiffer.

DEAR ANN LANDERS: I need the advice of an adult who doesn't know me. Please don't let me down. Last night I was at my girl friend's house. (We have been best friends ever since third grade. We are both 14 now.) She made me promise I would never tell a soul if she let me in on her big secret. After I promised, she took a key out of a hiding place and opened a cedar chest. She started to show me her "fun stuff." I nearly keeled over. This girl has shoplifted at least $300 worth of merchandise. What scares me is that she has plenty of money and can buy anything she wants.

Another queer thing, Ann, there wasn't one article in that chest that she can use. She has dozens of packages of fish food and she has no fish—needlepoint canvasses and thread and she doesn't even know how to sew. She has shoplifted an electric heating pad, carpenter tools, fishing equipment, corn and bunion plasters—the craziest stuff you can imagine. The price tags are on everything. She likes to look at this junk and recall the fun she had getting it out of the store.

I now know there is something wrong with her, but I don't know what to do about it. I have promised not to tell, but maybe I should—for her own good. Please advise me, Ann. I am—SCARED SICK

DEAR SS.: A promise is a promise. You must not betray your friend. But you must somehow get across to her that she is sick and needs help. If she gets caught she could be in serious trouble. She must tell everything and asked to be taken to a doctor.

In the meantime, here's a word for you. DON'T go shopping with this girl. If she is caught stealing and you are with her, you could be in trouble, too.

ALL THIS BIG DEAL ABOUT WHITE COLLAR CRIME— WHAT'S **WRONG** WITH WHITE COLLAR CRIME?

WHO ENJOYS HIS JOB TODAY? YOU? ME? **ANYBODY?** THE ONLY SATISFYING PART OF ANY JOB IS COFFEE BREAK, LUNCH HOUR AND QUITTING TIME.

YEARS AGO THERE WAS AT LEAST THE HOPE OF IMPROVEMENT—EVENTUAL PROMOTION — MORE IMPORTANT JOBS TO COME. ONCE YOU CAN BE SOLD THE MYTH THAT YOU MAY MAKE PRESIDENT OF THE COMPANY YOU'LL HARDLY EVER STEAL STAMPS.

BUT NOBODY BELIEVES HE'S GOING TO BE PRESIDENT ANYMORE. THE MORE PEOPLE CHANGE JOBS THE MORE THEY REALIZE THAT THERE IS A DIRECT CONNECTION BETWEEN WORKING FOR A LIVING AND TOTAL STUPEFYING BOREDOM.

SO WHY **NOT** TAKE REVENGE? YOU'RE NOT GOING TO FIND **ME** KNOCKING A GUY BECAUSE HE PADS AN EXPENSE ACCOUNT AND HIS HOME STATIONERY CARRIES THE COMPANY EMBLEM.

TAKE AWAY CRIME FROM THE WHITE COLLAR WORKER AND YOU WILL ROB HIM OF HIS LAST VESTIGE OF JOB INTEREST.

©1960 Jules Feiffer

Term-Paper Hustlers

What old grad can forget the scourge of the term paper: those sunny afternoons in the dusky stacks, the night-long bouts with procrastination, the notes on white index cards that convey recrimination rather than inspiration?

Thousands of collegians in the Boston area, that's who. The reason appears under several names: International Termpapers, Inc., Universal Termpapers, Termpapers Unlimited and Quality Bullshit. Since September these new, aboveground organizations have turned out more than 4,000 term papers for students willing to pay $3 a page for standardized material and $6 a page if the paper is custom-made.

For off-the-rack themes, a buyer with the money first checks topics in stock, then tells his instructor that he has "chosen" to "write" about one of them. Up-to-date offerings include "Black American Heroes," "Nixon's Influence on the 1970 California Election," "Problems and Possible Solutions to Air Pollution." One service cheerfully composed a theme titled "Why I Wouldn't Use a Professional Term Paper Writing Service."

By the end of the spring rush, according to an exposé of the industry in the Boston *Globe,* the term-paper entrepreneurs expect to have produced 10,000 essays for a gross of $250,000. Several are setting up branches in other New England states, New York and California.

Glut of Longhairs. Ghostwriting on a modest scale has been a campus ploy for many years. But turning the practice into big business has taken men of vision like Ward Warren, 22, a senior at Babson College near Boston. Last fall Warren sank $25,000—earned in the delicatessen and the snack bar he owns—into Termpapers Unlimited. He now says that he is close to breaking even. "The secret of my success," he says earnestly, "is that my employees really believe in what they're doing. Also, there are a lot of brilliant, long-haired people out of work around here, and I rely on them." Indeed, the nationwide Ph.D. glut has produced a readymade crop of writers, including, the hucksters claim, some instructors at Harvard and M.I.T. Most of the firms remove from their files any paper that gets less than a "B" from two professors; they also say they keep track of where papers are submitted to make sure the same instructor does not get telltale duplicates.

Business comes mainly from what the entrepreneurs call "proletarian" campuses, where students have few hard-to-fake seminars with their professors—the University of Massachusetts, Boston University and Northeastern. One customer is a father who is trying to assure academic success for his two children by contracting to have all their papers written by the pros.

Best in Years. The pros have snowed the profs. One returned a paper with the remark: "Best paper seen in years." The Babson faculty has pronounced Warren's activities "very distasteful," but the college plans no action against him on the theory that his customers are guilty of plagiarizing—not he. Harvard Dean of Students Archie Epps has asked university lawyers how the school can proceed against the sharpsters. In fact, the colleges are virtually powerless to prove a given paper was plagiarized.

Meanwhile, the entrepreneurs are in some disagreement over the ethics of their work. Warren claims that customers use his products only as reference sources. "Listen," he insists, "I've taken surveys of 400 of my clients, and the overwhelming majority say that they don't plagiarize." One professor cites the case of a senior she confronted who confessed "four years of successful plagiarism, parental pressure and a conviction of his intellectual incapacity for college." Richard Mari, 26, a former technical writer for General Dynamics who heads Quality Bullshit, says that plagiarism is the whole point. "The kids have so many term-paper assignments now that they're an obstacle to a degree rather than a learning technique. As long as we're operating to help people, the business is not only justifiable, it may even be commendable."

Doctoral Dissertations For Sale

Students Clamor for Ghosted Research Papers

By Richard S. Johnson
FROM DENVER

"Nota: We do not condone Plagiarism."

This mocking legend, its pretentious use of a Latin word and its deliberate misspelling suggesting pseudoscholarship, is inscribed on a sign in the offices of a Denver ghost-writing company that expects to sell more than $100,000 worth of term papers, masters' theses, and doctoral dissertations during this academic year.

The company, Research and Educational Associates, Ltd. (REA), was formed here last Feb. 1 and already has 500 student clients. It has hired business managers to open offices in East Lansing, Mich.. where there is a 100,000-student population, and in Cleveland. Chicago, and Washington, D.C., all cities with major universities. Its founders also are negotiating with a prospective business manager in Tucson, home of the University of Arizona.

If all goes well, REA's founders expect to double or even triple this expansion before the third academic quarter begins next spring. Moreover, they see in academic ghostwriting a base for a potential multimillion-dollar business in providing information and literary services.

REA is a limited stock company with five youthful shareholders: Charles Johnson, Robert Pike, Paul Relyea, Marge Smith, and Larry Groeger. Johnson, a 30-year-old former college teacher, began the business part-time a year ago, when he was working on a Ph.D. degree at the University of Denver, "because I was tired of being a ribbon clerk in a department store."

The research and writing is supervised by Groeger, 20, an undergraduate philosophy major at Denver's Metropolitan State College. Groeger cheerfully admits that REA stole its misspelled slogan from a Boston group that he says grossed more than $250,000 last year ghosting for Harvard students. But REA's sights are already higher than that, Groeger says: This year it'll offer the first nationwide academic ghost-writing service.

Volume in the Denver area alone during the 1971 spring term was sufficient to convince REA's officers that they can gross a minimum of $100,000 by May 1972. And that should be, they think, a modest beginning.

'Absolute Security'

Yet, says Groeger: "We're not out to make it rich. We operate as a service. We all have a human-resources orientation." REA says that a client needn't sign a contract, and that the company doesn't permit clients to remain dissatisfied—particularly since the value of word-of-mouth advertising is obvious. Groeger says that REA guarantees absolute security of its records and anonymity for its clients.

Groeger can recall only one client whose experience with an REA-produced paper was unhappy. The student ordered a paper for a graduate seminar in philosophy, but "the subject was a very sophisticated one and he didn't understand the paper," Groeger says. "Others in the seminar shot him down." After that, REA began counseling clients on the various possible interpretations of "their" papers.

One of his favorite former college teachers takes a dim view of his occupation, Groeger says. So does his mother. But he himself finds no ethical problems in helping students plagiarize their way to academic degrees.

"Early in life I saw that the real ethos of America is, 'Anything you do is okay if you don't get caught,' " he explains. "I became acquainted with bureaucratic discrepancies in the university, and I saw the double standard that pervades the real world of politics and business." To Groeger, trading deals and favors isn't a moral or ethical matter; it's "just the way the world operates."

'You've Ruined My Week End'

Despite his criticism of the academic establishment, Groeger is considering teaching at the university level some day. He says that some of his philosophy teachers at Metropolitan State College here understand and sympathize with his ghostwriting activities.

But Groeger's department chairman, Dr. William E. Rhodes, didn't know of REA's existence until a reporter asked about it. "You've ruined my week end," he groaned. "I'm the last one to know, apparently."

Dr. Rhodes says that he is "totally unsympathetic" with academic ghostwriting and that he will debate its ethics with Groeger. "It poses a profound moral and ethical problem, both for Larry and his customers—and even more so for members of the faculty who would countenance this." Plagiarism, Dr. Rhodes adds, "undercuts the whole notion of a free and responsible society.

"I would oppose just as much a secret-police agency in the college" to stop plagiarism, Dr. Rhodes continues. "All of this would destroy the integrity of a free and responsible community."

From *The National Observer*, October 30, 1971.

19

The Right to Know vs. Rubies

THE WORD from Boston is that the Justice Department is trying to get an indictment against Neil Sheehan, the New York Times reporter who first wrote the story of the Pentagon papers. The charge being sought is that Sheehan knowingly transported stolen property across state lines.

There may be a technical point of law involved, but in equity and intent this is blatant nonsense.

This is not to say that Sheehan or any other newspaperman is immune from prosecution for violating the law. As Tom Winship, editor of the Boston Globe, said when his newspaper published the Pentagon papers, he was prepared to bear the consequences, whatever they might be. This was the same position taken by civil rights leaders in the South who knowingly broke state laws. They were willing to go to jail to demonstrate to the nation that the state laws were in violation of the Constitution.

To get a conviction against Sheehan, Justice is going to have to prove first that a crime was committed, and then that Sheehan did it. Assuming that Sheehan did what he is suspected of doing, Justice is still going to have trouble proving a crime. *Were the documents stolen? We don't know. They were certainly copied, but that's different. Documents aren't like a ruby necklace, nor was copying them like infringing on a copyright, which denies to its owner something of value.*

A theft implies a victim. Who was the victim? The answer is that there wasn't any.

The papers were the result of work done at government expense. The papers belong to the people. And what Sheehan did was not take the papers from the people, but the precise opposite. He and his presumed accomplices took copies of the papers from those who were hiding them from the people and delivered them to their rightful owners.

If anyone could be said to own them more than anyone else, it might be Robert McNamara, who commissioned them while secretary of Defense. Mr. McNamara is on record that the papers should have been given to the public long before.

It is interesting to note that Mr. Sheehan is apparently not to be charged with violating national security, which was the first reaction from the Nixon administration. The reason is simple: Experts from Dean Rusk, secretary of State at the time, on down say that no security was violated.

To argue that Mr. Sheehan committed no crime and violated no security in this case is not to provide the press with an absolute blanket of privilege. We recognize the necessity for some government secrecy and we recognize the dangers to security. On the whole, the media's record is exemplary. It is far better, for example, than the record of government officials who pepper their memoirs with classified material to justify their stewardship.

If anything, this is the issue which Sheehan has raised. The people have the right to know the people's business, not just that part of it some bureaucrat wants them to know. With common sense, publication of the papers will lead to sensible use, rather than abuse, of classification codes. This in turn will better serve the public interest.

US Army in lowest esteem

by Richard Scott in Washington

A former NATO Supreme Commander in Europe and United States Army Chief of Staff, General Ridgway, has said: "Not before in my lifetime has the army's public image suffered so many grievous blows and fallen to such low esteem in such wide areas of our society."

The general was commenting not only on the My Lai massacre but on the indictment of the Sergeant Major — the most senior non-commissioned officer in the army — and that of several other senior NCOs on charges of embezzlement of NCO club funds overseas; on the award of a battlefield decoration to a senior officer for acts he had never performed; and on pending charges against the former Provost Marshal General of the army.

General Ridgway, now retired, said that during visits to the army and navy war colleges in the past six months he had been told by officers that in order to gain army promotions "it was essential to make a record in a combat unit. To do that your unit had to have a fine record judged by a 'body count' of enemy dead. To achieve these results the unit commander could not tell the truth, the whole truth, and nothing but the truth." He had to repudiate the West Point code — "Don't lie, cheat or steal."

The general, who was addressing former West Pointers, made a strong plea for a return to undeviating acceptance of this code. He had no doubt in the response of the army officers, but was less certain of that of its "civilian secretaries, its Commander-in-Chief, and the appropriate committees of the Congress."

Top page, from the *Detroit Free Press*, July 17, 1971.

Above, from *The Guardian*, London, April 10, 1971.

Term Paper Mills: A Booming Business

By M. J. WILSON
(Newsweek Feature Service)

"WHY SHOULDN'T I buy a term paper?" says a student at New York University. "I'm an English major, assigned a paper on physics, a subject I don't know anything about, and don't want to know anything about."

"Even if I write a paper myself," says a University of Maryland coed, "the professor isn't going to read it. How can he? He's got about 300 people writing papers for him. He'll just farm it out to some graduate student."

Ann Landers

DEAR ANN LANDERS: Our 12-year-old son is selling his homework and my husband thinks it is just terrific. He keeps saying, "That kid will make it big one of these days."

Albert has fixed prices (from what I gather when he talks on the telephone.) He gets a dime for an arithmetic assignment and 25 cents for a book review. The boy is doing a very good business. He bragged at dinner tonight that he has saved up $21.

I think this is disgraceful but whenever I open my mouth I am shouted down. My husband insists that Albert has ingenuity, is smart and is making his brains pay off. If I am wrong, please tell me. If my husband is wrong, please tell him. I'm beginning to doubt my own sanity.

— CHICAGO MOTHER

DEAR MOTHER: You are not wrong and I hope you'll keep talking.

In this age of tax-chiseling, padded expense accounts and political pay-offs, it's a small wonder a kid would take to selling his homework. Someone should explain to the boy that it is admirable to help friends with their homework by showing them how to do it. But a person who sells "help" is supporting dishonesty in them and behaving dishonestly himself.

I grew convinced that *truth, sincerity* and *integrity* in dealings between man and man were of the utmost importance to the felicity of life, and I formed written resolutions (which still remain in my Journal book) to practise them ever while I lived. Revelation had indeed no weight with me as such; but I entertained an opinion that tho' certain actions might not be bad *because* they were forbidden by it, or good *because* it commanded them, yet probably those actions might be forbidden *because* they were bad for us or commanded *because* they were beneficial to us, in their own natures, all the circumstances of things considered. And this persuasion, with the kind hand of Providence, or some guardian angel, or accidental favourable circumstances and situations, or all together, preserved me (thro' this dangerous time of youth and the hazardous situations I was sometimes in among strangers, remote from the eye and advice of my father) without any *wilful*, gross immorality or injustice that might have been expected from my want of religion. I say *wilful* because the instances I have mentioned had something of necessity in them, from my youth, inexperience, and the knavery of others. I had, therefore, a tolerable character to begin the world with; I valued it properly and determined to preserve it.

Above left, from Newsweek Feature Service.

Above right, courtesy of Ann Landers and Publishers-Hall Syndicate.

Left, from *The Autobiography of Benjamin Franklin*.

Ellsberg and the Pentagon Papers

On Stealing Government Documents

By REP. JOHN ASHBROOK (R.-Ohio)

It is amazing how the major media have chosen to overlook one important aspect of the recent Pentagon Papers affair. That is the simple fact that, by his own admission, Daniel Ellsberg just plain stole the government documents in direct violation of law and in violation of his trust as a government employe. If his is to be condoned, where does it ever stop?

I have never been impressed with the validity of the argument that the individual can decide what law he wants to obey and selectively break it whenever it fits his fancy. Historically, the true martyr often felt compelled by act of conscience to violate the law and then pay the penalty. The modern chicken martyr on the other hand has chosen to violate the law but then tries to evade paying the penalty. The Rev. Martin Luther King was a great exponent of deliberate civil disobedience but when he was found guilty of breaking the law he invariably attacked the system as racist.

Now there seems to be an effort to build Daniel Ellsberg into some kind of a Robin Hood hero. This he is not, in my judgment. The news media seem to think that the public's right to know is more important than the logical contention that there are some things that must be discreetly held back. Would the New York *Times* print the invasion plans for Normandy the day before the troops left England? Would it be feasible to tell in advance that the government is planning a devaluation of currency? (Wouldn't the speculators have a holiday?)

Three governments have already protested to our government that they no longer feel they can confide or discuss sensitive problems due to the lack of security and the problems of having some unfaithful employe think he knows best. For example, we are involved in trying to work out some of the really major differences between Israel and the Arab nations. It would absolutely torpedo these negotiations back home if some State Department employe were to tell the New York *Times* and it were to print that "Mrs. Meir is prepared to concede on point X" or to print that "Despite Sadat's public pronouncements, he has indicated that he will compromise with Israel on point X." Such a disclosure would galvanize their position from which they could not retreat.

It sounds simplistically accurate to generalize that everything that goes on in government should be in the public domain but this defies common sense. I personally believe there is too much cover-up and feel that the government has in the past misled and continues to do so in some areas. I don't think that the press has a right to every news item that some disloyal employe would slip to it, however.

The press also takes a singularly one-sided approach to the whole issue of the public's right to know. Capitol Hill reporters write most of their articles on the basis of what "a well-informed observer says" or "a senator who does not want to be identified" or "a usually reliable source." What about the public's right to know where this reporter got his information or if there was, in fact, any source other than the fertile mind of the reporter himself? No, they say. We have an absolute right to keep our sources sacred. Yet they think the government doesn't have any such right. CBS alleges its right to clip news items, rearrange them, present its own propaganda view and then tells a congressional committee they have no right to see the raw, unedited transcripts. The public's right to know stops rather abruptly where their own self-interest is concerned.

Somewhere between full disclosure of everything on one side and censorship and cover-up on the other there should be a reasonable balance. It is hard to find this in a free society, to be sure, but this effort must be made. To follow the New York *Times*' logic to its ultimate conclusion, they or the individual simply knows what is best and will judge. Julius and Ethel Rosenberg had a "right" to give our atomic bomb secrets to our enemy. The government has no right for predetermined withholding of any news item. By the way, it was interesting to note that Cyrus Eaton, a pro-Red fellow Ohioan, let the cat out of the bag. Hanoi knew all of these things all along, says Eaton. Why? Well, some individual privy to them probably thought it was Hanoi's right to know and the government had no right to withhold the information.

Where does this strange reasoning end? You can only guess.

Reprinted with permission from the July 24, 1971, issue of *Human Events*, 422 First St., S.E., Washington, D.C. 20003.

Ethics and Big Business

In presenting a moral argument one is usually trying to demonstrate that a particular action is right, wrong, permitted, not permitted, etc. In many cases the agent is an individual person. However a moment's reflection reveals that moral judgments are frequently passed on the actions of groups. Nations are castigated for wars, business concerns are blamed for injustices, and clubs are responsible for unjustified discrimination, to cite only a few familiar examples. Moral judgments like these are more complex because their subjects, though easily named—e.g., the United States, General Motors, the local chapter of ΣAE—are more elusive than those of moral judgments whose subjects are individual persons. This very elusiveness suggests to some that a group cannot be held responsible for an action, that the responsibility for actions can lie only with individual persons.

We cannot stop ascribing responsibility to groups, however, unless we can provide some means for determining which members of a group are responsible for a certain event or state of affairs and which are not. Consider a large company whose New York plant dumps pollutants into the Hudson River. Precisely which of the number of employees, officers, and stockholders are responsible for that action and which are not? Without some non-arbitrary criterion for establishing individual responsibility, we have no reason to stop ascribing responsibility to groups. In addition to the problem of pinpointing individual responsibility within a group, it is also often necessary to distinguish degrees of responsibility. We should not always expect to find among the members of a large organization (such as Dow Chemical) that one member is responsible for a particular action, while another is not. Some people are more responsible for certain acts than others; in short, there is a continuum of responsibility within the group.

It should also be noted that moral duties can be said to be owed to groups; for example, a person may have a duty to do his best for his employer. If his employer is General Motors, it will be just as difficult to identify any individual to whom he owes this duty as it is to find any individuals who bear the responsibility for the policies and actions of the company. When we recognize that each of us is a member of many different organizations, we can begin to appreciate the complexity of our moral relationships to others. And we also become more aware that "conflict of interest" is a moral as well as political problem.

Above, from *The Rat*, Underground Press Syndicate.

Labor's Double Standard?

Organized labor relies heavily on the support of society at large. Its clout would be appreciably diminished if it did not resort to a variety of social pressures to sign up workers as members. In any office or shop where a union is recognized as bargaining agent by the employer, the individual employee most likely does not have a truly free choice on whether or not to join the union. Labor's rationale for coercion is that everyone who benefits from collective bargaining should contribute to it.

Our society has accepted this infringement upon individual freedom, for better or worse, feeling that the benefits outweigh the loss of liberty. Unfortunately, however, labor seems lately to be reluctant to recognize its debt to society. Unions still have a long way to go in eliminating racial discrimination, but they are resisting government proposals designed to help correct biased policies and practices.

The nation's construction unions issued a strongly worded statement last month saying they would fight government-imposed quotas on non-white workers in apprenticeship programs. We agree that quotas are probably not the answer. But isn't it merely something of a twist on the quota principle that enables the unions to achieve a de facto closed shop? If the government shouldn't force the unions to take in applicants it doesn't want, why should the unions be allowed to force into membership workers who don't want to join? □

Right, copyright 1971 by *Christianity Today*; reprinted by permission.

Lockheed's Little Helpers

ANYONE who credits Congress with a collective ethical principle is hard put to prove his point, since ethics usually finishes among the also-rans on Capitol Hill. It is especially difficult to find anything resembling a principle in congressional approval of a $250,000,000. loan guarantee to Lockheed Aircraft Corp. But let's try, very hard, to uncover what our lawmakers were trying to tell us in their handling of that political-economic-diplomatic squabble.

If one can believe the proponents of the loan to Lockheed, a basic goal was to save jobs. President Nixon, in hailing the passage of the bill, said it would "save tens of thousands of jobs that would otherwise have been eliminated." Unquestionably that will happen. But the inequities of saving 60,000 jobs at Lockheed while permitting thousands of other workers to become jobless every month because of business failures are so clear that even congressmen and the Nixon Administration can't help but comprehend them.

Perhaps, then, the idea was to preserve jobs of workers in "big" companies. How big? Companies with 20,000 employes? Or 10,000? Where does one draw the line in deciding which jobs are worth saving?

If that's not the answer, maybe the goal was to "help ensure that the nation's largest defense contractor . . . will continue serving the nation's needs," as Mr. Nixon declared. That brings the Government's emphasis out of saving jobs and into saving companies. Again, apparently size has something to do with it, because Congress is unlikely to rescue a filling-station operator who is going bankrupt or, for that matter, a small defense contractor.

The real reason could be related more to diplomacy than to economics. The British government, after all, was threatening to allow *its* principal industrial weakling, Rolls-Royce Ltd., to go out of business unless the United States bailed out Lockheed. Rolls-Royce makes the engines for the TriStar airbus, the commercial jet being developed by Lockheed; the partnership of the two companies in this shaky project seems singularly appropriate, like putting a Studebaker engine in an Edsel.

All of those reasons for helping Lockheed seem unconvincing, so maybe there is something else. We must try not to be cynical, but the phrase "political expediency" does come to mind. Lockheed has huge plants in California and Georgia, where thousands of Lockheed employes vote. It would have been too much to expect Senators Tunney and Cranston, California Democratic liberals, and Senators Talmadge and Gambrell, Georgia Democratic not-so-liberals, to oppose the bill. And, indeed, they voted for it. One wonders whether the Nixon Administration had some similar vote-getting goals in mind in its strong support of the bill.

That's a nasty thought, not to be dwelled on. It's much better to think of politicians as being motivated by high principles. So if your candy store is going bankrupt, don't call the banker, call your senator or representative. Ask him to apply the "ethics" of the Lockheed "principle" to your little store. But be prepared for a going-out-of-business sale.

—*JAMES G. DRISCOLL*

From *The National Observer*, August 9, 1971.

Cans.
Bad Guys or Good Guys?

A can is a nice thing when you want a soda or a beer. But it doesn't do much for a landscape or a highway. We know that better than anyone because we make cans. So here's the story. Both sides.

Cans are bad guys.

Cans are all over the streets and highways. Cans cause litter.

Cans are bad guys.

Returnable bottles were better. Return to returnables.

Cans are bad guys.

You use them once and throw them away. They can't be recycled.

Cans are good guys.

Out of all the litter on the streets and highways, over 83% isn't cans.

Still, somebody has to do something. So we've been working with people who are developing a fantastic machine that can actually pick the litter off the roads. We call it the octopus.

One more thing about litter: Please don't. People litter. Not cans.

Cans are good guys.

The can is one of the safest, cleanest, cheapest containers ever invented. If we return to returnables, prices will go up. Because everything is set up for non-returnables, and it will cost money and jobs to change it.

Besides, people don't return returnables. That's why cans happened in the first place.

Cans are good guys.

We've already set up recycling centers for used cans. (All used cans. Steel and aluminum. Beer and soda and food.) More are coming. This costs us money, but it doesn't cost you anything. You bring us the cans and we'll recycle them.

We know it would be easier and better if all you had to do was throw your cans in a garbage pail. So we're supporting the development of automated machines that can pick cans out of the rest of the garbage. And we hope that eventually every can in every city will be recycled and used to make new cans. You won't see it tomorrow. But you will see it. We promise you that.

We have more to lose than you do.

The Can People
We care more than you do. We have to.

Courtesy of the Carbonated Beverage Container Manufacturers Association.

The Can People: American Can Company, Continental Can Company, National Can Corporation, The Heekin Can Company.

Now...A Word from the Strikers...

Western Union Can <u>Easily</u> Afford Fair Pay and Security

That's What This Strike Is All About!

SOME MATTERS OF PRINCIPLE

Of course we're sorry that our strike, by closing down every Western Union telegraph office in the nation, has caused inconvenience to the general public. But the root cause of this shut-down lies in Western Union management policies that forced us, as self-respecting citizens, to go on strike.

Three very important principles are involved in this walkout. For instance:

☐ Must working men and women forever take second place to computers and new technology? Don't we deserve to be treated as well as machines? Should we be expected to subsidize machines?

☐ Does a prospering company like Western Union have a moral right to talk out of both sides of its mouth at once . . . to boast about high profits when it speaks to stockholders, to cry poverty when it talks to its employees?

☐ Does Western Union truly serve the communications needs of the nation when it rushes ahead with programs to curtail telegraph service to the public, to close many hundreds of present telegraph offices, to slow down still further the transmission and delivery of telegrams?

We think not.

Yet these matters of principle are all involved in this strike.

Courtesy of United Telegraph Workers, Western Union Division.

Walter
Goodman
STOCKS
WITHOUT
SIN

Still, for the sake of argument, what if it should somehow happen that virtuous actions are not rewarded in this life? "I don't notice that DuPont stock has tripled since they announced they're going to spend $300 million against pollution," remarks a veteran fund manager. Having lately, and belatedly, doubled its anti-pollution budget, the St. Regis Paper Company experienced a 51 per cent decline in profits in the first quarter of this year. Or what if companies that behave in unvirtuous ways make money? "What has been the cost to corporations of discriminating against blacks?" asks Phil Moore as though the answer were evident. Well, the nation is paying for it all right, but was discrimination really all that unprofitable all those years to companies that relied on a supply of low-paid workers to do disagreeable jobs?

A rough study at Princeton University, where students protested against the school's investments in South Africa, indicates that those objectionable stocks had almost a 3 per cent higher average rate of return than other securities in its portfolio. (Incidentally, it would cost Princeton an estimated $5 million in brokerage fees to get out of South Africa altogether.) In its 1971 proxy statement to General Motors, the Domestic and Foreign Missionary Service of the Protestant Episcopal Church urged that GM wind up its $125 million of manufacturing activities in South Africa because apartheid "will inevitably lead to turmoil and instability . . . and consequently to the destruction of foreign capital invested there." However, the church went on, GM should get out of South Africa even if it entailed a loss because "only those corporations which conduct themselves in a socially responsible way will be able to survive profitably, in the long run . . ." The Will to Believe survives among Episcopalians. At least it did before GM's annual meeting, where their proposal won 1.29 per cent of the shares voted.

And what of the managers of trust funds and pension funds? Should they be permitted to risk my money in behalf of their principles? The laws governing fiduciary relationships do not encourage experimentation, even for reasons of conscience. The Wall Street rule for persons legally charged with the management of other people's money runs as follows: "Invest funds in a company with the aim of gaining the best financial return with the least financial risk for the trust beneficiaries. If you later come to disagree with the company's management, sell the stock." This rule, we may assume, is used by many trustees to go along mindlessly with management and avoid the wear and tear of decision-making. Nevertheless, there remains a real legal question. David Silver, general counsel of Investment Company Institutes, a trade group, observes, "If a fund sells a share in a company that it thinks is à good investment because it doesn't like its hiring policies in South Africa, there could be a shareholders' suit."

But even if there were no legal problem, might

there not be a moral problem for the prudent trustee? Peter L. Bernstein, chairman of the board of Bernstein-Macauley and chairman of the investment policy committee of CBWL-Hayden, Stone, confesses that he feels some inner pressure to invest the funds in his charge in mortgages in minority areas, with the prospect of a lower return than they might bring elsewhere. But if he should succumb to that small voice, he observes, it will not be he who pays the price, but his clients: "Sorry, fellas, you've been elected to bear the cost." Why should this particular group suffer this special tax? Moreover, Bernstein points out that in a market economy, if capital flows not toward profits but toward social priorities, "we lose a rational measure of how to allocate capital." That, he acknowledges, suggests the limits of a market economy—and awakens in him stirrings of sympathy for radicals who would scrap the whole thing.

Not all investment advisers are as diffident as Mr. Bernstein. "We're making moral judgments all the time," Donald Weeden, chairman of Weeden & Company, told the *Institutional Investor*. "As individuals, we have been picked for our overall sensitivity to what's been going on." Now, no offense to Mr. Weeden, but I don't know any investment adviser whom I would care to have act in my behalf in any matter except turning a profit—and I'm not sure about that. The value of these specialists, I believe, lies in their limitations; they ought not allow themselves to see so much of the world that they become distracted.

Perhaps, though, fund managers might poll their investors and let them make their own decisions when confronted by a conflict between profit and principle. Under a recent SEC decision, shareholders can vote on whether fund managers should consider the social policies of a corporation before investing in its stock. During the latest GM go-around, in May, the Dreyfus Leverage Fund, holder of 25,000 shares of GM stock, solicited the opinions of shareholders on several of the insurgent proposals. In every case, most people voted with GM management and against the insurgents, whereupon Dreyfus voted its proxy *in favor* of the proposal requiring GM to publish detailed information on pollution and so forth. "We had to vote for that proposal," explains a fund spokesman, "because we believe in it." Mutual fund democracy?

Suppose that in a fit of social consciousness, American Motors should decide to put out a two-year model? And suppose everyone knew that the company's sales would sink in the second year? How many fund managers would hold onto their shares of American Motors? How many investors would stay with funds that operated in that public-spirited way?

Why, after all, should one expect selflessness from the widow dependent on her capital, the father concerned for his children's education, the speculator looking for gain—all those stock marketeers who have spent a lifetime trying to make money make money? We may be certain that any stock whose value drops to a tempting low because the Episcopal Church or a Boston synagogue sells it will be quickly picked up by investors of all religions who don't care what a company does, much less the country where it does it.

U.S. Interests in South Africa

In your article "U.S. Business in South Africa" (BUSINESS AND FINANCE, March 29) you attribute to a Ford Motor Co. spokesman that "U.S. corporations should not interfere in the domestic affairs of the countries in which they do business." Supposedly this is a counterargument to the demand that Ford withdraw its investment in South Africa's apartheid.

The hypocrisy of such an argument is obvious, but its perversity is made manifest in a later article in the same section in which you report Henry Ford II's interference in British affairs. Capitalist Ford presented Prime Minister Edward Heath with the economic ultimatum that until "stability" returned to Britain, he would not make further commitments in that country.

The roots of such a double standard can lie only in the profitability found in fascist but stable South Africa and not found in Britain's experiment in social and economic justice. What are America's priorities? Profitability and repression, or freedom, justice and equality? And why are the latter not the priorities of U.S. business abroad?

ALAN J. ERICKSON
Nashville, Tenn.

Eco-Guerrilla Warfare

The capers of the Chicago Fox (THE CITIES, Jan. 11) make me think of a scenario that could pose some problems far more significant than the identity of the stain on the rug at U.S. Steel.

Suppose an eco-guerrilla ran a hose from an industrial smokestack into the company president's office. The fumes then kill the executives and a few secretaries. The environmental prankster is caught soon afterward.

Would he be charged with murder? Presumably he would. However, if he could be found guilty of murder for pumping industrial fumes into an office, what about the company that is releasing the poisons into the air in the first place?

Three cheers for the Fox if his actions force people to contemplate deeper implications of the muck on the rug.

JEFFREY C. BAUER
Colorado Springs, Colo.

Left top page, letter to the editor of *Newsweek* by Alan J. Erickson, April 19, 1971.

Left, letter to the editor of *Newsweek* by Jeffrey C. Bauer, February 8, 1971.
Above, right from *The Rat*, Underground Press Syndicate.

An experiment in South Africa

Polaroid sells its products in South Africa as do several hundred other American companies. Our sales there are small, less than one half of one percent of our worldwide business.

Recently a group has begun to demand that American business stop selling in South Africa. They say that by its presence it is supporting the government of the country and its policies of racial separation and subjugation of the Blacks. Polaroid, in spite of its small stake in the country, has received the first attention of this group.

We did not respond to their demands. But we did react to the question. We asked ourselves, "Is it right or wrong to do business in South Africa?" We have been studying the question for about ten weeks.

The committee of Polaroid employees who undertook this study included fourteen members – both black and white – from all over the company. The first conclusion was arrived at quickly and unanimously. We abhor *apartheid,* the national policy of South Africa.

The *apartheid* laws separate the races and restrict the rights, the opportunities and the movement of non-white Africans. This policy is contrary to the principles on which Polaroid was built and run. We believe in individuals. Not in "labor units" as Blacks are sometimes referred to in South Africa. We decided whatever our course should be it should oppose the course of *apartheid.*

The committee talked to more than fifty prominent South Africans both black and white, as well as many South African experts. They heard from officials in Washington. They read books, papers, testimony, documents, opinion, interpretation, statistics. They heard tapes and saw films.

They addressed themselves to a single question. What should Polaroid do in South Africa? Should we register our disapproval of *apartheid* by cutting off all contact with the country? Should we try to influence the system from within? We rejected the suggestion that we ignore the whole question and maintain the status quo.

Some of the black members of the study group expressed themselves strongly at the outset. They did not want to impose on the black people of another country a course of action merely because *we* might feel it was correct. They felt this paternalistic attitude had prevailed too often in America when things are done "for" black people without consulting black people.

It was decided to send four of the committee members to South Africa. Since this group was to include two black and two white members, it was widely assumed they would not be granted visas. They were.

It was assumed if they ever got to South Africa they would be given a government tour. They were not.

It was assumed they would not be allowed to see the actual conditions under which many Blacks live and would be prevented from talking to any of them in private. They did see those conditions in Soweto and elsewhere. And with or without permission they met and talked to and listened to more than a hundred black people of South Africa. Factory workers, office workers, domestic servants, teachers, political leaders, people in many walks of life. They also talked to a broad spectrum of whites including members of all the major parties.

Their prime purpose in going to South Africa was to ask Africans what they thought American business should do in their country. We decided the answer that is best for the black people of South Africa would be the best answer for us.

Can you learn about a country in ten days? No. Nor in ten weeks. But our group learned one thing. What we had read and heard about *apartheid* was not exaggerated. It is every bit as repugnant as we had been led to believe.

The group returned with a unanimous recommendation.

In response to this recommendation and to the reports of the larger study committee, Polaroid will undertake an experimental program in relation to its business activities in South Africa.

For the time being we will continue our business relationships there (except for sales to the South African government, which our distributor is discontinuing), but on a new basis which Blacks there with whom we talked see as supportive to their hopes and plans for the future. In a year we will look closely to see if our experiment has had any effects.

First, we will take a number of steps with our distributor, as well as his suppliers, to improve dramatically the salaries and other benefits of their non-white employees. We have had indications that these companies will be willing to cooperate in this plan.

Our business associates in South Africa will also be obliged (as a condition of maintaining their relationship with Polaroid) to initiate a well-defined program to train non-white employees for important jobs within their companies.

We believe education for the Blacks, in combination with the opportunities now being afforded by the expanding economy, is a key to change in South Africa. We will commit a portion of our profits earned there to encourage black education. One avenue will be to provide funds for the permanent staff and office of the black-run Association for Education and Cultural Advancement (ASECA). A second method will be to make a gift to a foundation to underwrite educational expenses for about 500 black students at various levels of study from elementary school through university. Grants to assist teachers will also be made from this gift. In addition we will support two exchange fellowships for Blacks under the U.S.-South African Leader Exchange Program.

Polaroid has no investments in South Africa and we do not intend to change this policy at present. We are, however, investigating the possibilities of creating a black-managed company in one or more of the free black African nations.

Why have we undertaken this program? To satisfy a revolutionary group? No. They will find it far from satisfactory. They feel we should close the door on South Africa, not try to push it further open.

What can we hope to accomplish there without a factory, without a company of our own, without the economic leverage of large sales? Aren't we wasting time and money trying to have an effect on a massive problem 10,000 miles from home? The answer, our answer, is that since we are doing business in South Africa and since we have looked closely at that troubled country, we feel we can continue only by opposing the *apartheid* system. Black people there have advised us to do this by providing an opportunity for increased use of black talent, increased recognition of black dignity. Polaroid is a small economic force in South Africa, but we are well known and, because of our committee's visit there, highly visible. We hope other American companies will join us in this program. Even a small beginning of co-operative effort among American businesses can have a large effect in South Africa.

How can we presume to concern ourselves with the problems of another country? Whatever the practices elsewhere, South Africa alone articulates a policy exactly contrary to everything we feel our company stands for. We cannot participate passively in such a political system. Nor can we ignore it. That is why we have undertaken this experimental program.

Polaroid Corporation

A public statement made by Polaroid Corporation, which appeared in the press in January of 1971.

JOHN R. RARICK
6TH DISTRICT, LOUISIANA

Congress of the United States

House of Representatives

Washington, D.C. 20515

COMMITTEE:
AGRICULTURE

January 13, 1971

Mr. Edwin H. Land, President
POLAROID CORPORATION
Cambridge, Massachusetts   02139

Dear Mr. Land:

Having shared your newspaper advertisement from today's **Washington Post,** "An Experiment in South Africa," with my morning coffee, I felt that I should drop you a line to express my disgust, or rather sympathy, at your naivete.

South Africa is a long way from Cambridge, Massachusetts, and from the United States. So it must be easy to make peace with your blackmailers by joining in their guerrilla warfare against another peaceful ally of the free world.

If it is to now be the policy of the Polaroid Corporation to embarrass the American people further in our international relations for your self-serving employee relations, when are you going to run ads expressing your company's abhorrence for the national policies and customs of other nations?

Is Polaroid going to employ some Arabs to investigate apartheid in Israel so you can denounce that country?

What about India with its caste system, where the untouchables are not to be seen in public even in the street by the higher caste? Of course, under your researchers' racist type examination, you must hire the lower caste to help formulate your policies.

Then we have the many African nations such as Liberia, Congo, Ethiopia, which still practice slavery. Most certainly you will want to alienate these nations as well as Zambia, which persecutes Jehovah's Witnesses, Indians, and all Moslems.

Finally, I notice nothing in your public relations propaganda which indicated that your company is cutting camera trade with Russia or its Communist satellites, which practice apartheid not only against the Zionist Jew, but other religious and ethnic minorities as well.

If you think life is so bad in South Africa, why is it that there are no lines of refugees or escapees fleeing that country? On the other hand, people fleeing from Communist countries at the risk of losing their lives and all of their belongings is a daily occurrence. I dare suggest that for a successful industrial organization, you people have been taken.

Yes, South Africa is a far piece from the United States, and as your article confesses, you have little if any business there anyway, so what do you have to lose in South Africa? Perhaps you are unaware that there are many Americans who are sick and tired of the Black Panthers and these revolutionaries being pampered and bank rolled by organizations such as yours.

It has hardly been a month since your $20,000 contribution to Boston's black appeal was sent to Cairo, Illinois to help destroy race relations in that community — the remainder was sent to Communist affiliated revolutionary troops in Africa, dedicated to kill white people and overthrow responsible governments.

I think that you will find that the people of South Africa have far more friends in the U.S. than your colored advisors have led you to believe. As for me, neither myself nor any member of my family will ever consider buying a Polaroid product, or using same. Until the day when South Africa manufactures her own cameras, I will confine my photography to the Zeiss of Germany, and Yashica. These companies are still interested in increasing sales and friendships — not alienating them.

Sincerely,
John R. Rarick
Member of Congress

JRR:cf

P.S.   Incidentally, I am writing the Internal Revenue Service to inquire for an opinion as to whether corporations which are forbidden by law from making political donations can write off full page newspaper advertisements such as this as operating expenses.

Courtesy of John R. Rarick, the representative from the Sixth District, Louisiana.

 **THE DOW CHEMICAL COMPANY**

Statement of Position on Napalm

The Dow Chemical Company endorses the right of any American to protest legally and peacefully an action with which he does not agree.

Our position on the manufacture of napalm is that we are a supplier of goods to the Defense Department and not a policy maker. We do not and should not try to decide military strategy or policy.

Simple good citizenship requires that we supply our government and our military with those goods which they feel they need whenever we have the technology and capability and have been chosen by the government as a supplier.

We will do our best, as we always have, to try to produce what our Defense Department and our soldiers need in any war situation. Purely aside from our duty to do this, we will feel deeply gratified if what we are able to provide helps to protect our fighting men or to speed the day when fighting will end.

(]966-67)

SECTION IV

War and Peace

There are three possible views concerning war: (1) There is no valid moral justification for waging war; (2) There is no valid moral objection to waging war; (3) There are some valid moral justifications for waging some wars and some valid moral objections to waging other wars. The first view is that of the pacifist. The second is advocated by those who assert that prudential, political, and/or legal considerations alone can be applied to warfare. Variations of the third view are probably held by most people, including selective conscientious objectors.

The selections in this section exemplify each of these positions. But even though most selections exemplify the third, there is disagreement even among these. Those who agree that some wars are morally justified disagree about *which* wars are justified. And these disagreements are not all moral disagreements. For example, there is *factual* disagreement about the Vietnam War: Is it a civil war? Is the United States bound by treaty to defend South Vietnam? Would a communist government in South Vietnam jeopardize vital United States' interests? Thus we see again that the adjudication of moral disputes does not simply depend on agreement about moral principles.

REFLECTIONS
THE LIMITS OF DUTY

"Let us follow the process of creating an evil more closely. A scientist who is doing his specialized duty to further research and knowledge develops the substance known as napalm. Another specialist makes policy in the field of our nation's foreign affairs. A third is concerned with maintaining the strength of our armed forces with the most modern weaponry. A fourth manufactures what the defense authorities require.

A fifth drops napalm from an airplane where he is told to do so. The ultimate evil is the result of carefully segmented acts; the structure itself guarantees an evasion by everyone of responsibility for the full moral act."

From an article by Charles A. Reich, appearing this week in The New Yorker. Yes, The New Yorker.

Above, courtesy of *The New Yorker*.
Right, courtesy of C. P. Sarsfield and *The New Guard*.
Below, a message from Pope Pius XII.

CEASAR'S DUTY

A nation is required to protect the lives of its citizens; it is not expected to do good to all the world, and those who would demand that it do are not fit citizens. Given a choice of having liberty or death, some would choose the latter, for there are fates worse than death. Letting it be known that death is not feared if life as one wants it connot be had, can sometimes be an effective measure of policy. It is sometimes known as calling a bluff. It draws a line, and though the price may be high, in time that line is usually respected. Some may die, even many, but their deaths win worthy goals for their successors. That is sometimes known as laying down one's life for his fellows. It is an act the benefits from which the pacifist is willing to accept without contributing his proportional measure.

In a remarkable allocution to Military Doctors (October 19, 1953), Pius XII said:

"Let there be punishment on an international scale for every war not called for by absolute necessity. The only constraint to wage war is defense against an injustice of the utmost gravity which strikes the entire community and which cannot be coped with by any other means — for otherwise one would give free course, in international relations, to brutal violence and irresponsibility."

Relating the principle of proportionality to modern times, he added:

"Defending oneself against any kind of injustice, however, is not sufficient reason to resort to war. When the losses that it brings are not comparable to those of the 'injustice tolerated,' one may have the obligation of 'submitting to the injustice.' This is particularly applicable to the A.B.C. war (atomic, biological, chemical)."

The movable small town

USUALLY WHEN I FIRST MET a general, he would take the trouble to explain that the Army was just like anywhere else, that it really wasn't so different from business, or law, or the electronics industry. At the end of a few months I came to understand that few generals believed that. Most of them take pride in the distinction between the Army and civilian society, the latter commonly referred to as "the outside" and thought to be inferior. An officer obliged to live away from an Army post is said to be "living on the economy"; the customary inflection of the phrase implies foraging in hostile country. The distinction rests upon the premise that civilian society is dominated by "the commercial values" (i.e., money and greed) whereas the Army is seen as being governed by the ideals of honor, duty, and country. The expression of the prejudice takes various forms.

Most explicitly it was the sentiment that Galloway had framed under glass and placed on the wall of his office at Fort Knox: "War is an ugly thing, but not the ugliest of things. The decayed and degraded state of moral and patriotic feeling which thinks nothing worth a war is worse . . . A man who has nothing which he cares about more than his personal safety is a miserable creature who has no chance of being free, unless made and kept so by the existence of better men than himself."

A massacre in Pakistan

Only now are we getting Pakistani facts to abet the fears. President Yahya Khan has striven to suppress these facts, filling his air waves and press with evasive propaganda, deporting every journalist he could find. But a few independent reporters escaped this net and their stories — just emerging — reek with horror: crowds indiscriminately machine-gunned; student hostels razed by shells; shanty towns burned and bombed; civilians shot dead in their beds. We do not yet know the fate of those arrested in the East, or the true level of resistance throughout the province. But we do know, first hand and reliably, that many unarmed and unready Bengalis have died.

From this point the whole complexion of the crisis changes. Before the troops moved, many leaders shared responsibility and blame, Sheikh Mujib and his wilder henchmen among them. But Yahya Khan's licensed mayhem has swept all this towards irrelevancy. While he negotiated with Mujib his generals planned carnage. His vaunted bluff sincerity (and the sincerity of Pakistan's brief return to democracy) lies tattered. Henceforth the country must be regarded as a particularly brutal and insensitive military dictatorship, its elected political leadership in prison, its majority party obliterated by decree. The "Guardian," with many others, has long believed that the balance of advantage lay with a united Pakistan. But unity can never come through murder, and unity is not worth the price of innocent lives. East Pakistan survives today only as occupied and exploited territory, living proof of every Bengali suspicion over the years. Mr Bhutto, who purports to be a national leader, "thanks God" for this miserable carnage. Yahya Khan hears none of Pakistan's friends who counsel mercy and morality even at this late stage.

But he must be made to hear. In contrast with Biafra, the rights and wrongs of East Pakistan are easily determined. Those — like America — who stock the Pakistan Army must realise to what uses their weaponry is put. Those — like China and Ceylon — who permit forces to ferry from the West must realise what acts and purposes those forces pursue. Those — like Britain — who retain some vestige of influence in the area should spend it openly and forcefully. The fate of Dacca is an arrogant crime against humanity and human aspirations: no one should stand mealy-mouthed by.

THE SOVIET MILITARY TAKES A LOOK

AT THE U.S. MILITARY

Translated from KRASNAYA ZVEZDA, Moscow

The American press in recent months has focused on the sad array of problems facing the U.S. military services, so it shouldn't be surprising that other nations have taken up the cry. The following article from Moscow's military journal *Krasnaya Zvezda* ("Red Star") doesn't spare us clichés or old-fashioned propaganda, but it is interesting nonetheless as an illustration of the current image of the American G.I. behind the Iron Curtain. For Capt. Yuri Romanov's view of poor old G.I. Joe, see the following report. Then turn to the review of a West German film on the American soldier on page 53 . . .

THE AMERICAN SOLDIER— who is he? What devilish machine turns him into a cynical killer, out to stifle the freedom of his own people and that of other nations?

In an attempt to deceive and flatter, Pentagon propagandists print lies about him in the *Army Digest:* "The American soldier has pride and he knows how to pray. He often gives away the chocolate bar from his K-ration, he smiles and waves to children weary from years of war."

Pentagon propagandists go on lying even though the entire world has seen the photographs of the Song My victims, has read the notorious caption: "The children, too." The photography of that Song My "hero", Lieutenant Calley, should bear a caption taken straight from the U.S. Officers Manual: "An officer is a gentleman . . ."

Bravo, gentlemen! Don't blame yourself if honest people all over the world identify invaders and cynical killers with Yankees in uniform.

The reason for this is obvious. The U.S. Army is an imperialist army. That is the only kind of army that can produce "heroes" like Calley. Yankees in uniform are dispatched to all corners of the globe to trample on freedom. They committed their bloodiest crimes in Vietnam. And they are ready to repeat these crimes in other "small wars" anywhere on the face of the earth.

But this is not all. They are ready to kill their own countrymen if ordered to do so by "the iron heel"—Jack London's name for the all-powerful American capitalist oligarchy. To wit the events in Newark and Detroit, at Kent State and in many other U.S. towns.

In 1970 the world learned about Song My and other atrocities. By a strange coincidence, 1970 also marked the 25th anniversary of the Nuremberg trials. In the years to come, of course, the imperialist press, particularly the American press, will be writing about "mistakes made by our Western allies" and about the "il-legality" of the Nuremberg decisions and sentences.

Isn't it possible that even then the American "iron heel" was thinking of ways to deceive the army and to use genocidal methods for their own mad plans of world conquest? At any rate, there is little difference between American occupants and aggressors in Indochina and *Sonderkommandos* and *Einsatzgruppen* [both were special troops under the Nazi regime] of the sad past. The difference may lie in the use of napalm, chemical weapons and bullet-proof vests. As for hypocrisy and double talk, Pentagon propagandists outdo their predecessors by a long stretch.

This is what the American soldier is really like—certainly not as the *Army Digest* pictures him.

"It is a soldier's honor and duty to defend American ideals," he is told. "Soldiers have to believe that they are fighting for a just cause." "American soldiers have to know what they are fighting for." These are quotes from official regulations. Just what are American soldiers fighting for? The answer should be "for the fortunes of the duPonts and the Rockefellers, who are the worst enemies of their own people and of all humanity," but, of course, the American soldier is not given this answer. He gets highflown

Reprinted from *Atlas* magazine. Translated from *Krasnaya Zvezda*, Moscow.

slogans, obvious lies and shameless rhetoric. One thing is important to notice: the dollar oligarchs know that they can no longer ask their soldiers to obey orders blindly, they can no longer proclaim such obedience as being synonymous with honor and duty.

Let's take a look at the machine that turns "honest" citizens into the final product—Yankee soldiers.

The American soldier is not only lied to and brainwashed, he is also corrupted and bought off. Take the case of the so-called volunteers—and there are quite a few of those in the armed forces of the United States. What they are really being paid for is killing Vietnamese, including children, ransacking villages, and destroying the Vietnamese countryside. It is particularly shameful that young college-trained Americans agree to become mercenaries. Everyone should know these facts: in 1968 more than half of all U.S. Army officers in active serv-

ice, including 168 generals, were college and university graduates. Officer rank was conferred upon many while they were still in college and members of ROTC. American imperialism takes advantage of the high cost of higher education in the U.S. For many young people with limited economic resources joining the ROTC is the only way to get a higher education. The U.S. military establishment knows how to profit from this situation.

This is one of the most monstrous methods of morally corrupting American youth: Do you have a yearning for learning? Fine. You'll get your education, but you have to join an ideological and military machine that is essentially hostile to science and enlightenment.

Do you want security in life? You will get it, if you agree to say that white is black and black is white; if you agree to become a professional soldier.

But that's not all. Deceit and

bribery is not enough. Young people are taught to hate—we will not exaggerate if we call it animal hatred. Everybody knows the formula. It consists of brainwashing via TV and the press. The entire atmosphere of the American way of life, with its cult of violence and cruelty, does its share of influencing young minds. Take, for example, a game currently popular with American children—shooting Viet Cong, which is their derogatory name for Vietnamese patriots. Less known but no less infamous is the practice of dressing the "enemy" in Soviet or Vietnamese uniforms during military training. The uniforms are intentionally made to look very ugly, with huge hammers and sickles or red stars on the helmets. Training films show officials dressed in such uniforms jeering at prisoners in fictitious P.O.W. camps.

"Training an army dog consists in teaching it to hate the enemy. For this purpose the 'enemy' must wear the uniform of the hostile army, and he must be cruel to the dog," says a military encyclopedia.

Sometimes it is argued that the commanders and not the soldiers are responsible for war atrocities. That is true, of course. The men in charge of the U.S., the men who train the soldiers and make them do what they do in Indochina and at home, are the embodiment of cruelty and hatred. They think they can deprive a people of freedom. But that people cannot envisage a future without freedom, and their struggle is supported by all of progressive humanity.

The whole truth is not yet out. The Nuremberg trials demonstrated that crimes against humanity and violations of international law cannot be excused on grounds of following orders from above.

There is no justification for American atrocities and there never will be. The crimes of the U.S. military will not remain unpunished.

Lieutenant Calley

From KOMSOMOLSKAYA PRAVDA, Moscow

The War: The Record and the U.S.

By W. W. ROSTOW

Rostow: Morality and the War

AUSTIN, Tex.—Mr. Reston's column of June 13, 1971, says this:

"One of the many extraordinary things in this collection is how seldom anybody in the Kennedy or Johnson Administrations ever seems to have questioned the moral basis of the American war effort." He mentions me among others who "concentrated on pragmatc questions . . . rather than whether they were justifiable for a great nation fighting for what it proclaimed were moral purposes."

Mr. Reston is quite wrong. The moral and other bases for the position I held—and hold—on American policy in Asia are set out in "The Prospects for Communist China" (1954); "An American Policy in Asia" (1955); "The United States in the World Arena" (1960); as well as in a good many other pieces, including a talk at Fort Bragg in June 1961 and a number of memoranda written as a public servant which have, somehow, not yet found their way into The New York Times. My colleagues can speak for themselves, but I am sure their views were as deeply rooted as mine.

I raise the matter now not in personal defense, for I feel no need for that. I do so because the relation of morality to the national interest has been a peculiarly difficult problem for Americans (as George Kennan, for example, has lucidly pointed out) and because the question is dangerously bedeviled in current discussions of foreign policy. For reasons that reach back to our birth as a nation, out of the ideas of the Enlightenment, we have tended to oscillate between highflown moralism and a highly pragmatic pursuit of conventional national interests.

There are moral issues involved in supporting the pursuit of the national interest—ours or anyone else's. And they are not simple.

First, and above all, is the question of pacifism. For any reasonably sensitive human being the rejection of pacifism does not come easy. War is ugly and sinful. But pacifism requires an acceptance of all the consequences of never fighting. And this most Americans, including myself, cannot do. That means, however, that all national policy—like the human condition itself—is morally flawed because it envisages war as an ultimate sanction and contingency.

Second is the question of whether the defense of American interests runs with or against the interests of those most directly affected. In Asia this has meant, for example, answering the questions: Did the South Koreans in 1950 and the South Vietnamese in 1961 and in 1965 want to fight for an independent destiny or did they prefer to go with the Communist leadership in Pyongyang and Hanoi? (I can attest that it was this question President Kennedy felt he had to answer above any other before making his critical commitments to South Vietnam in November-December 1961.)

Third is the tactical moral question of conducting war, if it comes, so as to minimize damage to civilian lives. The history of war suggests this is never easy nor wholly successful; but it is clearly a part of the problem and a legitimate claim on the nation and its armed forces.

Fourth is the broad question of whether the raw power interests of the nation, in general, are decent and morally defensible in at least relative terms. I have for long taken the power interest of the United States to be negative: to prevent the dominance of Europe or Asia by a single potentially hostile power; and to prevent the emplacement of a major power in this hemisphere. These objectives demonstrably accord with the interests of the majority of the peoples and nations of Europe, Asia and Latin America. We could not have conducted our post-1940 foreign policy if this were not so. This convergence of our interests with theirs is reflected in treaties and other agreements which have been approved in accordance with our constitutional arrangements and those of other nations. In the world as it is, I find our power interests, as I would define them, to be morally legitimate.

Fifth is the moral question of the nation's word, once given. For a great nation to make the commitments we have to Southeast Asia involves a moral commitment to stay with them. I believe it immoral to walk away from our treaty commitments, which other nations and human beings have taken as the foundations for their lives in the most literal sense.

I do not detect any thoughtful weighing of these inherently complex moral considerations in Mr. Reston's casual *obiter dicta*. What I do detect is a slipping into *realpolitik* in the next column. What he implies is that, for reasons he does not explain, the fate of South Vietnam ceased at some point to relate to the fate of Southeast Asia as a whole. Mr. Reston appears to have unilaterally repealed the domino theory. As late as 1969, when I last toured Asia, there was great and widespread anxiety from Tokyo to Djakarta about the consequences of premature American withdrawal from the area. And I would guess that anxiety is at least as high today. This is not a moral but a factual question and a matter for judgment on the basis of evidence. We ought to be able to discuss it in a mature and dispassionate way.

In many years of debate about Southeast Asia, I have studied with care and sympathy the views of those who arrived at judgments different from mine. The issues at stake are such that, as Mr. Rusk used to say, they ought to be approached on our knees. My most profound objecti n to those who would withdraw our commitment to the defense of the area is the sanctimony with which they sometimes clothe their positions.

It is time for all of us to recall these words of Dean Acheson: "On one thing only I feel a measure of assurance—on the rightness of contempt for sanctimonious self-righteousness which, joined with a sly worldliness, beclouds the dangers and opportunities of our time with an unctuous film. For this is the ultimate sin."

W. W. Rostow is former White House adviser to President Johnson.

An hour's torture

Although military b r u t a l i t y should not be kept secret, as was the case at first with the My Lai killings, neither does the solution lie in inviting thousands of spectators to watch soldiers torture prisoners to death.

Yet this is exactly what took place in Dacca Dec. 18, perpetrated by Bangla Desh soldiers, the "moral" side in the India-Pakistan war which the U.S. was severely criticized for failing to support.

It was not merely a public execution, like the town-square hangings in frontier America; instead, it came close to the ferocity of human dismemberment by lions 2,000 years ago in the Roman Coliseum.

The AP report, carried in The Republic, described how in almost an hour of sadism, with 5,000 cheering spectators at Dacca's race course, four men suspected of sympathizing with Bangla Desh's enemies were beaten and stabbed to death.

A youngster, believed to be related to one of the victims, flung himself on a prostrate figure. Bangla Desh soldiers and the crowd efficiently battered and trampled him to death.

None of the military leaders present was able to cite any specific c h a r g e s against the four men, who had been beaten for half an hour, struck with rifles, karate-chopped in t h e genitals, kneed in the abdomen, burned with cigarettes, shot, and repeatedly stabbed with bayonets, which were twisted and turned in their gaping wounds.

The Indian government, which toppled East Pakistan's former leaders, decided that foreigners would somehow be offended by this lively display. And so officials of India's Overseas Communication Service, which transmits wirephotos for news services, rejected five graphic Associated Press photos of the sadism, declaring, "We do not consider them to be in our interests."

That's beyond dispute. They are neither in the interest of Bangla Desh nor of India. Nor in the interest of those who chant that the U.S. is the most barbaric nation in the world. Nor of those who portrayed the Bangla Desh - India alliance as morally superior to the authoritarian Pakistan g o v e r n ment.

We have all heard about dictatorships torturing opponents in secret cellars. But when the public is i n v i t e d to cheer calculated vengeance, it is hard to distinguish between the democrats and the totalitarians.

U.S. Chaplains Under Attack For Supporting Vietnam War

In an interview in his office last month, the Army Chief of Chaplains, Maj. Gen. Francis L. Sampson, a Roman Catholic who will complete his four-year-term next month, said violence was an evil "but the man who doesn't resist the violent man becomes culpable, it seems to me." He added:

"In the case of nations, innocent friends who are being attacked by aggressive nations, it seems to me if we made a commitment of friendship to a country, we owe it our support."

Not Applicable

The commandment against killing, he said, is actually a prohibition against murder and therefore is no applicable to wartime.

Above *The Arizona Republic*, December 23, 1971.

Above right, © 1971 by the New York Times Company. Reprinted by permission.

Right from *National Review*, April 20, 1971.

Dist. Publishers-Hall Syndicate

A G.I. Writes Home About 'A Little Turkey Shoot'

At right is the first page of a letter written on July 4, 1969, by an American soldier in Vietnam to his family. Its content—the reference to the use of CS, a riot control gas, to drive Viet Cong troops out of their bunkers into the open where they become easy targets for American small arms ("a little turkey shoot")—demonstrates a contradiction of the most recently stated U.S. policy on gases of this kind, which prescribes their use in circumstances "when they will help save lives." Evidently the firing on the troops flushed out by the gas was continued from gun ships—helicopters carrying men armed with automatic weapons.

U.S. policy statements on the use of riot control agents have themselves been marked by inconsistencies. However that may be, not one of them gives support to the use described in the letter. This is from the most recent statement, issued by the Pentagon in September: "Riot control agents are particularly useful in reducing civilian casualties when the enemy has infiltrated into population centers or built-up areas, or is believed to be holding civilian hostages. In short, riot-control agents are used when they will help save lives."

In a covering note sent with his son's letter, his father wrote: "Please understand that the letter is written in typical G.I. lingo, and don't be shocked at the casual mention of death. These boys have been brainwashed to the point where they actually believe in what they're doing. I would have it no other way because it is the only hope I have of getting my son home alive. He has to fight to live. I have noticed though, in some of his latest letters, signs of doubt. And I'm glad he is ready for his rest period. They are not much good for the front after that, so the army postpones it as long as they can."

The soldier's name is being withheld at his father's request.

Top page, © 1971 Jules Feiffer.
Above and right from *War/Peace Report*, November 1969.

4 July

Dear Mom, Dad, ████████

Well I hope you all have a groovy 4th, I am. Right now I'm sitting atop bunker #18 on LZ Grant & I'll be on Grant for seven to ten days. I don't know how you'll be celebrating the fourth, but our company did theirs on the second. I didn't make it back out in the field in time but they had a real groovy time. They walked into about 600 to 1000 gooks and didn't have anybody killed. They took about a dozen wounded but none too bad. Two small helicopters got shot down and they had two killed & four wounded. Our company tried going in six times & each time they were driven back. So they called in some brand new gas masks & then drop a ton or so of CS gas (Riot control) and had a little turkey shoot. Killed about 40-50 but they drove the gooks out of the bunkers & the gun ships have been having fun ever since.

I spent three days in Tay Ninh for my headache (slight concussion) and I've been put in for a purple heart.

Yet, granted this principle of having no clear principles, how do we determine the point at which we should abandon principle? Where does consistency become an "illegitimate extension"? In Vietnam, for instance, Schlesinger himself did not become aware of the illegitimacy until well into Johnson's regime; he was still defending the war during the successful antiwar "teach-ins." Now he tells us that we "went too far" in Vietnam, but his norms seem merely quantitative — he falls back on the "just war" concept of proportionality: "I do not see that our original involvement in Vietnam was per se immoral. What was immoral was the employment of means of death out of all proportion to rational purposes." It was not wrong to kill Vietnamese (or Americans); but we should not have killed *so many*. Bombs away, but sparingly. It is easy to see how such a view leads men imperceptibly — one bomb at a time, as it were — into situations that are not, for a long time, repugnant to their original principles, but which become, at some stage of the carnage, more than they can stomach.

Henry Niles started up the businessmen's protest in mid-1966. A Quaker convert, and father-in-law of vintage New Left activist Staughton Lynd, his entire family had long been active in movements for peace.

"I felt that in 15 minutes of atomic war the Baltimore Life Insurance Company could lose practically all of its assets, most of its customers and most of its prospects," he tells other businessmen, with an ironic dash of enlightened self-interest. "All that I had been doing in 25 years to build this company would be wiped out." Military spending, even without atomic war, "could cause such inflation that the value of the life insurance policy would decline seriously."

If all the professions that have participated in Vietnam are honest with themselves, and are prepared to examine the notions upon which their involvement was predicated, it can provide an opportunity for this country to attain a wiser sense of direction, and to evolve a higher system of accountability in humanitarian terms for decisions that in the past have been justified solely by vague national security principles.

Albert Speer, sentenced to twenty years' imprisonment by the Nuremberg Tribunal, addressed himself to the old

Above left, from *Nixon Agonistes* by Gary Willis, Houghton Mifflin Company, 1970.
Left from "Businessmen Against the War (Sic)," by Steve Weissman, in *Ramparts*, December 1970.
Below, courtesy of James Reston, Jr., and *Saturday Review*, January 9, 1971.

excuses of not knowing about Nazi atrocities or not participating directly in them. In his remarkable memoirs, *Inside the Third Reich*, he wrote:

I no longer give any of these answers. For they are efforts at legal exculpation. . . . In the final analysis I myself determined the degree of my isolation, the extremity of my evasions, and the extent of my ignorance. . . . Whether I knew or did not know, or how much or how little I knew is totally unimportant when I consider what horrors I might have known about and what conclusions would have been the natural ones to draw from the little I did know. Those who ask me are fundamentally expecting me to offer justifications. I have none. No apologies are possible.

Americans now know enough about Vietnam to draw some natural conclusions. The question is: Will they do it?

talk
of the
world

American campuses may have been too wintry, antiwar groups too weary, but in the rest of the world, the news of the invasion of Laos reverberated at a screechingly high pitch for nearly a month. . . . The fact that uniformed American soldiers were not involved in the ground fighting didn't do much to ease feelings; Vienna's moderate *Kronen Zeitung* put it this way:

The Americans technically may not be the burglar, but they play the role of the man on whose shoulders the burglar stands when climbing the wall. They also supply the burglar's tools, they have worked out the plan, they keep a lookout and they give him covering fire.

Assuredly, the action had its supporters; Paris's center-right daily, *Le Figaro:*

The truth is that the neutrality of Cambodia and Laos has been constantly violated by Hanoi, whose forces have never left those kingdoms despite the Geneva Accords of 1962 . . .

London's conservative *Daily Telegraph:*

It is the height of hypocrisy for the North Vietnamese and the Russians to accuse America, with such a show of righteous indignation, of violating Laotian neutrality.

But Munich's *Süddeutsche Zeitung* snorted:

In Laos, one side is as bad as the other. . . . The Ho Chi Minh trail itself contravenes Laotian neutrality, while the U.S. has bombed it for many years!

Nevertheless, an impartial observer of the world press would probably concede that the boos drowned out the cheers; the foreign minister of Sweden, Torsten Nilsson, said simply:

Now the U.S. has invaded another small nation. Such contempt for the integrity of a small nation must be condemned.

Hong Kong's independent weekly *Far Eastern Economic Review* referred cuttingly to what it termed a policy of "Indosinicization", adding:

It does not seem to have occurred to Nixon that France gained in prestige and influence after ceding independence to Algeria, or that Britain went on to its peak of imperial power after admitting defeat at the hands of the American revolutionaries.

From *Atlas*, April 1971.

Thinking Out Loud

The Editor

True Christian believers hate war without being pacifists. A pacifist is one who does not believe there is ever a justifiable war. But even a casual study of the Old Testament Scriptures reveal that God has helped His people through many military conflicts.

However, these wars have always been *defensive* wars — never aggressive wars. Always the occasion for warfare was the invasion by a foreign power, or the deliverance from bondage of nations which held God's people in captivity.

An apparent exception was the invasion by the Israelites of the land of Canaan, under Joshua. However, it must be remembered that Israel's mission was to "re-possess" their own land, a land which had been given by God to Abraham and his posterity. They did not invade territory belonging to other nations. So that, strictly speaking, it could not be considered an aggressive action. Through the performance of many miracles God enabled them to repossess their own land.

The only justification the United States has for engaging in a military contest with another nation is when that nation either attacks our country or endangers our security. On the basis of this truth, we were not justified in launching the campaign in Vietnam.

Above, courtesy of Dale Crowley in *The Capital Voice*, June 1, 1971.
Right, copyright 1971 Christian Century Foundation. Reprinted by permission from the April 7, 1971, issue of *The Christian Century*.

A Call to Penitence and Action

This editorial concerning the observance of Holy Week and the meaning of the crucifixion and the resurrection of Jesus Christ is being published jointly by The Christian Century, Christianity and Crisis, Commonweal *and the* National Catholic Reporter.

✝ ON GOOD FRIDAY of what we dare to call this year of our Lord 1971 countless people in Indochina — God's children — are crying out, inchoately or articulately, "My God, my God, why hast thou forsaken me?" To offer a human answer to such a cry is never easy. This year it is poignantly hard for Americans, because many of earth's millions raise the cry out of their perception of oppression by our government, our economy and our armed forces. Especially in southeast Asia, American military might is repeating the crucifixion of Christ.

Let no one say that we are confusing religion and politics. Christ was crucified by soldiers of an imperial army in a conquered land under a ruler who enforced distorted law and maintained an oppressive order. It is Christ who has taught us that what we do to the least of his brothers we do to him. There was no clear separation of religion from politics on Golgotha, and there can be none today.

Even so, we do not make our charges glibly. In a world where people must make perplexing moral decisions, most Christian traditions take account of occasions when love has its "strange" work to do — a work of enforcement, pressure, even violence. Conscientious convictions may differ on the justification of coercion and war in specific circumstances. Too often, when men should recognize conflicts of judgment they impute bad faith. All these reservations we take seriously.

But in this second decade of war in Vietnam we are convinced that the American church has been too patient — not too polemical — toward national leaders. We Christians have been too tolerant of American men of power, too forgetful of foreign victims of such power. Too often we have been manipulated into ineffectiveness by a sophisticated political machinery.

We voted, we petitioned, we paraded, we shouted. In one way or another we supported a few of our young men who risked their freedom in efforts to stop this war. But they have borne more than their share of the burden. It is time for the rest of us to give our hearts and voices to an accusation that even a purposefully deaf government will hear.

ABORTION PASTORAL

VARIATIONS ON A THEME

Few of the many comments on the unfortunate contrast between the strong stand of American bishops on the matter of abortion and their silence on the question of Vietnam have been as striking as that of one priest of the archdiocese of New York. After reading from the pulpit Cardinal Cooke's pastoral letter marking Right-to-Life Sunday and preaching on its contents, the priest added that "respect for life in one direction demands respect for life in another." He reread the letter with only slight modifications such as those below. He made no other remarks, nor were any necessary.

My Friends in Christ:

Today, America needs to be reminded of the guiding principles upon which it was founded. Respect for all human life is fundamental to our national existence. In recent years, however, we have seen a steady erosion of respect for life in our society. The ~~New York State Abortion Law of 1970~~ [war in Vietnam] has drawn our society far down the road to open contempt for human life. Since I wrote to you on behalf of the Bishops of the State last December, we have seen the situation grow worse daily. New ~~abortion clinics~~ [fronts] have opened with increasing frequency. Both as Catholics and as citizens we must speak out against this tragedy of ~~abortion.~~ [war]

Some say that Catholics should not speak on this issue. "~~Abortion~~ [The war] is only a ~~social~~ [political] matter," they claim; "religion should not enter into it." Such a position disenfranchises men of certain religious convictions. It says, in effect, that certain citizens may not have a voice on particular issues.

Anyone who is convinced, be he Catholic or not, that ~~abortion~~ [the war in Vietnam] is an attack on human life has the right and the duty to say so. Every human person is a member of society and has a serious social responsibility to shape the values of that society as they are expressed in its laws.

~~In New York State,~~ we have moved far beyond a mere debate on personal values. ~~One hundred thousand unborn children~~ [Hundreds of thousands of lives] have been destroyed in ~~New~~ [Indo-china] ~~York alone. New York is already the abortion capital of the nation.~~

Not only Catholics, but men and women of many diverse religious backgrounds believe that, by the ~~Abortion Law of 1970, New York State~~ [war in Vietnam, the United States] has alienated what the Declaration of Independence calls the "inalienable" right to life.

We urge each person, young or old, who believes in the right of every ~~child to be born,~~ [person to life] to enter the public forum and work for the ~~repeal~~ [end] of this tragic ~~law.~~ [war.]

There are bills in ~~Albany~~ [Congress] right now that would stop this slaughter of the innocent ~~unborn.~~ I suggest that you write, phone, telegraph and speak to all our ~~state's~~ [nation's] lawmakers and make your support of life known to them in a very clear manner.

I join in prayer with you that the tragedy of ~~abortion~~ [the war in Vietnam] may be removed from our society.

Faithfully yours in Christ,

TERENCE CARDINAL COOKE,

Archbishop of New York

From *Commonweal*, May 14, 1971.

SECTION V

Atrocities, War Crimes, and the Calley Case

No one seriously doubts that the deliberate killing of a hundred or more defenseless men, women, and children is an atrocity. Yet the My Lai affair was as controversial as any event in recent years. No doubt many factors contributed to this confusion, but we suggest that conceptual difficulty was one of the most important elements of the controversy. What exactly did Lt. Calley *do* at My Lai? How much responsibility does he bear? Should he have been tried? Having been found guilty, should he be punished? Failure to distinguish these four questions has made rational evaluation of the whole affair difficult, if not impossible.

These questions are logically connected. One cannot, for example, profitably ask the last three questions without having answered the first one. It is possible to agree that Lt. Calley *did* issue certain orders and shoot certain civilians. But there is a sufficiently weak sense of "did" which permits two individuals to agree that he did these things without necessarily agreeing that he is criminally or morally responsible for having done them. This point can best be illustrated with an example such as the following: A hunter thinks he sees a deer in the distance and shoots it. When he reaches the fallen body he discovers—to his horror—that it is one of his friends wearing a deer costume. Clearly we can agree that the hunter shot his friend without agreeing that he is a murderer or that he is morally responsible for his friend's death. Of course we may, upon further investigation and consideration, decide that he *is* morally culpable, but we may also determine that he is not. The important point is that we can only raise questions of responsibility and culpability once we have determined what was done.

Without a voluntary confession by the agent, it is often quite difficult to

46

ascertain exactly who did what in a given situation. The question of responsibility, however, is even more difficult to resolve in principle. This is partly due to the serious obstacles to acquiring sufficient empirical knowledge about the motivation of the agent. In addition, thorny theoretical questions concerning free will and responsibility come into play. We cannot stress too strongly that the categories "completely responsible" and "not responsible at all" simply mark the two ends of a spectrum. We should not assume that the resolution of the responsibility issue in any particular case will fall at either of the two extremes.

Lastly, we face the questions of trial, conviction, and punishment. Obviously, a man should not be brought to trial if there is no reason to believe that he is responsible for the commission of some criminal act. But is this sufficient for morally justifying his trial? It is at this point that the issue of the just administration of the law arises. A law can be itself unjust, or it can be just but unjustly administered. In the present case, rules outlawing indiscriminate killing of the innocent are clearly just in content. But if there has been a widespread violation of this rule (as many people have claimed), is it right to pick out just one person for trial? Why him? Why not others?

At best, we have only begun to probe the complex conceptual issues involved in the My Lai affair. Many important questions have not even been raised, let alone discussed (such as the question of the chain of responsibility running all the way up to the president). This is another instance of the way in which practical moral concerns lead directly to difficult factual, conceptual, and theoretical questions which the morally sensitive person cannot avoid.

Calley Admits My Lai Killings

Left, courtesy of Associated Press News-features, February 24, 1971.
Bottom left, from *Newsweek*, March 29, 1971.
Below, from *The National Observer*, April 5, 1971.

FT. BENNING, Ga. (AP) — Lt. William L. Calley Jr. admitted Tuesday that he fired at a handful of Vietnamese civilians in My Lai nearly three years ago, and decreed the mass execution of others. But he said he felt he did no wrong.

"I never sat down and analyzed whether they were men, women and children—they were enemy not people," Calley told the court-martial jury of six superior officers trying him on charges of premeditated murder of 102 My Lai villagers on March 16, 1968.

"It was a group of people who were the enemy, sir," Calley testified at another point. "I was ordered to go in there and destroy the enemy. That was my job that day. That was my mission . . .

"I felt then and still do that I acted as I was directed and that I carried out orders I was given. And I do not feel I was wrong in doing so, sir."

Calley said he fired fewer than 18 rounds from his M16 automatic rifle during an infantry assaut on My Lai. Among his targets, he added, were Vietnamese men, women and children in a ditch. He denied a sizable number of other civilian murders charged against him.

Latimer pleaded with the jury of career officers to consider the Army itself. "I'm proud of the United States Army," he told them. "It grieves me to see it being pulled apart from within . . . An acquittal will help the Army. It will show the judicial process protects a man who makes an error in judgment . . . There ought to be a difference between errors in judgment and criminality."

Then came Daniel's final, stinging rebuttal. Calley, he declared, had been "judge, jury and executioner" at My Lai. "There has been talk of the accused as a poor kid sent over there, but there hasn't been anything said for the victims. Who will speak for them? . . . Would any tribunal in this world have found one of those children guilty of any offense and then ordered his execution?" He concluded pointedly: "You gentlemen are the conscience of the United States Army. You are the conscience of this country. Your duty is clear . . . to find the accused guilty as charged."

The next afternoon Mr. Latimer pleaded for his client's life in his maundering, cliche-ridden style: "Lieutenant Calley, outside of a normal traffic ticket, was a good boy. . . . He stayed that way until he got in that Oriental environment . . . . Maybe you can say he used bad judgment and became too aggressive and went too far . . . . But who taught him to kill, kill, kill?"

Then Rusty Calley, standing at the microphone that his 70-year-old advocate always had to use to magnify his weak voice, addressed the jurors. His voice quavered uncontrollably, and whatever had kept a maelstrom of emotions from gushing out all these months seemed about to give way at any moment:

"I'm not going to stand here and plead for my life or my freedom. . . . I have never known a soldier, nor did I ever myself, ever wantonly kill a human being in my entire life. If I have committed a crime, the only crime that I have committed is in judgment of my values.

"Apparently, I valued my troops' lives more than I did that of the enemy . . . when my troops were getting massacred and mauled by an enemy I couldn't see, I couldn't feel, and I couldn't touch—that nobody in the military system ever described as anything other than communism. They didn't give it a race, they didn't give it a sex, they didn't give it an age; they never let me believe it was just a philosophy in a man's mind. . . . Yesterday you stripped me of all my honor. Please, by your actions that you take here today, don't strip future soldiers of their honor."

WAR CRIMES
"Forgive Us Our Sins . . ."

Conspicuous Disparity. Thoughtful people throughout the Western World realized that not merely eleven wretched lives were at stake, but Western democracy's moral position in the inevitable trials of history. Their doubts about Nürnberg's justice were perhaps best summed up by two British publications. Said London's *Economist*:

"The result of the Nürnberg trial has been a well-deserved fate for a group of evil men . . . yet the force of the condemnation is not unaffected by the fact that the nations sitting in judgment have so clearly proclaimed themselves exempt from the law which they have administered." Said the *Manchester Guardian Weekly:* "Behind [the Nürnberg case] lie the outraged feelings of whole peoples whose memories carry a far heavier load than ours. . . . If they demand a brutal penalty which is yet hopelessly inadequate we may not gainsay them. . . . [But] there are many features of this process which do not sit lightly on a civilized conscience. . . . Certainly, if we had been defeated . . . we should have had some difficulty in justifying Hiroshima. . . . There needs to be a consistency between the law of the judges and the conduct of the powers [behind the judges]. There exists a disparity which the world must notice. . . . The Nürnberg judgment will look well or ill in history according to the future behavior of the four nations responsible for it. . . . If they behave as nations have invariably behaved till now, it will seem no more than the quirk of an oddly assorted bunch of victors. . . ."

The doubts had their answerers. Most defenders of Nürnberg fell back on the U.S.'s Robert Jackson, who at the trial's start had summed up the still precarious but deeply urgent aspirations of millions in the memorable sentence: "If there is no law now under which to try these people, it is about time the human race made some."

Right, letter to the editor of *The Guardian*, London, by Hilda Morris, April 17, 1971.
Above, Reprinted by permission from *Time, the Weekly Newsmagazine.* Copyright Time, Inc., 1946.

Sir,—The case of Lieutenant Calley is tragic in every one of its many aspects. It would be even more tragic if it were buried in the legal and military annals without helping the world to draw the only certain conclusion that can be drawn from it: that war itself is the ultimate atrocity.

An army at war can and must have only one aim, to gain victory. To do so, it must destroy as many enemy lives as possible and, at the same time, try to preserve the lives of its own personnel. The idea that unarmed civilians should be spared was never very firmly established, except on paper. It was finally demolished with the advent of aerial bombing and the kind of jungle warfare which the Americans and their adversaries are conducting in Vietnam. In these circumstances, every civilian is a potential victim and a potential enemy.

The principles laid down in Nuremberg, too, are paper precepts and bear no relationship to the realities of war. Supposing they had existed when the first nuclear bomb was to be dropped on Hiroshima, and the US airmen had refused to inflict on unarmed civilians a new weapon whose effects were largely unknown. They would have been told that their mission might save thousands of American lives. How were they to decide whether they were committing a crime or doing a favour to their countrymen? Which, in fact, did they do?

It should be glaringly obvious by now that no military man, from the general to the private, can conduct a war according to the Nuremberg principles. They may have been well-intentioned but in effect they were but another attempt to gloss over the basic truth that humane warfare is a contradiction in terms.

If that truth can now be established in the minds of men everywhere, the sufferings of My Lai and the anguish of Lieutenant Calley will not have been in vain.—Yours sincerely,

Hilda Morris.
Peace Pledge Union
6 Endsleigh Street
London WC1

NATIONAL REVIEW

APRIL 13, 1971
Vol. 23   No. 14

The Calley Trial and After

BULLETIN

Whatever was to happen to William Calley, one result of the first Mylai trial was certain in advance: the United States Army was going to be found Guilty. The Army couldn't win. If Calley had been let off: a whitewash. If he had been (as he has been) condemned: a scapegoat for the higher brass. That's the way the media set it up and, in the courtrooms of our global village, the media, as we all know, are prosecutor, judge and jury.

Surely there is something essentially wrong in the way the Mylai episode is being handled. Of course there was also something very wrong about the episode: Horrible things happened at Mylai, and there seems little doubt that William Calley did at least some of them. But what happened *in* the Mylai episode is a different matter from what happened and is happening *to* the Mylai episode—in myriad news dispatches, the hour upon hour of TV shots and radio-TV commentary, the thousands of articles, speeches, sermons, the scores of books, the meetings, conferences and now the seemingly endless—and relentlessly publicized—session of one, two . . . and how many more trials.

One thing most wrong is a distortion so extreme that it brings a total falsification. Objectively viewed, the Mylai episode—however horrible—is a trivial incident within a large and complex whole. That whole includes the torturing and assassination by the Vietcong and the North Vietnamese of an estimated fifty thousand South Vietnamese civilians; it includes thousands of booby traps, set or triggered by children and women as well as men, that mangled young Americans, Australians, Koreans and South Vietnamese; it includes, also, bombings by American aircraft that have killed far more noncombatants than all the Mylais there may have been—as did bombings by American, Russian, British and German aircraft in World War II. But besides all the local and immediate combat facts it includes an array of political, social and philosophical facts extending on a global and historic scale. Our intellectuals and verbalists seem to be divorcing themselves from history in order to revel in an obsessed orgy of Guilt.

Horrible and obscene things happen in war, in every war; and in peace, too, and in the course of each individual's life and dying. Human existence bears no resemblance to the projections of sentimentalists and utopians. But to dwell exclusively on the horrors and obscenities is the road not to vision but to madness. Nor is it necessary that *everything* be brought at all times into the open for everyone to see. Not every diner need keep always in mind the horrors of the slaughterhouse. The civilized man believes that even in war a line must be drawn somewhere. Under a global searchlight may not always be the best place for drawing it. There is something to be said, often, for the old-fashioned rite of the drumhead court-martial.

It has been generally remarked that this Vietnam conflict is the first TV war, and therefore the first in which war's horrors have entered mass consciousness. We are told that this will make war impossible since the masses, being conscious now of the horrors, will not permit war. Both premise and conclusion are faulty. It is not the war that is being presented on a global screen, but only a cross-section of horrors and sensationalized happenings drawn by camera crews and reporters functioning freely on our side of the line. There are no freely ranging crews or screens or networks on the enemy's side. The televised war of horrors exists not for the global village but only for the side that is the more civilized, democratic and technologically advanced. If the continuous televising of this war is, in fact, leading the audience to renouncing war, this will not at all mean no more war. If civilized men, overcome by war's quota of sensationalist horror, no longer can fight, then they will inevitably be enslaved, or destroyed, by the uncivilized, who can.

From *National Review Bulletin*, April 13, 1971.

Americal GIs Say 'We've All Done It'; About Calley

CHU LAI, Vietnam (AP) — Enlisted men who tasted combat in the Americal Division, the outfit of Lt. William L. Calley Jr., believe he got "a bum rap for something we've all done at one time or another," as one of them put it.

Among 30 enlisted men interviewed before Calley was sentenced to life Wednesday, there was not one who agreed with the jury's decision that he committed premeditated murder at the village of My Lai. Many of them had been in combat in the same hostile hills.

Calley's brother officers— those who will talk for the record— concede he "had a fairer trial than the people of My Lai." But some feel life imprisonment is too harsh a penalty for Calley. One said Calley's superiors should be punished.

Blames Higher-Ups

"A lot more people, especially the higher-ups, should get burned also," said Capt. Laurence A. Snyder, 28, of Wayne, N.J.

"I've met some of the brass involved in the My Lai incident. I've been on various investigative committees myself, and I just don't think they worked hard enough.

"How could something like this happen without the brass knowing? Somebody must have kept their ears closed, that's all."

Said Pfc. Gary Cooper, 22, of Brookhaven, Miss.: "They shouldn't do anything like this to Calley. These people out here will kill you for anything—food, money or cigarettes. Any GI that's been in the bush will tell you Calley was just doing his job. If he's a war criminal, then everyone in Vietnam is a war criminal."

Of 10 officers interviewed at division headquarters here, only two felt the verdict was justified. One of those two, a major, preferred to remain anonymous because "mine is definitely a minority opinion around here."

Agrees With Verdict

The other officer, Lt. Tom Schmitz, 23, of Niagara Falls, N.Y. was blunt: "He was found guilty, and I think it was right. Our job is not to come over here to murder civilians."

Pfc. Alan Aspholm, 20, of Manson, Iowa, one of those who survived the disastrous attack on Fire Base Mary Ann on Sunday, said: "I've seen women shooting at me. Out by Landing Zone Young we chased two dinks down a hill and one of them turned out to be a woman carrying an M16.

"You mean I'm not supposed to shoot someone like that? Calley was all right."

Observed Lt. Louis R. Ogus, 23, of New York City: "If I walked into a village and I received fire from there in the last hour, and if I saw a Vietnamese running or making some fast move, I'm afraid I would have done the same as Calley."

Above, courtesy of Associated Press Newsfeatures, April 1, 1971.

Right, courtesy of John Ciardi and *Saturday Review*, May 1, 1971.

Manner of Speaking

John Ciardi

Cases of Conscience

A MORAL ALPHABET: Individual A is found guilty of having massacred individuals B-through-W, twenty-two in all, including men, women, children, and babes in arms. The original charges against A cited 102 counts of murder. The jury was eager to disbelieve the charges. "I am assured," said one juror, "that every member of the jury was hoping against hope that we could find something somehow that would allow us to find [A] innocent." It was in that frame of mind that the jury sifted the original charges down to twenty-two counts of murder on which the evidence permitted no doubt.

Various veterans have come forward to announce that their wartime actions made them as guilty as A and that they, too, should be tried. One retired general declared that he had once given a "no prisoners" order (meaning "shoot them if they surrender"). [Moral question b]: Is the refusal to take prisoners in a combat situation in which no men can be spared to guard them analogous to the act of herding civilians into a ditch and there gunning them down?] Air Force veterans have cited the fact that they bombed civilian population. [Moral question c]: In an age in which wars are won and lost on the production line, is a civilian who manufactures a shell less an enemy than the soldier who fires it? d): If non-producing civilians are killed by the bombs aimed at disrupting war production, whose responsibility is it for not having evacuated them to safer areas? e): Is such bombing, in any case, analogous to the act of rounding up and shooting presumably allied civilians? f): It is possible that B-through-W were being forced to shelter the enemy at night, as they were forced to submit to our forces by day, but in that case what is their guilt, and who is authorized to decide it and to kill them for it?] A former special forces officer came forward to confess that he had, on CIA orders, murdered something called "a triple agent." [Moral question g]: Can any governmental organization be so far above legal scrutiny that it can order a man's death without trial and shut off inquiry in the name of national security? Particularly when the circumstances make it readily possible to hold the suspected agent incommunicado until such time as he can pose no threat?]

51

Most Feel Calley Was Scapegoat

The Veterans of Foreign Wars thought the Calley verdict was terrible. For different reasons, so did a number of antiwar groups.

The Establishment right, in the person of Rep. Barry Goldwater Jr. (R-Cal.), thought the trial "should never have taken place" at all. On the liberal Establishment left, the view was more that the trial was not really that important at all when measured against the vast immorality of the war.

The man in the street seemed divided on the verdict, though whether for or against it most Americans seemed to share the conviction that Calley was a "scapegoat."

Singling Out

The soldiers on a local Army base were equally divided: some dismayed at the "unfairness" of singling out Calley, who after all they said, had only obeyed a commonplace order in Vietnam; others pleased at the demonstration that, order or no order, there were some things a soldier did not do with impunity.

And a Buddhist monk who is secretary-general of an anti-government faction in Vietnam asked for leniency for Calley and compensation for the victims. "One more death will not help anything," said Thich Huyen Quang.

Above and top page right, reprinted by permission of *New York Post.* © 1971, New York Post Corporation

Above right, letter to the editor of *Newsweek* by Paul Gillette, May 3, 1971.

In Washington, the Citizens Commission of Inquiry oin U. S. War Crimes, an anti-war group, was no more elated than the VFW, calling the conviction "part of a cynical attempt to scapegoat low ranking military personnel in order to deflect attention away from those actually responsible for atrocities in Indochina—the U. S. military and civilian leadership."

Goldwater, meanwhile, thought that "to air our dirty laundry in front of the world is not being very smart . . it degraded Americ a)n the eyes of the world."

But from the GOP left, former Sen. Charles Goodell said: "Nothing will be solved by the Calley verdict." And Sen. George McGovern, a liberal Democrat, warning against being distracted by the verdict, said: "Policymakers at the very highest levels of our government have been ordering procedures in Southeast Asia that I personally find contrary to principles of humane conduct."

That theme was echoed again and again by members of the public interviewed at random, whether they sided with Calley or not. "From my observation, I'm convinced he was guilty and should be punished," said John Dunn, 63, a retired construction engineer. "But I think they should go all the way up the line and locate the ultimate responsibility."

A few, of course, disagreed. "This is a war they're fighting, not a goddamned tennis match," snapped John De-Maze, a bus driver, as he sipped a beer in an Eighth Av. bar.

At the Fort Hamilton Army Base in Brooklyn, Vietnam veteran Spec 4 Robert Meyer summed up the feeling of many enlisted men when he said: "I think it was unfair because . . . he was over there to do a job."

"People who came back that I spoke to feel he should be considered innocent, because this one person didn't do anything a lot of others didn't," noted Sp. Barry Bahl.

But Sgt. Robert Lipscomb, a black Vietnam veteran had a sharply different view.

"It's great," Lipscomb said of the verdict. "This will help the Army have control over its people, or else you'd have soldiers running amok, killing whoever they want. It's only the gooks they're killing, they say, but when you think in those terms the next step is killing the niggers or anybody different."

■ American sympathy for Calley testifies to strong undercurrents of racism. If the lieutenant had murdered 22 Caucasians we would feel little sympathy for him. But because they were Vietnamese—Orientals, slopes, gooks, subhumans—we are outraged not so much by their deaths as by the fact that Calley, a Caucasian, might have to spend a few years in jail for killing them.

PAUL J. GILLETTE

Carbondale, Pa.

WILFRED BURCHETT

America's Genocide in Indochina

I think Lieutenant Calley is probably one of the wisest young white men in America: He now understands that you don't have to be black to be a nigger in this society. Lieutenant Calley bought the whole program. He wore the uniform, he had the bars, he carried the flag, and he went out to do the job they told him to do—killing, even killing innocent men, women, and children. But when the system felt it would rather create a nigger than put the military high command and the civilian leadership on trial, they turned on Lieutenant Calley.

We've understood that right along, because when this system cannot deal with its problems, it says, "Look! Black Panthers! Angela Davis! Activists! Campus Unrest!" And so the silent majority gets diverted from the problems of this country to look at scapegoats. Calley's a scapegoat, and they hope that you'll look at Calley so that you won't look at the people who established the policy in Indochina that allows us to kill, kill, kill.

Above, Congressman Ron Dellums as quoted in *The Progressive*, June 1971. Right from the quarterly magazine, *New World Review*, Spring 1971.

AFTER having very carefully studied every scrap of evidence on which I could lay my hands, regarding the trial of Lieutenant William L. Calley, I have decided that the prosecution has no case at all. Calley was a "good" officer, loyally obeying orders from a chain of command that reached right back to the Commander-in-Chief of the US Armed Forces, the President of the United States. And as he prayed to the Almighty before the main executions, Calley was obeying even Superior Forces which the president also recognizes. There is no reason why, for his performance at My Lai, his name should not be put down for another of those two million medals which, the press informs us, have already been awarded to Vietnam war veterans. The only formal criticism that a military court could have of Calley's conduct was that he revealed that dogs and pigs— in addition to babes and grandmothers—were also included in the "body count" statistics. But apart from that lapse, Calley should be decorated for faithfully applying official policy, as laid down by successive US presidents. That is to exterminate by any means whatsoever the political opposition, actual and potential, to the type of regime the government of the United States decided was suitable for South Vietnam. Calley's method of suppressing the political opposition was relatively simple and straightforward—grenades and machine-gun bullets.

Calley, as he testified, saw his victims. In fact he loved them. He found them to be "very wonderful people" and he appreciated that the word "kill" was never used. "Waste them" was the more delicate expression and he felt he could be sentenced to death for disobeying orders "to waste" the citizens of My Lai. "The defense contends," according to a UPI report from Fort Benning, where Calley was being tried, "that Lt. Calley did not consider the villagers to be human beings, but only enemy with whom he could not talk or reason." Actually the original charge sheet had admitted that the My Lai victims were in fact "Oriental human beings" so Calley was one step behind low-level official formulations, but otherwise he was well in step with top-level policies, expressed in more lofty philosophical terms. Charles Wolf, Jr., for instance, in a paper highly appreciated at the White House as far back as May 1965, had refuted the idea that US policies in Vietnam should be aimed at winning popular support. Wolf's conclusion, at the time the US invasion force was being built up for its first big battles, was that "the primary question **should be whether the proposed measure is likely to increase the cost and difficulties of insurgent operations, rather than whether it wins popular loyalty and support. . . ." To hell with trying to win "hearts and minds," says Wolf in effect, "let's go after the bodies."

That was the policy that Calley was implementing. Calley saw his victims, even if briefly, face-to-face, huddled together on the ground before his grenades tore them to pieces; lined up against a ditch before their bloodied bodies were hurled into it by his firepower and orders. But what about the technicians of "Mitey Mite," blowing high concentrations of CS poison gas at two pounds per minute into sealed-off, underground shelters, killing, as cruelly and inevitably as the Zyklon B death machines in the Nazi gas chambers, those who seek shelter from US bombs and shells? Come out like men (not to mention women and children) to a clean death from our bullets, or die like rats, poisoned in your holes—that is the alternative given by the gas experts. To hide from bombs is evidence of guilt and any GI can act as judge and executioner. Calley is a clean killer in comparison. Who has heard of any "Mitey Mite" operator being brought to trial? One has seen filmed scenes of them dragging out gassed babies and piling them up for the body count!

Accountability for My Lai Extends to All of Us

AS THE TRIAL of Lt. William Calley grinds on its painful course, the evidence mounts that he was as much a victim as a villain.

This in no way excuses the charges against him—the mass murder of 100 civilians and the individual murder of two others—that morning in the war three years ago. Nor, under the Nuremberg doctrine which American prosecutors propounded for the trial of the Germans, can he be excused by proving that he was only acting under orders.

The Nuremberg doctrine specifies that an individual's behavior is his own responsibility, for which he must be held accountable.

But there are circumstances which show clearly how Calley got into his present predicament. They are an indictment of the military system and of the rest of us who, through approval, ignorance or apathy, let it happen.

Taken to its logical conclusion, as Gen. Telford Taylor, one of our Nuremberg prosecutors, took it in a book he wrote recently, accountability extends all the way to the White House.

Calley was hardly the Army's brightest soldier. He graduated 666th out of 731 students in his high school class. He dropped out of junior college with failing grades, and when he finally got through Officer Candidate School, he graduated 119th of 156.

Still, he was smart enough to learn his lessons. And one of the lessons he learned best was to obey orders. His orders that day, he sincerely feels, were to "waste" the Vietnamese.

"Lt. Calley," his attorneys announced a few days ago, "states that he did not feel as if he was killing humans, but rather that they were the enemy with whom he could not speak or reason."

On the witness stand this week, Calley said that originally he had intended to save some Vietnamese civilians for a later attack on a neighboring hamlet called My Lai I.

"It was understood when we made our final assault on My Lai I, we would have had civilians pulled in front of us," he said. The purpose? "Clear the minefields."

Considering that Calley has been judged sane and "normal in every respect," it is only fair to ask where he got such ideas—that the Vietnamese weren't humans, that they could be "wasted" without a second thought, and those saved could properly be used as human detonators.

It came from the Pentagon psychology, in which Orientals are "gooks" or "slopes." It manifests itself not only in the William Calleys, but in an official policy that decrees free fire zones for artillery, indiscriminate bombing raids, search and destroy missions, defoliation, and a scorecard based on body counts.

It is fair to ask, as Newsday asked the other day, whether we would destroy Indochina and its people so viciously if the people were Europeans or ethnically like us.

The next question, then, is that if U.S. policy does not consider these people human, what must the Indochinese think of us? It would be too much to expect them to view us with anything but hatred.

From the *Detroit Free Press*, March 1, 1971.

Hersh: Now Try the Leaders

By DICK BELSKY

"If the Army thinks it has the answer to My Lai by finding Calley guilty of premeditated murder, it's wrong. He's not important. He's just the guy who happened to be on trial."

—*Seymour Hersh, Pulitzer Prize-winning author of My Lai 4, who first broke the story of the massacre.*

Seymour Hersh feels a little sorry for Lt. William Calley today—sorry because it was Calley's cooperation that enabled him to write about what happened when Charlie Company swept through My Lai on March 16, 1968.

"I think" said Hersh, in a telephone interview from Washington, "that Calley was a victim of My Lai just as much as those he shot."

Hersh recalled that it was his conversations with Calley in the fall of 1969 that convinced him the rumors he had been hearing from Pentagon sources about a massacre were true.

Who Else Is Guilty?

"I found Calley down at Fort Benning and asked him about it," Hersh said. "He confirmed everything. He enabled me to write it. It could have been Mitchell (S. Sgt. David Mitchell, acquitted of My Lai massacre charges) or anyone else. But it was Calley.

"If they're going to charge Calley with premeditated murder, the next step is to initiate a million court martials. I think he was guilty of murder. But for the premeditation I think we have to look to the Pentagon and the White House and people like John Kennedy and Lyndon Johnson.

"They were the men who tried to computerize the war, and make the body count all-important. That's where we have to find the premeditation, not in William Calley."

Hersh feels the judicial machinery of the court martial itself was relatively adequate, but he says the basic issues were not really touched on.

'The Real Story'

"I just think the whole procedure—isolating Lt. Calley —is sort of grotesque. What about the racism, what about the fact that Calley had no chance to make a moral judgment, what about all the other brutality?"

"I remember talking to one soldier who told how horrified he was during his first week in Vietnam when he saw an armored personnel carrier go by with 40 human ears on the antenna. He said everyone who had just gotten there said: 'My God.' A week later they were doing the same thing.

"That's the real story of My Lai, and that never really came out in the Calley court martial."

Laws of War

Twenty-five years ago I defended General Yamashita who, after a military trial in Manila and hearing before the United States Supreme Court, was hanged as a war criminal.

Prof. Telford Taylor (NATIONAL AFFAIRS, Feb. 22) is correct when he says that Gen. William Westmoreland, Army Chief of Staff, could be found guilty of the My Lai atrocities under the rules of Yamashita's case.

This is because the statement you quote from Army general counsel Robert E. Jordan III—"a commander cannot be held to be a murderer merely because one of his men commits murder"—does not square with the law. The fact that General Yamashita had no knowledge and indeed could not have known of the atrocities in the Philippines was held immaterial. He was declared a "war criminal" and while that may not be identical to a charge of "murder," the penalty was equally final.

The late Justice Frank Murphy objected to this idea of "command responsibility" and in his dissenting opinion he prophesied that "the fate of some future President of the United States and his Chiefs of Staff and military advisers may well have been sealed by this decision."

Must we try General Westmoreland and former President Johnson for these capital crimes? A better answer would be a frank admission that we were wrong in deviating from the concept that we punish men for committing crimes, not merely for holding jobs. Inherent in convictions for "violations of the laws of war" is the assumption that there are good and bad ways to kill; that it is criminal to shoot unarmed civilians on the ground but legal to bomb them from the skies. If we won't quit trying to solve disputes by killing people, let us at least recognize war for what it is and stop such hypocrisy.

A. FRANK REEL

New York City

■ Calley was doing what he was ordered to do, so why convict him? If he were a high officer's son, the Army would find a way to pardon him.

PAM SEAMAN

DeTour Village, Mich.

Beyond the Calley Verdict

In a courtroom at an Army post in Georgia yesterday, a young officer was formally found guilty of an appalling war crime. It remains for the nation that convicted him to judge the other officers—civilian as well as military—responsible for the continuing crime of the Indochina war and the barbarism countenanced in high places.

No one with even a cursory acquaintance with the testimony in the case of Lt. William Calley Jr. can seriously doubt that he was guilty of the massacre of South Vietnamese civilians at My Lai in 1968. The horrifying record was simply overwhelming; the outstanding question was whether these homicides could be justified in some way as consistent with "orders" from higher commands.

That was not and is not an irrelevant question. To have acquitted Calley would have appeared to be condoning the murders and proclaiming the cheapness of Asian life. But to deny the responsibility of the "chain of command," reaching to the loftiest levels, is to accept the contorted view that the conviction of Lt. Calley somehow brings this monstrous case to a quiet and satisfying close, with justice done at last.

It is not yet clear what Calley's sentence will ultimately be—death or life imprisonment. In any event, long appeals will ensue. But it has been apparent from the outset that neither the Dept. of Defense nor any civilian administration could exculpate itself, no matter what the verdict.

It is not only Lt. Calley who lived by the doctrine that the extermination of unresisting civilians — men, women and children—was "no big deal." On the contrary, this attitude was exactly that of the men of high affairs who, after blundering into war in Indochina and discovering that neither political nor military butchery was successful, nevertheless sought—and still seek—to wash away blood with more blood.

The arguments on the sentencing of Lt. Calley begin today. The arguments on the verdict have barely started; unless they lead to full exploration of the role of men far more eminent than William Calley—whether before military or Congressional tribunals, or both — the United States will have lost both conscience and honor as surely as it has lost its way in Indochina.

ON THE RIGHT

Calley

By WILLIAM F. BUCKLEY JR.

4) As regards the question of ultimate responsibility, the public is entitled to be confused. We hanged Admiral Yamashita after the Second World War, and if we applied rigorously the logic of that execution, we would have a case for hanging General Westmoreland. That would be preposterous and cruel. So that we learn, gradually, what some people knew and warned against in 1945: victors' justice.

We are overdue for shame in our complicity in the Nuremberg-Tokyo trials. But whatever we do to amend these doctrines, it is inconceivable that we should come up with new rules of war that permit to go unpunished such an act as Lieutenant Calley was found guilty of, and I for one am proud of a country that makes such activity punishable by imprisonment or death.

Moreover, the Nuremberg trials after the second world war made clear that the Nazi high government officials. the brass as well as the **individual soldier** were all indeed guilty of the most barbaric war crimes.

What about Calley, is he guilty? We think he is profoundly guilty. He admitted committing the murders. Though Calley was operating within the genocidal framework of the war policy itself and though he had specific orders (from above) to murder at My Lai. we think **Calley had a choice!**

Men in Calley's own company. we must remember. refused to commit the same atrocities at My Lai. Why didn't Calley?

Lieutenant Calley and the President

The furor over the Calley verdict was in its way almost as appalling as Mylai itself, and President Nixon's intervention did not improve matters.

As Telford Taylor wrote in LIFE last week, the verdict was harsh, but acquittal would have been a disaster: here was a responsible officer, not even in the position of being fired upon, who callously mowed down women and children. The sympathy that welled up across the nation was in large part grounded on the notion that Calley was, if not singled out (after all, Mylai is a low point, even in this cruel war, for avoidable cruelty), being made the scapegoat. Others above him were lightly rebuked, or charges against them dismissed. Besides, wasn't Calley, like everyone else in the armed forces, fighting a ruthless enemy?

Such feelings are understandable, but sympathy did not stop here. For some of the doves, Calley was merely a cog in a machine gone mad; everything about the war is wrong, and in the words of a distinguished Washington clergyman: "Calley is all of us. He is every single citizen in our graceless land." On that line of reasoning, responsibility is everyone's and therefore no one's.

Perhaps this kind of masochism, this increasing feeling of national shame and revulsion at the war, helped generate that other excessive response in so many Americans: the sense that Lieutenant Calley was merely doing his duty, a wronged patriot, perhaps even a hero, for whom flags should be lowered and folk ballads sung. George Wallace rushed to make him an honorary lieutenant colonel in the Alabama National Guard. Not to be outdone, President Nixon freed Calley from the stockade while his lawyers appealed his case and was cheered for it in Congress (several of the Democratic presidential aspirants in the Senate were not exactly profiles in courage either).

But this was not to be the President's only intervention. In San Clemente, the press was summoned to be told that whatever course the military appeals took, the President would personally review the case finally in a "nonlegal, nontechnical" fashion. Since the President has such authority anyway, calling it to everybody's attention seemed a presidential play to the political constituency Nixon so often cultivates, and earned an eloquent rebuke (see box) from Captain Aubrey M. Daniel III, who prosecuted Calley. To the officers who must conscientiously pass on Calley's case on appeal, the implication was clear that if they didn't mitigate the lieutenant's life sentence, the President would. In a President who as a lawyer so often speaks out for law and order, in a Commander-in-Chief who should be concerned with the calm, orderly processes of the Uniform Code of Military Justice, Nixon's action was reckless and dismaying.

Excerpts from a letter to President Nixon from Captain Aubrey M. Daniel III, the prosecutor in the Calley trial:

. . . How shocking it is if so many people across this nation have failed to see the moral issue which was involved in the trial of Lieutenant Calley—that it is unlawful for an American soldier to summarily execute unarmed and unresisting men, women, children and babies.

But how much more appalling it is to see so many of the political leaders of the nation who have failed to see the moral issue or, having seen it, compromise it for political motive in the face of apparent public displeasure with the verdict. . . . I have been particularly shocked and dismayed at your decision to intervene in these proceedings in the midst of the public clamor. . . .

Your intervention has, in my opinion, damaged the military judicial system and lessened any respect it may have gained as a result of the proceedings. . . .

For this nation to condone the acts of Lieutenant Calley is to make us no better than our enemies and make any pleas by this nation for the humane treatment of our own prisoners meaningless.

From *Life* magazine, April 16, 1971.

THE BATTLE HYMN OF LT. CALLEY... AND THE REPUBLIC

• • • • • • • • • • • • •

MICHAEL NOVAK

The sleeper in the Calley case is the link between populism and the lesson learned in the Hitler period. It is not enough for a Christian or any moral man merely to be patriotic, or obey orders, or give his conscience over to a bureaucracy. Each man must reflect, choose and pay the consequences. Populism in this case might carry large numbers of "little people" into a tradition of personal responsibility and dissent. Not a few in the South, traditional breeding ground of professional soldiers, have said in recent days that they would now prefer their sons to be draft-dodgers and deserters rather than fall into Lieutenant Calley's shoes. . . . Yes, that's the moral point. That's what the brave young men in the Resistance and among the deserters were trying to say all along. History is already vindicating them.

■ The American people, of course, did not pause to think of the consequences of a "not guilty" verdict. They failed to see that such a verdict could give a U.S. soldier in Vietnam a psychological immunity to the atrocities he committed. Nor did they reason that Hanoi's attitude toward our POW's could worsen. They could execute all American prisoners and idolize the executioners as heroes, imitating America's elevation of Calley to hero status.

RONALD TEEN

Las Vegas, Nev.

DEAR ABBY: I'd like to make a comment on the My Lai incident: I served in Viet Nam at the same time as Lt. Calley. (Same division, same brigade, but different battalion.) What that man and his men are being tried for was, and probably still is, an everyday occurrence over there. I have seen so many of those peaceful people murdered, raped and beaten I thought I'd go crazy before I got out of that country.

No single similar occurrence in my unit was on so large a scale as My Lai, but if I were to total all the men, women and children we shot because they looked like V.C. in the age group between 15 and 40 or were too scared to stand still when we approached, you could double the number as were killed at My Lai.

I am not defending Lt. Calley, I am only saying that if the Army and the people must judge that man and his men then they had better judge me and the three million other men that pulled time in that hell-hole.

I learned one thing. Life over there is worth no more than the time and effort it takes to pull the trigger.

BEEN THERE

DEAR BEEN: Thank you, soldier. And to the American people as a whole, I say, "Judge not lest ye be judged ."

Above left, from *Commonweal*, April 30, 1971.

Left, reprinted by permission of the Chicago Tribune—New York News Syndicate, Inc.

Above, letter to the editor of *Newsweek* by Ronald Teen, April 26, 1971.

Conscientious Objectors, Draft-Dodgers, and Military Obligations

The very statement of the problem of conscientious objection raises the basic question "What is conscience?" Is it an inner voice that whispers moral advice, and causes us mental (or spiritual) discomfort when we act wrongly? If it is, why believe that it is a reliable source of advice? When two individuals' consciences issue conflicting moral guidance, how is the resulting disagreement to be resolved? Are some consciences better guides to what is right or wrong than others? Or is an appeal to conscience really a metaphorical way of talking about acting in accordance with reasoned moral beliefs, as opposed to acting from habit, from command, or on impulse? Or is the concept of "conscience" so confused and muddled that it is of no use in determining the proper course of action in particular situations?

Even if we can ultimately resolve such questions, we shall still be a long way from solving the moral problems raised in the arguments in this section. Additional questions concerning civil disobedience and the justifiability of war must be faced, as well as the problematic issues of freedom and responsibility. If, for example, most people clearly are not *totally* responsible for the moral beliefs they hold, then a person who acts in a particular way for "reasons of conscience" *might* be seen as having been compelled in some morally interesting way to so act. Enough has been said for us to see once again that moral problems do not come neatly labeled and that the more important they are, the more difficult they seem to be.

ADVICE TO A DRAFTEE

by Leo Tolstoy

In my last letter I answered your question as well as I could. It is not only Christians but all just people who must refuse to become soldiers — that is, to be ready on another's command (for this is what a soldier's duty actually consists of) to kill all those one is ordered to kill. The question as you state it — which is more useful, to become a good teacher or to suffer for rejecting conscription? — is falsely stated. The question is falsely stated because it is wrong for us to determine our actions according to their results, to view actions merely as useful or destructive. In the choice of our actions we can be led by their advantages or disadvantages only when the actions themselves are not opposed to the demands of morality.

We can stay home, go abroad, or concern ourselves with farming or science according to what we find useful for ourselves or others; for neither in domestic life, foreign travel, farming, nor science is there anything immoral. But under no circumstance can we inflict violence on people, torture or kill them because we think such acts could be of use to us or to others. We cannot and may not do such things, especially because we can never be sure of the results of our actions. Often actions which seem the most advantageous of all turn out in fact to be destructive; and the reverse is also true.

The question should not be stated: which is more useful, to be a good teacher or to go to jail for refusing conscription? but rather: what should a man do who has been called upon for military service — that is, called upon to kill or to prepare himself to kill?

And to this question, for a person who understands the true meaning of military service and who wants to be moral, there is only one clear and incontrovertible answer: such a person must refuse to take part in military service no matter what consequences this refusal may have. It may seem to us that this refusal could be futile or even harmful, and that it would be a far more useful thing, after serving one's time, to become a good village teacher. But in the same way, Christ could have judged it more useful for himself to be a good carpenter and submit to all the principles of the Pharisees than to die in obscurity as he did, repudiated and forgotten by everyone.

Moral acts are distinguished from all other acts by the fact that they operate independently of any predictable advantage to ourselves or to others. No matter how dangerous the situation may be of a man who finds himself in the power of robbers who demand that he take part in plundering, murder, and rape, a moral person cannot take part. Is not military service the same thing? Is one not required to agree to the deaths of all those one is commanded to kill?

But how can one refuse to do what everyone does, what everyone finds unavoidable and necessary? Or, must one do what no one does and what everyone considers unnecessary or even stupid and bad? No matter how strange it sounds, this strange argument is the main one offered against those moral acts which in our times face you and every other person called up for military service. But this argument is even more incorrect than the one which would make a moral action dependent upon considerations of advantage.

If I, finding myself in a crowd of running people, run with the crowd without knowing where, it is obvious that I have given myself up to mass hysteria; but if by chance I should push my way to the front, or be gifted with sharper sight than the others, or receive information that this crowd was racing to attack human beings and toward its own corruption, would I really not stop and tell the people what might rescue them? Would I go on running and do these things which I knew to be bad and corrupt? This is the situation of every individual called up for military service, if he knows what military service means.

I can well understand that you, a young man full of life, loving and loved by your mother, friends, perhaps a young woman, think with a natural terror about what awaits you if you refuse conscription; and perhaps you will not feel strong enough to bear the consequences of refusal, and knowing your weakness, will submit and become a soldier. I understand completely, and I do not for a moment allow myself to blame you, knowing very well that in your place I might perhaps do the same thing. Only do not say that you did it because it was useful or because everyone does it. If you did it, know that you did wrong.

In every person's life there are moments in which he can know himself, tell himself who he is, whether he is a man who values his human dignity above his life or a weak creature who does not know his dignity and is concerned merely with being useful (chiefly to himself). This is the situation of a man who goes out to defend his honor in a duel or a soldier who goes into battle (although here the concepts of life are wrong). It is the situation of a doctor or a priest called to someone sick with plague, of a man in a burning house or a sinking ship who must decide whether to let the weaker go first or shove them aside and save himself. It is the situation of a man in poverty who accepts or rejects a bribe. And in our times, it is the situation of a man called to military service. For a man who knows its significance, the call to the army is perhaps the only opportunity for him to behave as a morally free creature and fulfill the highest requirement of his life — or else merely to keep his advantage in sight like an animal and thus remain slavishly submissive and servile until humanity becomes degraded and stupid.

For these reasons I answered your question whether one has to refuse to do military service with a categorical "yes" — if you understand the meaning of military service (and if you did not understand it then, you do now) and if you want to behave as a moral person living in our times must.

Please excuse me if these words are harsh. The subject is so important that one cannot be careful enough in expressing oneself so as to avoid false interpretation.

April 7, 1899 LEO TOLSTOY

Spread of objections of conscience

must be halted

One thing must be made plain from the very beginning — demands for a defence tax (Wehrsteuer) must be accompanied by demands for a better army. Defence tax can only have a sound purpose if it is considered as a way to adapt general conscription to the age in which we live.

All considerations must be based on the duty of protecting the community. Providing external security is a binding commitment on everybody. This can be achieved in a number of ways. One of these is by becoming a soldier.

What we now understand by defending our country has been largely freed of the pathos of a personal sacrifice of life and limb.

NATO armies are trained for war, it is true. They must be able to fight. The martial spirit must not be extinguished.

But their military role is given a political interpretation. The army is a means of preventing war. It has to exist as a threat to others. Its deterrent effect is one of the cornerstones of the strategy of maintaining peace.

Diplomatic flexibility, political will, industrial power, technical organisation, economic opportunity and treaties of alliance are the other factors of our strategy.

Conscription and the soldiers thus provided are essential to external security. Soldiers are important but they do not stand at the centre of planning for this work-sharing strategy. Not all the young people liable for conscription are calles up. A selection can be made among them.

Conscription must be interpreted differently than was once the case. It is no longer the reservoir for a large armed body. It must be compared with the readiness of the modern industrial nation to contribute to external security in a large number of fields.

In times of peace a measurable form of action for the security of the community is the financial contribution of the individual in preserving the common good.

Everyone pays for our external security by paying taxes. Those who do military service in addition are taking over further burdens.

Starting from the fact that everyone has to pay taxes and that events do not force everyone to do military service, a person cannot fail to come to the conclusion that a person who does military service should pay less.

Nobody will underestimate the technical difficulties involved in shifting various parts of the tax burden. The first thing to do is to work out the financial value of the service period.

The period during which a person is freed from paying taxes need not necessarily be the same as the time he spends in the reserves. How are people who want to serve yet are not recruited to be treated?

But really all these questions can be answered during the course of events. The main point to be recognised when discussing the problem of a defence tax is that the contribution to external security can take a number of forms.

Military service too must be viewed as a special type of defence tax. At the same time it must be freed from the myth that it is a *levée en masse*.

The old idea of the indissolubility of the right of the citizen to be provided with defence and his duty to provide it is no longer relevant in an industrial nation. We have become more sober. We are satisfied by the duty alone.

This type of attitude makes it easier for a government to approach the ideal production State. Even the mention of "military autonomy" could not be used to prevent modern interpretations of the role of army and State.

If military defence tax is to be understood as compensation, it is easy to draw up laws to satisfy the moral and political demands of soldiers for balanced personal treatment in a democracy.

The way would also be cleared for greater justice in the armed forces. The chance that often decides whether a person is conscripted or not has done a lot to contribute to the disinclination toward doing armed service.

Conscientious objection may be traced to the recognition that modern European war is no longer a battle between knights but a military form of mutual extermination. A sensitive conscience must be respected.

But a large number of young conscripts know that their role is to provide security. Many have understood what deterrent strategy entails.

The suspicion is therefore justified that there is a link between conscientious objection and the injustice surrounding conscription. There is no other explanation for the flood of applications to be excused military service on the grounds of conscientious objection.

11,446 applications have already been received in the first quarter of 1971. Six thousand applications were made during the whole of 1967, twelve thousand in 1968 and nineteen thousand in 1970.

It is estimated that by the end of 1971 more than 100,000 applications will have been made since the Bundeswehr was set up.

The Bundestag could not ignore this fact during its debate on the subject. Unorthodox action is necessary if the situation is to be changed.

Adelbert Weinstein
(Frankfurter Allgemeine Zeitung für Deutschland. 12 May 1971)

Originally published in *Frankfurter Allgemeine Zeitung*, May 12, 1971.

And What About Situation Ethics?

By FR. A. H. GOLDSCHMIDT, S.A.C.

Probably nothing has done more harm to many consciences than the present emphasis on situation ethics or conscience morals as it is sometimes called. Speaking about situation ethics I do not mean a philosophical system that still recognizes a set of fast outside norms and rules. I only mean situation ethics as it is currently widely promulgated and preached; a situation ethics that ignores and rejects practically all laws and norms outside one's conscience. In other words I mean that kind of situation ethics which emphasizes that the conscience of each individual is the sole and supreme norm and arbiter of man's behavior. And it is this type of situation ethics that has produced profound bewilderment and perplexity in the minds of many. Confusion has seized the minds of a great many people. I think this is really the mother heresy of our time. Hand in hand with this new teaching goes the minimizing and de-emphasizing of every outside standard or law — be it God's law, the Ten Commandments or any sound natural law. The jargon is: "only follow your conscience"; "do what you think or feel is the right and best thing to do!" Well, Mr. Hitler did just that, and the results were a little bit awkward, weren't they! The harm that has been done by the pseudo-writers, teachers and preachers cannot be measured!

Situation ethics teaches that the given situation is the supreme law, and that personal feelings and considerations are the final norm for behavior. It is the theory of Heidegger, Paul Sartre and others.

Their principal thesis is: "Man is free to choose irrespective of moral or ethical principles." Any law, divine or natural must be ignored. Only what advances man, his position, his ideals and his gains in the exclusively existing mundane realm has value. A business man may employ any tactics and any means as long as he is successful businesswise. There are no norms from the outside. The situation is the supreme law.

Just imagine what would result from such a philosophy! Each one would be allowed to act and behave freely by the dictates and the whims of his conscience, regardless of the weal and woe of his fellowmen. Each one's conscience is supreme! In the final analysis this would dispense with all authority, with all rules that would guarantee safety for the community. It would spell anarchy. Would this make for a happy society?

But don't get me wrong. I do not mean to say that conscience has no significance at all. By no means. It does play an important part in our lives. What I mean to say about conscience is that it must be informed. It must conform to eternally fixed standards — norms that lie outside man. It must harmonize with God's eternal laws. It cannot be a conscience independent of these laws. It cannot be a biased and prejudiced conscience, merely guided by momentary situations. Conscience must be in conformity with objective truth, justice and love. It must be in harmony with the very nature of all things. I am speaking of normal conditions. However, there may be a case where a man is sincerely convinced and having no doubt whatsoever that he must act as he sees it, although he may be objectively wrong. This man must obey his conscience. St. Paul writes in this sense: "Whatever is done in bad faith (or conscience) is a sin." (Rom. 14:23) Similarly, St. James (4:17). The man would be in bad faith if he acted against his conscience. If, however, one has a doubt about a certain matter, he would have to make every effort as far as he can to clear up the doubt before he acts.

From *The Wanderer*, September 10, 1970.

COMING TO A DECISION

Up to this point these pages have been impersonally concerned with facts. An effort has been made to avoid the present. But the times cannot help but intrude. In Vietnam, Thailand, Cambodia, Laos, Peru and Guatemala, Americans are fighting wars large and small. The threat of other wars is constantly present. Even where there are presently no bombs falling and no napalm-charred bodies, there is a more subtle violence, institutionalized and gunless—what some have termed the violence of the status quo. This is the form of violence which allows exhaustion to rob men and women of half their lives in order that a relative handful may live in luxury and which gives arms production priority over health and education.

The draft is the most serious and immediate point of contact most Americans have with the machinery of war, an institution compelling us to confront the life-and-death realities from which millions of others have no hope of escaping. Point after point decisions have to be made, and by no means easy ones: to register, or not to register; to fill out, or not to fill out draft forms; to accept or reject various classifications; to report—or not to—for draft board hearings, physicals, induction itself, and there whether to take the step forward into uniform.

Making a responsible decision is no easy matter. Not only must decision be an act of intelligence and will, it must be rooted in man's most crucial and mysterious faculty, that of conscience. It is not unlikely that great courage may be required.

At least it is now clear that none of us can any longer accept as God's will what congressmen, generals and draft officials might wish of us. Unthinking obedience has at last been made to stand without a virtuous or even patriotic facade; our concepts, both regarding love of man and love of native land, have been considerably enriched and expanded. In the words of the Fathers of the Second Vatican Council, we have learned that "Man's dignity demands that he act according to a free choice that is personally motivated and prompted from within, not under blind internal impulse nor by mere external pressures." (*Constitution on the Church in the Modern World*, Section 17.) We have come to realize, though sometimes at great cost in suffering, that freedom and happiness ultimately spring from the individual's willingness to take responsibility for the use of his life.

The study and listening, the prayer and meditation that go into the decision-making process need hardly be described here. Obviously the peacemaker is first of all one who can listen and is eager to learn, one who is willing to try and see the world as others see it, no matter how incomprehensible other cultures or persons may seem.

But what is more difficult to speak of is the centrality of love, a much-abused word. "Love in practice is a harsh and dreadful thing compared to love in dreams," Dostoevsky wrote. Where love is, no token response will suffice. It is the opening of one's whole self to the pressing needs of others. It is to understand that French proverb which declares, "When we die, we carry in our clutched hands only that which we have given away."

The Council Fathers speak of this activized love in the *Constitution on the Church in the Modern World:*

"This Council lays stress on reverence for man; everyone must consider his every neighbor without exception as another self, taking into account first his life and the means necessary to living it with dignity, so as not to imitate the rich man who had no concern for the poor man Lazarus.

"In our time a special obligation binds us to make ourselves the neighbor of every person without exception, and of actively helping him when he comes across our path . . ." (Section 27.)

That in the end love is the measure, there is no doubt:

"Come you blessed of my Father and take possession of the kingdom prepared for you from the foundation of the world. For I was hungry and you gave me food, thirsty and you gave me drink; I was a stranger and you brought me home, naked and you clothed me, sick and you cared for me, a prisoner and you came to me . . . Believe me, what you did to the least of my brothers, that you did to me." (Matthew 25.)

Against the invitation to love and care stand the ceaseless commands of those—and they are found in every country and across all ideological frontiers—who believe power comes out of the barrel of a gun. Their commands—to burn, to starve, to make homeless and naked, to imprison, to march in step, to obey without pause—remain eternally in conflict to the ways of mercy, peace and justice.

The rewards for a life founded in the works of mercy are not pictured in magazine advertisements. The "reward" granted Jesus, though turned into an ornament and made synonomous with comfort and respectability, is still the criminal's cross. And for all the reverence showered upon those who have taught the way of liberation and the power of love, few are yet free enough to follow that path no matter where it may lead. For us, as for the disciples at the foot of the cross, the resurrection still seems incomprehensible.

THE UN-JUST WAR C.O.

"It wasn't I who persecuted the Jews," the planner of German death camps, Adolph Eichmann, told his jurors. "That was done by the government. Obedience has always been praised as a virtue. I accuse the rulers of abusing my obedience."

Millions today realize that there is often an unbridgeable chasm between conscience and obedience—even between common sense and obedience. The realization has been stimulated in large measure by public horror at the crimes committed by otherwise good and decent citizens—all acting under the seal of obedience and patriotism—during recent times just as during the era of Adolph Eichmann.

On the floor of the Second Vatican Council, Bishop John Taylor of Stockholm emphasized the particular responsibility of Christians to place intelligence and conscience above the demands of authority:

"In view of the monstrous crimes committed by both sides in war and Christians' past involvement in these through unquestioning submission to authority, Christians confronted today by the possibility of even more terrible crimes cannot surrender their moral judgment on wars to civil authorities. They have instead the responsibility, in justice and charity, to examine the orders of authority and to bear witness, as conscience demands, to the peace of Christ and the sacredness of human life."

The American Catholic bishops, in a pastoral letter of November, 1968, have called for laws recognizing the objector to particular wars.

"As witnesses to a spiritual tradition which accepts enlightened conscience, even when honestly mistaken," they declared, "we can only feel reassured by this evidence of individual responsibility and the decline of uncritical conformism . . . if war is ever to be outlawed, and replaced by more humane and enlightened institutions to regulate conflict between nations, institutions rooted in the universal common good, it will be because the citizens of this and other nations have rejected the tenets of exaggerated nationalism and insisted on principles of nonviolent political and civic action in both the domestic and international spheres."

Citing the present legal provisions for conscientious objection to war in general, they go on to say, "We consider that the time has come to urge that similar consideration be given those whose reasons of conscience are more personal and specific."

Yet despite the lengthy procession of Catholics who have for one reason or another refused to take up the sword—or wear a military uniform or take a military oath—the question continues to be asked: Does a Catholic have the right to withhold his services from the government in its wars or preparations for war? Can a Catholic be a conscientious objector? Can a Catholic be a draft resister?

UNQUALIFIEDLY YES

The constant teaching of the Church regarding the primacy of conscience, the Church's consistent application of this teaching in defense of Catholic conscientious objectors and, not least, the continued presence of such objectors throughout Church history would indicate that the answer is unqualifiedly yes.

In defining conscience, the Fathers of the Second Vatican Council wrote into the *Constitution on the Church in the Modern World* the following:

"In the depths of his conscience, man detects a law which he does not impose upon himself, but which holds him to obedience. Always summoning him to love good and avoid evil, the voice of conscience when necessary speaks to his heart: do this, shun that. For man has in his heart a law written by God; to obey it is the very dignity of man; according to it he will be judged. (Rom. 2, 15-16.) Conscience is the most secret core and sanctuary of man. There he is alone

Left and above, from the booklet *Catholics and Conscientious Objection*, published by The Catholic Peace Fellowship, 339 Lafayette Street, New York, N.Y. 10012.

with God, whose voice echoes in his depths. (Pius XII, March 23, 1952.) In a wonderful manner conscience reveals that law which is fulfilled by love of God and neighbor. (Matt. 22, 37-40; Gal. 5, 14.) In fidelity to conscience, Christians are joined with the rest of men in the search for truth, and for the genuine solution to the numerous problems which arise in the life of individuals and from social relationships. Hence, the more right conscience holds sway, the more persons and groups turn aside from blind choice and strive to be guided by the objective norms of morality. Conscience frequently errs from invincible ignorance without losing its dignity. The same cannot be said for a man who cares but little for truth and goodness, or for a conscience which by degrees grows practically sightless as a result of habitual sin." (Sec. 16.)

Addressing themselves more specifically to the problem of war, in the same document, the Council Fathers called for legal recognition of the rights of conscientious objectors to war: "It seems right that laws make humane provisions for those who for reasons of conscience refuse to bear arms, provided, however, that they agree to serve the human community in some other way." (Sec. 79.)

A Thorny Question: Selective Conscientious Objection

A MORAL DILEMMA

Thus there is a real moral dilemma involved for the conscience of the individual as he faces the question not only of the justice of a particular war, or the justice of his own society, but the justification of his own actions in the light of what he claims to believe. If he holds that his own society is basically immoral, is there any way in which he can justify drawing benefits from it?

And if he believes he must make war against his society through encouragement of revolutionary activity, is he not acting in contradictory fashion to claim any kind of immunity from it by asking for provision for conscientious objection, whether selective or absolute? Is he not asking a society which he believes to be basically immoral to act in a moral way in connection with what he holds to be his own rights? Either he is wrong in regarding the society as fundamentally immoral, in which case he can of course appeal to its sense of fairness and morality in considering his plea for conscientious objection; but he must then give up his revolutionary attitude towards it. Or if it is truly immoral, he has no reason to expect that it should act morally towards him. This basic contradiction in making use of the legal processes of a society at the same time that one regards that society as essentially illegitimate, is what dilutes the moral credit of many of these conscientious objectors.

MORAL RESPONSIBILITY

In any case of selective conscientious objection, there exists the question of one's moral responsibility for the welfare of the society from which one has drawn so many benefits of both a material and a cultural nature — the argument which Socrates uses in justification of the Laws of Athens in the *Crito*, when he is being urged by his friends to escape from the condemnation which has been passed upon him by his own city. There is often an assumption in revolutionary circles that the person in revolt somehow sits enthroned in judgment above the society of which he is a member. This is to ignore the facts of cultural formation and the way in which the individual is dependent upon society for his personal development. Thus, if one condemns things taking place in the society in which he lives, this can not be justly done unless one is aware of his responsibility for trying to purify the society of its faults — he must not permit himself to condemn it outright as something completely alien to himself.

Above, *The Wanderer*, April 22, 1971.

65

Former Senator Gruening on the Need to End the Draft Now

The opposition to letting the draft expire, as it already has, on June 30, last, is based on dire predictions. One columnist labels the prospect of non-resumption of the draft as a "catastrophe" and forecasts that in that event the United States would become a second-class power in six months! And some of the same prophecies of doom have characterized the eloquence of draft supporters in the White House, the Pentagon and the Congress. Our nation has now been without a draft for two and a half months and the foundations of the Republic, however, impaired by economic problems, by mounting inflation, mounting unemployment, mounting pollution and mounting crime, have not been noticeably impaired by the draftless interlude.

Is it not high time that the Congress faced the human aspects of the basic moral issues involved in human liberty? For a century and three quarters our country was free of a peacetime draft. It was imposed only in time of war, in times when our nation was seriously threatened—the Civil War and World Wars I and II. It was not until a quarter of a century ago that, for the first time, Congress adopted peacetime conscription, thus reversing a hallowed tradition. One which had long established the difference between America, the land of freedom and the Old World. Since then we have steadily become a more and more militaristic nation. Our military costs—so-called "defense"—have mounted to astronomical levels to the neglect of our vital domestic problems, solution of which would restore the strength, unity and well-being and confidence of our people previously enjoyed. Despite these war outlays, the people feel less secure than when we did not have the greatest Navy, Air Force and "defense" establishment on the earth.

It was the draft that made it possible for our leaders to deceive the American people into the longest, costliest, least justifiable and most unpopular war in our history. Even though the Tonkin Gulf Resolution based on spurious incidents has been repealed, the war goes on at costs not yet computable, and the resumption of the draft would be another potent factor in keeping the monstrosity going. It is at the root of our unprecedented domestic troubles.

We have been told by the White House for four and a half years that the war is about to be ended. "Winding down the war" is the phrase echoed on the Hill. Every so often the President announces the withdrawal of more thousands of troops. Why then is it necessary to draft more kids and send them in the opposite direction to engage in senseless slaughter?

The draftee is the victim of unique discrimination. Those in the various armed services, Army, Navy, Air Force, Marine Corps, who enlisted voluntarily know that they would have to go when they are ordered to go. The draftee on the other hand is subjected in the vast majority of cases to the involuntary servitude which our Thirteenth Amendment prohibits.

By now our young people know that our nation was lied into this war. (Some of us knew it before the publication of the Pentagon papers.) Quite properly then object to being compelled to fight in a war in which no vital American interest is in jeopardy, to kill people against whom they feel no grievance, participate in what has become a mass slaughter of civilians, and maybe to get killed or maimed in the process. But if they refuse to go, if they follow their consciences, they face imprisonment at hard labor with all the disastrous consequences for their future.

This is an infamous dilemma to which no citizen of a people that calls itself "free" should be subject. This issue transcends all others. It is crucial. Upon its solution will depend in large part whether our long great peace-loving society will return to what we have loved and cherished, or whether we shall slide further into the abyss into which misleadership has plunged us.

A heavy responsibility rests on every senator. He will have to decide whether or not he will sentence more young men to fight and possibly die or be maimed and kill others in an utterly discredited cause.

ERNEST GRUENING.

Washington.

The writer is former U.S. Senator from Alaska.

The extension of the draft into a universal invasion of privacy would be a disaster. Even if we were not at war, the draft would be under attack today because it goes so profoundly against conscience. Coercion will no longer work; the same person who will volunteer to teach a child in the ghetto will bolt when drafted to do the same thing. The enactment of Universal National Service would convince millions of young Americans that they had been sold into indentured servitude, and could precipitate the kind of rebellion that many people fear. To predict this reaction is not extreme in light of what the commission said about the draft:

Compelling service . . . undermines respect for government by forcing an individual to serve when and in the manner the government chooses, regardless of his own values and talents. . . . The draft erodes ideals of patriotism and service by alienating many of the young men who bear its burden. American youths are raised in an atmosphere where freedom and justice are held dear. It is difficult for them to cope with a situation which falls far short of these ideals just as they enter adulthood. The draft undermines identification with society just at the age when young men begin to assume social responsibility. It thwarts the national desire of youth to commit themselves to society.

Mandatory National Service is immoral, impractical and arrogant.

The recommendations of presidential commissions have not had a good track record, but if we can salvage nothing else from the report of the Commission on an All-Volunteer Armed Force let us heed its low-key but imperative statement: "The cure for inequity is not its extension."

Above, letter to the Editor of *The Washington Post* by Ernest Gruening, September 21, 1971.

Principles carry heavy price

Young Steven Claude Murray's refusal to be inducted for military service, for which he could draw a five-year prison term when sentenced by federal Judge William Copple in September, is one of those agonizing dilemmas that has become increasingly familiar in recent years.

The 23-year old former Eagle Scout, who graduated with honors from Camelback High School before going to Occidental College and the University of Arizona, explained his "personal pledge of noncooperation" w i t h Selective Service this way in a letter to President Nixon, prior to his actual refusal to serve: "I have come to believe that all men are brothers quite literally . . . To carry a draft card is to place the needs of the state above those of the individual and to sign my most precious possession, my life, over to the s t a t e to be used where, when, and how it chooses."

Such a blanket rejection of conscription, while based on idealistic notions of world brotherhood and nonviolence, does not address itself to the question of the obligations a man accepts when he freely avails himself of the civilizational life made possible by the existence of the state.

Personal moral convictions are compromised, even degraded, if they are invoked to justify a one-sided repudiation of the contract of civil society. A person is guilty of moral insensitivity if he is moved to evade the draft because of a personal belief about the iniquity of a citizen's military obligation, when the very structure of our freedom depends from moment to moment on the vigilant maintenance of Armed F o r c e s that only the American state can provide. Nevertheless, one must grudgingly admire the person who willingly accepts the consequences of his noncooperation, rather than flees to Canada or exile elsewhere.

What is in store for Steven Murray is not yet known. He is already suffering in the grim surroundings of prison life while he undergoes a three-month period of observation and study before final sentencing. The immediate effects of his action will be anguish and heartbreak for his f a m i l y and friends and serious damage to his own previously bright future.

And so Steven Murray will go to jail in defense of his principles. No doubt he regards that as the lesser of two evils. It is our duty to respect that choice. Nevertheless, we must wonder whether the young man — all young men, in fact — truly understands the nature of our political order and the obligations of citizenship in a free society.

It is one thing to take a stand on principle after a careful assessment of all the issues. It is yet another to be led to take a position at the urging of self-appointed spokesmen for what is moral and ethical. And the tragedy of public debate today is that youngsters like Steven Murray all too often are victims, even though willing victims, of political pitchmen who goad them into adopting an ill-thought out stance that they may come to regret forever more.

Draft Defiance

On Monday, March 8, heavyweight champion Joe Frazier decisively beat Muhammad Ali, whose life in and out of the ring has been disrupted for more than three years by his efforts to avoid the draft. Curiously, that same day the Supreme Court rendered a decision that, while it did not concern Ali directly, did speak to the issue of selective conscientious objection.

Guy P. Gillette and Louis A. Negre had argued that they were opposed in principle not to all war but to the one being waged in Viet Nam. The court ruled that conscientious objectors, religious or otherwise, must be opposed to "participation in war in any form." Objection to a specific war affords no grounds for relief from military service. The vote of the court was 8 to 1.

The decision of the high court is sound if for no other reason than that the alternative would be chaotic. However, it still leaves unanswered the question of what Christians ought to do if they conscientiously believe that a particular war is immoral. No one can dispute the fact that some wars are immoral and offensive to Christian conscience. Any Christian who feels this way about a particular war should obey his conscience and refuse to serve. When God's law and Caesar's are at variance, then God's law must prevail. The Christian who so determines must then face and accept whatever penalty he is required to pay for his refusal to obey Caesar's law if he wishes to stay within Caesar's domain. This is suffering for righteousness' sake. He is free not to obey, but he is not free to run away from the consequences of his disobedience. Nor is he free to presume that his decision is infallible and that other Christians who see matters differently are necessarily wrong.

Gillette and Negre, who did not base their cases on Christian grounds, lost their fight. Now let them pay the price for their convictions. Muhammad Ali lost a boxing match the same day. It remains to be seen whether he soon will lose a second and perhaps greater battle over the draft. □

■ New York Congresswoman Bella Abzug recently appeared before the House Armed Services Committee, where she harangued against continuing the draft, characterizing it as "immoral." Rep. Abzug found her congressional peers less easily finessed than the New York electorate, however. Why, asked Rep. O. Clark Fisher (D., Texas), is it immoral? Because, replied Mrs. Abzug, it violates "freedom of individual rights." "Do you apply that same standard . . . to Israel?" asked Rep. Fisher "What other countries do is a matter of national policy for them to decide," she answered. "I see," said Fisher dryly. "Then you feel it is a matter for each country to determine based on the problems and responsibilities they are confronted with. Your revulsion against conscription is not universal. Morally you think it's wrong only in the U.S." Replied Mrs. Abzug: "Yes, that is my view."

Above, from *National Review*,
April 20, 1971.

Left, copyright 1971 by *Christianity Today*; reprinted by permission.

Top page, from *The Arizona Republic*, June 13, 1971.

Exile Or Prosecution
Draft-Dodgers' Choice

A MAN who renounced his U.S. citizenship four years ago to avoid the draft has now come face to face with the consequences of his act. A Supreme Court decision has confirmed that he is a "man without a country" and faces deportation.

Although Thomas Glenn Jolley took the unusual step of formally foreswearing his birthright, he is not alone in being divorced from his native land as a result of his determination to escape military service. American draft-dodgers and military deserters in Canada, Sweden and elsewhere are more or less in the same boat. Although they may still claim U.S. citizenship, they must choose between self-imposed exile or a return to America to answer for violations of the law.

There is a notion arising that because U.S. forces are being withdrawn from Vietnam, the moral stigma and legal consequences attached to desertion or draft evasion are somehow lightened. Arguments are advanced that it is wrong to exact justice for violations of the Military Code or the Selective Service Act that were committed in the name of "protest" during the height of the Vietnam war. President Nixon has been urged to grant amnesty to t h e s e offenders. One Democrat c a n d i d a t e for president, Sen. George McGovern, has even made amnesty for draft dodgers a plank in his platform.

Moral issues do not change with headlines, nor does the meaning of our laws. Amnesty for these offenders would make a mockery of the sacrifice of all those who have obeyed the call to national service and fulfilled their enlistment oath, and all who would be asked to do so in the future. The dignity of the law, including the obligation of each citizen to obey it, has been abused enough in our c o u n t r y without the body blow that would be dealt it by such an amnesty.

"To err is human, to forgive divine." What of those young men who were led into a disgraceful act by the deceptive counsel of others, who now with greater maturity can recognize their folly and are filled with regret? They deserve sympathy, and justice is certainly not without mercy. The road is open to each to satisfy both his conscience and the law by returning to his country and pleading his case before a court. It is the function of our courts to determine degrees of guilt or innocence in individual cases.

Some organizations continue to try to coax young men who are wavering in their sense of duty across an awful line that is so difficult to recross. It would be a pity if more should be pulled into the moral abyss of desertion by a meaningless and grossly irresponsible offer of "sanctuary" by that radical-dominated council.

The fact is that there can be no real sanctuary for deserters or draft evaders—in Canada or elsewhere — nor should the prospect of amnesty be held out to ease the burden they must bear. Having turned one's back on a moral duty, there is no refuge — except to turn around and confront the consequences of one's own behavior.

Above, from *Illinois State Journal*, November 26, 1971.

Right, letter to the editor of *Illinois State Journal* by James Krohe, Jr., December 6, 1971.

Raps Draft-Dodgers Editorial

Journal Editor:

I've just finished reading your editorial of November 26 e n t i t l e d "Draft-Dodgers' Choice."

I must take exception to the opinions there expressed concerning the issue of amnesty for these young men who have flown the country to escape the Vietnam draft.

In that editorial you posed this question, "What of those young men who were led into a disgraceful act by the deceptive counsel of others, who now with greater maturity can recognize their folly and are filled with regret?" To that I pose this question: What of those young men who followed the deceptive counsel of men like yourself, who for years have confused morality with a shop-worn and dubiously legal "duty," and have been forced out of ignorance or deceit to resort to sloganeering to justify a war that was at best a mistake, and at worst a crime against principle?

It is true, as you stated on the 26th, that "some organizations continue to try to coax young men who are wavering in their sense of duty across an awful line that is so difficult to recross."

One of these organizations is the U.S. Army. Another is the Copley Press. Both have been tiresome in their attempts to convince the public to forsake its moral responsibility and to support a war that should never have been fought.

"Having turned one's back on a moral duty, there is no refuge" is an opinion you share with the many thousands of young Americans who have chosen exile or imprisonment as the only possible alternative to a war that is both politically suicidal and morally repugnant.

James Krohe Jr.
Springfield

The process of the law

An important function of law is to help people settle into predictable social relationships so that they will know what is expected of them and what, in turn, they can expect from other people. To this end, law establishes norms, standards, and codes of conduct.

Laws are subject to revision and redefinition by the bodies charged with giving them form—that is, through the interpretations of the judiciary and the prescriptions of legislatures.

If lawmaking bodies decide that certain strictures have ceased to apply, then a revision is formally codified, and people again know how they stand in relation to others.

Were it left up to each man to decide how every law is to be observed, society would cease to cohere and people would ram into one another like random molecules. If each individual decided whether the law applied to him when it forbade t h e f t, forgery, drunken driving, and all the other statutory offenses, no individual would be safe in his person.

And yet we sometimes hear, for instance, that an individual must take a "moral" stand against the law providing for the military draft, because it is "immoral."

We ourselves believe that the government should not exert a prior claim to a person's services through compulsory federal service—whether w i t h the military draft or with a proposed "civilian" draft for such things as the Peace Corps or VISTA.

However, the logic of this anti-compulsion position is not helped when draft protesters dump themselves on courtroom floors, such as a 20-year-old Scottsdale man did recently when he was sentenced to prison for refusing to be drafted.

In fact, the man had not pursued the legal course open to him because he had not sought to qualify as a conscientious objector, an honorable classification to anyone who claims it truthfully.

Instead, he made the predictable statement about not surrendering his conscience to legislation.

The fact is, however, that the weak, the defenseless, and minorities are among those most often protected precisely because citizens are willing to abide by laws laid down to regularize societal behavior—because people are willing to "s u r r e n d e r their conscience," as the Scottsdale man might archly phrase it, for others' good.

Those who say they have the "right" to defy "immoral" laws often seem to be unaware that they encourage others to disobey all law, just and unjust. And a lawless society, or one where citizens pick and choose which laws to obey, is an uncivilized society.

Which Side Needs the Pardon?

The amnesty question is a thicket of thorny moral issues. One school would interpret amnesty as a generous pardon from the state for youthful transgressions. Others insist that it is the government, not the exiles, that should be seeking pardon. In their view, amnesty would be a "mea culpa" from a guilty government, a sort of official act of contrition for the war. Most of the exiles themselves feel strongly that they have done nothing wrong. "It's not a question of the government forgiving us," contends Rick Thome, a deserter now living in Vancouver. "The United States has to be willing, for once, to admit it made a mistake."

Top page, from *The Arizona Republic*, December 10, 1971.
Above, from *Newsweek*, January 1971.

A Time to Close the Book

Indeed, the broadest support for amnesty seems to come from those who take it literally—the word comes from the Greek for "forgetfulness." Amnesty in this sense would be a recognition that the moral equations on Vietnam are too complicated and too painful to keep endlessly computing. It might very well include not only draft evaders but also deserters, since the difference between them is often only one of class: the better educated and more sophisticated evade, the others don't know what they're getting into until they are already serving. And some make a case for covering American troops who have been convicted of war crimes as well—on the argument that a true national reconciliation must include all who have been caught up in the special pressures and dilemmas that Vietnam has produced.

Civil Disobedience– The Individual versus the State

"Give unto Caesar that which is Caesar's and unto God that which is God's." This is one of the oldest statements of the view that man has two kinds of duty—moral and legal. This particular statement seems to imply that this is a simple dichotomy, that all cases fall clearly into one category or the other. But, unfortunately, situations frequently arise in which an individual discovers that his moral duties conflict with his obligations to the state, and vice versa. When confronted with such a conflict in duties, many people act on the assumption that moral duties are superior in the sense that conflicts between moral and legal obligations should be resolved in favor of the former. This is in part what is expressed in the famous dictum "An unjust law is not a law." This view is far from universally accepted and the selections in this section will focus on this basic disagreement as manifested in a variety of concrete cases.

"Why should one obey the law?" is not a legal question. No one can seriously wonder whether there is a legal duty to do one's legal duty. Actually, the question is a moral one, which can be rephrased as "Does anyone have a moral duty to obey the law?" Bear in mind that "One ought to obey all laws" and "There are no laws one ought to obey" do not exhaust the possibilities. In seeking to answer this question one should not fasten his attention on legal prohibitions to killing, stealing, slander, and the like. For these laws prohibit actions that people ought not to perform anyway, whatever the legal situation may be. The most important class of laws to pay attention to in trying to answer our question, then, includes those laws which enjoin or proscribe actions that one presumably would have no moral obligations to do or forbear doing independently of a law's existence. That is, to show that one has a moral obligation to obey the law, one has to show that the fact that a law says "Do A" can and does make it a man's moral obligation to do A.

There is a close connection between showing that a particular government is, morally speaking, a good thing and showing that one ought to obey its laws. Many arguments try to show that one ought to obey the laws of a government on the grounds that disobeying them jeopardizes the existence of something valuable or good. What makes a government *worthy* of continued existence is a difficult question, but it is one that frequently cannot be avoided. A good way to see the importance of this question is to examine the premises (explicit and implicit) of the arguments in this section. It will become readily apparent that a crucial premise or assumption for many of the arguments is that the maintenance of the legal and political system of the United States is a desirable end. Some people would claim that it is unpatriotic to ask "Why?" of this premise; but such an attitude seems to reflect a deep-seated fear that the question is not answerable. Surely, if a given system of government *is* good and ought to exist, then reasons can be given for supporting it.

If one concludes that civil disobedience is morally justifiable in certain situations, questions must still be faced as to what form the disobedience should take—violent or nonviolent. It should be noted that violent civil disobedience on a large enough scale is civil *war*, and thus arguments concerning these issues will be closely related. Another question that can be raised on this topic is whether an individual should *always* be punished for violating a law, even if he was morally justified in violating it. That is what is being asked in the debate over amnesty for draft-evaders who moved to Canada rather than participate in what they considered an immoral war. Is this a moral or legal question, or is it simply a matter of politics?

In Congress, July 4, 1776,

THE UNANIMOUS DECLARATION OF THE THIRTEEN UNITED STATES OF AMERICA,

When in the Course of human events, it becomes necessary for one people to dissolve the political bands which have connected them with another, and to assume among the Powers of the earth, the separate and equal station to which the Laws of Nature and of Nature's God entitle them, a decent respect to the opinions of mankind requires that they should declare the causes which impel them to the separation.

We hold these truths to be self-evident, that all men are created equal, that they are endowed by their Creator with certain unalienable Rights, that among these are Life, Liberty and the pursuit of Happiness. That to secure these rights, Governments are instituted among Men, deriving their just powers from the consent of the governed, That whenever any Form of Government becomes destructive of these ends, it is the Right of the People to alter or to abolish it, and to institute new Government, laying its foundation on such principles and organizing its powers in such form, as to them shall seem most likely to effect their Safety and Happiness. Prudence, indeed, will dictate that Governments long established should not be changed for light and transient causes; and accordingly all experience hath shown, that mankind are more disposed to suffer, while evils are sufferable, than to right themselves by abolishing the forms to which they are accustomed. But when a long train of abuses and usurpations, pursuing invariably the same Object evinces a design to reduce them under absolute Despotism, it is their right, it is their duty, to throw off such Government, and to provide new Guards for their future security.—Such has been the patient sufferance of these Colonies; and such is now the necessity which constrains them to alter their former Systems of Government. The history of the present King of Great Britain is a history of repeated injuries and usurpations, all having in direct object the establishment of an absolute Tyranny over these States. To prove this, let Facts be submitted to candid world.

SCIENCE

Concerning Dissent and Civil Disobedience

What rights are exercised, and what rights are violated, when students forcibly occupy a campus building, when participants in the Poor People's Campaign march to the U.S. Capitol with the intention of being arrested there, or when critics oppose the war in Vietnam? Abe Fortas, newly appointed Chief Justice of the Supreme Court, has written an admirably brief and clear explanation* of the constitutional principles involved.

The need to understand the principles will continue. The war in Vietnam is not the first and may not be the last unpopular war. Much has been achieved in the removal of racial discrimination, but the much is still too little. Justified student complaint must be distinguished from disruptive intent. The dean of Howard University's Law School has described the dilemma of his students in wanting to follow the law yet wanting to change radically our legal and social structure. The reformer's appetite is increased, not satisfied, by moderate initial success. The need to understand the principles involved will not soon disappear.

The rights to dissent, to advocate social change, to oppose government policy and practice, to change government itself—all these, if carried out by peaceful means, are protected under the Constitution. Fortas writes: "Nowhere in the world—at no time in history—has freedom to dissent and to oppose governmental action been more broadly safeguarded than in the United States of America, today."

But the right to dissent runs into another right. "The Constitution seeks to accommodate two conflicting values, each of which is fundamental: the need for freedom to speak freely, to protest effectively, to organize, and to demonstrate; and the necessity of maintaining order so that other people's rights, and the peace and security of the state, will not be impaired." It is actions, therefore, rather than motives or thoughts that must be judged. No matter how nobly motivated, actions that endanger others or infringe their rights are unlawful and subject to punishment.

Yet sometimes one feels it his duty to disobey a law he considers immoral, and Justice Fortas writes: "I am a man of the law. I have dedicated myself to uphold the law. . . . But if I . . . had been a Negro living in Birmingham or Little Rock or Plaquemines Parish, Louisiana, I hope I would have disobeyed the state law that said I might not enter the public waiting room reserved for 'Whites.' "

If the route of disobedience is taken, the consequences must be accepted. Acting in the great tradition of true civil disobedience, Dr. Martin Luther King warned that Negroes would disobey unjust laws, and then insisted that the disobedience be open and peaceful and that those who disobeyed accept the consequences. It may seem unduly harsh to fine or jail a person who violates a law he believes immoral or unconstitutional, but this is the rule of law—the rule of law that is essential to the procedure we have developed to protect dissent and to encourage peaceful change. The objectives of a particular movement or protest may be of great importance for the quality of our lives, but preservation of the procedure is our guarantee of future change and improvement.

In a time of troubled disagreements, when the term *civil disobedience* is widely misapplied, Mr. Fortas offers help to protestors and activists in understanding their rights and the limitations on those rights, and a guide to other persons in formulating standards for judging the actions they watch with fear, with wonder, or with sympathy.—DAEL WOLFLE

*Abe Fortas, *Concerning Dissent and Civil Disobedience* (New American Library of World Literature, New York, 1968), 64 pages, paper, 50¢.

Above, "Concerning Dissent and Civil Disobedience," by Dael Wolfle in *Science, 161,* p. 9, July 5, 1968. Copyright 1968 by The American Association for the Advancement of Science.

Right, letter to the editor of *Science* by Donald A. Strickland, September 13, 1968.

It is surprising to encounter solecisms in Wolfle's editorial. Justice Fortas, whose recent essay *Concerning Dissent and Civil Disobedience* stimulated the editorial, is permitted such legerdemain: Fortas is a lawyer, and lawyers are trained to confound and to employ logic dialectically.

1) The freedom "to speak freely and protest effectively" (*ex Fortas*) is activity and entails further activities. So it makes no sense to say that exercises of First Amendment rights must be judged by the consequent actions "rather than motives or thoughts." To imagine such a disjunction between motives, thoughts, and behavior is not only to subscribe to a passé legal fiction, but also to consign science and the intelligentsia to the status of a bauble.

2) Actions which "endanger others and infringe on their rights" are of course, *ex def.*, "unlawful" if reference is to positive law. (That is not quite accurate, since official action that endangers people *is* lawful, except in cases where subsequently it is officially decided to have been unlawful.)

3) To assert next that "the [legal] consequences must be accepted" by those who disobey laws which they deem to be immoral is to beg the question altogether—the question being, under what circumstances, if any, should the law be set aside to satisfy the claims of morality? The reasoning of the editorial could not distinguish Eichmann from Dr. Spock, because it values legal coercion for its own sake.

4) "The rule of law" is offered as the logical and ethical underpinning of this line of thought. To be sure, the rule of law is not a term of art among jurists. It is a political slogan which celebrates the values of compliance and due process. What it means is that disputes should be settled according to rules agreed upon in advance of the dispute, administered impersonally, and stated sufficiently precisely for people to be able to anticipate the risks of liability. Hence, "the rule of law" is procedural, has no substantive contents, and cannot possibly be relevant to political disputes in which the interpretation on validity of a particular law is in issue. . . .

Those who agreed with the sentiment behind Wolfle's editorial will be protesting to themselves that it was never intended to be understood in this way. That means that it was never intended to be understood, period; it was meant to be agreed with.

DONALD A. STRICKLAND
*Department of Political Science,
Northwestern University,
Evanston, Illinois 60201*

A Government of Laws, and Not of Men

Wolfle's editorial "Concerning dissent and civil disobedience" (5 July, p. 9), represents . . . unreal thinking. If one may disobey the law according to one's personal feelings then the only wrong that can be adjudged against Sirhan, Ray, or Oswald for their alleged offenses is that of resisting arrest, of "not accepting the consequences."

Personal physical violence is not included? Then how about destroying a man's home or business? No? How about just partially destroying them? How about hindering his means of livelihood? Where should the line be drawn?

The fact is that the basic statement is wrong. One is morally obligated to change a law he feels is wrong, not disobey it. As long as there are any legal means by which the law may be changed one must use them. The mere fact that a majority of people do not support the change gives no license to disobey, but only to work to make a majority see the need for the change.

No, I submit that "civil disobedience" in this country is wrong, a truly immoral act, and will remain so as long as we have a freely elected form of government and legal redress in the courts.

LESLIE M. BAGNALL
Department of Mechanical Engineering,
Texas A&M University,
College Station 77843

The editorial stated that "the term *civil disobedience* is widely misapplied." That term can be defined as the refusal to obey civil laws, especially, as Webster's puts it, "as a nonviolent collective means of forcing concessions from the government." The alleged crimes of Messrs. Sirhan, Ray, Oswald, and Eichmann are in a different domain.

Bagnall briefly, and Rhine more fully, hope we can rely on majority rule. So does the true civil dissenter (but not the violence monger who may come along at the same time). He accepts the principle of majority rule; he wants the majority to change a law; when he concludes that other means of persuasion will not succeed, he uses civil disobedience to emphasize and dramatize his case. He is saying, "I believe this law to be morally wrong. I believe it so strongly that I violate the law and expect to be punished. But I hope thereby to convince you that the law is wrong and that you should change it." Although he is violating a particular law, he accepts what Strickland called "rules agreed upon in advance" or the editorial called "the rule of law."

The sentiment behind the editorial was, I thought, clear and cogent. It is the desirability, in a period of much controversy—which concerns a variety of issues and is expressed in a variety of ways—of understanding the constitutional principles concerning dissent and civil disobedience, and of discriminating among the various means by which disagreements are expressed. I am sorry Strickland misunderstood.

DAEL WOLFLE

Lewis H. Lapham

THE EASY CHAIR
The longing for Armageddon

Above left, letter to the editor of *Science* by Leslie M. Bagnall, September 13, 1968. Above, letter replying to critics of editorial by Dael Wolfle in *Science*, September 13, 1968.

Left, from *Harper's*, August 1971.

• The man who burns his draft card falls into a similar error. The action loses its validity because it fails to contain the element of risk. If the man hires competent attorneys, he almost certainly will beat the rap; if he doesn't hire competent attorneys, then he is a fool. If he beats the rap, then another man (less idealistic and less rich) will be drafted to make up the consignment. Which means that the burner of a draft card, amid enthusiastic liberal applause, has merely engaged a substitute for a sum far higher than the $300 commonly paid during the Civil War.

THE ETERNAL CASE AGAINST INJUSTICE

By JACQUES MADAULE

Friends of mine have been very shocked when, in a moment of discouragement, I have told them that the petitions we sign and the demonstrations we stage against this or that injustice, against a death sentence, for example, are totally useless and probably do not have any effect upon the outcome. After all, there were demonstrations galore for Sacco and Vanzetti, and the Rosenbergs, and Julian Grimau —and they changed nothing.

There were slightly happier endings to the Burgos and Leningrad trials, inasmuch as no one was hanged, but all the demonstrators and petitioners may not have influenced the issue. What makes me think so is that in Yaoundé and Conakry, very soon afterwards, the public killings went on and no one batted an eyelid. Neither does a week go by without bringing more ghastly evidence of torture in Brazil year in, year out, and for how many years?

Perhaps we ought to throw up our hands in despair and call the whole thing off, since they are always the same people making the same useless fuss. Governments could perfectly well forecast, with all their computers, the world's precise reaction to this or that particular misdeed. The only astonishing thing is that, despite all their marvellous machines, they persist in acting irrationally, putting their political opponents to death and systematically torturing political prisoners.

Of course, one could retort that they are counting on the effects of terror and that unhappily this is not a completely irrational premise. My answer would be that for all Brazil's Gestapo tactics the regime's opponents still manage to pull off a spectacular kidnapping from time to time; and the police can no more find the missing diplomat than the opposition can stop torture. The dénouement comes with the inevitable exchange of the hostage against a score or two of prisoners, a scene out of a familiar ballet.

It adds up to this: we hear about all kinds of the world's wrongs, we protest and demonstrate indefatigably, and we ignore the very patchy results we tend to obtain. Protests and demonstrations do not seem to lessen the sum of suffering, of the universal bane of mankind, as Péguy's Joan of Arc said, particularly since we cannot protest or demonstrate against everything.

Surfeit of causes

You can spend days and nights signing protests, you can always be up at the front of the demonstrations, even so there will always be someone to ask why you failed to protest against this abomination or demonstrate against that horror, and what principles determined your choice of good causes. If you answer, "public opinion," you will be reminded how dextrously all sides manipulate it.

All of which is almost unanswerable—short of saying that there is a lot of wrong with the world, that no one person can hope to put it all right, but that it is still necessary, even vital, to keep fighting, and break down the conspiracy of silence that so many find so convenient.

Should the day ever come when not a voice raised because it seems there is no point in doing so, then the condemned and tortured will suffer and die in abominable loneliness. The real reason why we petition and demonstrate is to show them there are others, in the world outside who have not forgotten them. It is to give them the feeling of a human presence, even if it is invisible.

I believe that in so doing we keep up the morale of those for whom we cannot do anything more. There are too many of them, in too many parts of the world, and the vision of so much horror everywhere makes even the most stout hearted lose hope —not to mention the huge, indifferent herd interested only in their personal affairs, people more inured than ourselves, people who have always known that protesting does not help and that injustice has always had its way since the world began.

Heaven preserve us from such niggardly common sense! One day, the sooner the better, we should perhaps tackle the root causes, rather than the periodic symptoms, of the evil which men keep doing to each other—as if disease and injury, death and natural disasters were not enough. What makes us take out our personal frustrations on our fellow beings as if they were to blame for them? One might think the pain we cause them compensates for the pain we feel ourselves. It is always dangerous to give one man power over another, in case he takes advantage of it. It is the principle of tyranny.

So let us give credit to those who are sincerely trying to lessen the sum of evil in the world, even if they feel a twinge of flattered vanity at seeing their names in print, or buy an easy conscience too cheaply. Only, let us also hope that they do not remain content with merely demonstrating. Let them think, hard, without prejudice, about the real causes of all this human wretchedness.

In that case their devotion will certainly not have been totally useless.

From the weekly English edition of *Le Monde*, February 17, 1971.

Web of barbarism

Random violence rightly horrifies civilized society. Man recognizes that uncontrolled, unchecked force represents a step back toward the beast. The social structure, therefore, organizes rules and patterns to suppress such outbursts.

In time of war, the lid comes partly off, as large numbers of citizens take up arms and become soldiers. But even then, societies still usually observe rules which aim at channeling violence so it does not become all-encompassing, and does not engender such hatred and destruction that it makes any chance of post-war recovery impossible.

For instance, it is regrettable but expected when soldiers are killed in battle. But when a civilian area is bombed, even if accidentally, society is disturbed that the combatants did not take greater care.

Deliberate attacks on civilians or civilian installations are rare in ordinary warfare, if only because military commanders naturally consider concentrations of enemy troops and arms to be immensely more appropriate and rewarding targets than unarmed civilian areas.

And yet civilian areas are precisely the target of the modern urban guerrilla, who deliberately chooses non-combatant men, women, and children for his victims. He lays his plans not in a moment of passion, miscalculation, or frustration, but with full and careful knowledge.

The urban terrorist thus introduces a barbaric level of violence into civilization.

The most arresting current example is in Northern Ireland, with bombings and counter-bombings, assaults and counter-assaults by extremist Catholics and Protestants who do not allow each other safety in a tavern or while Christmas shopping.

Surely it is the height of man's overweening moral arrogance for him calculatedly to blow up a store packed with shoppers (killing four persons, including two children), as occurred Dec. 11 in Belfast, or to touch off a bomb and destroy 16 lives in a pub, as happened a week earlier.

Something is morally amiss with the world's violent radicals—as exemplified so well by Ireland's IRA and Quebec's FLQ—when they decide that their social goals are attainable at the cost of lives of housewives and children.

Individual tragedy means nothing to terrorists who claim to seek that elusive ideal, the perfected social order. What a travesty that the victims of their delusion are innocent bystanders.

Left, from *The Arizona Republic*, December 21, 1971.

Below, courtesy of Hallowell Bowser and *Saturday Review*, March 20, 1971.

Against Provocation

" "Agent provocateur" is a fancy term for a quite ugly kind of spy. Unlike ordinary spies, the provocateur does not join a "suspect" group to keep close tabs on its activities; instead, his aim is to stampede the group into doing something rash, egregious, and incriminating.

When challenged about using such provocative, para-legal tactics, the "fuzz and feds" claim they are just needling extremists into attempting now, in a botched, premature way, anti-Establishment exploits that they would have brought off with devastating success if allowed more lead time.

This is, of course, thin reasoning. As "red squad" people well know, an impassioned-cause group is like a Navy blimp that is riding free just a few feet off the ground. The blimp may weigh many tons, but a good hard shove by a determined man can warp the craft around and send it floating off in any direction the shover chooses. When an undercover agent gives a volatile splinter group a hefty push, the group is likely to go kiting off in an ideological direction astonishing to the onlooker.

But why push for empty violence that only enrages both the public and the police? Why not try instead to provoke—or evoke—positive, fruitful activity? Roger Baldwin may have hit on part of the explanation when, thirty-odd years ago, he wrote in the *Encyclopedia of the Social Sciences*, "Sometimes the political police have provoked or committed crime . . . to make a showing of the need for their services and thus to wrest from a hesitant government increased funds and larger powers."

—HALLOWELL BOWSER.

Arrogance, Not Freedom, Tested

Before he became disillusioned by the misbehavior of the media of his day, Thomas Jefferson said that if he were forced to make one choice only, he would select a free press over government.

If the New York Times, the Washington Post and the Boston Globe are sustained in their thesis that they can at their own discretion publish any top secret documents that they can acquire, the nation may face a Jeffersonian choice.

Freedom of the press is really not the issue that the three newspapers have brought before the nation as the federal government seeks to recover top secret documents that were stolen from the Pentagon files.

No responsible person is against freedom of the press or the legitimate right of the public to know the decisions of its governments. By the same token, no responsible citizen challenges the principle that some things that government does must be kept secret in order to protect our nation.

Thus the willful publication of stolen, secret material must be considered in another light, particularly in view of the current newspaper tactics. When the New York Times was enjoined from further publication after publishing three articles, the Washington Post printed the next two. When the Washington Post was enjoined, the Boston Globe presumably completed the series. At no time did any of the newspapers make

Clearly the challenge is to the institution of government itself. What the three newspapers are saying is that the judgment of the press — and that could be anybody with a mimeograph machine — supersedes that of the elected and appointed representatives of the people.

Moreover, those newspapers are saying that the means justifies the end — that if they regard their goals as moral, they can break the law to attain those goals. In this respect, their argument is little different than that used by the anarchists who take to the streets. A comparable principle would be that false testimony and tainted evidence could be used in court so long as it results in the guilty being punished.

Reason alone dictates that this concept cannot be sustained if the United States of America is to survive. If the United States could no longer have secrets, or if stolen secrets were fair game for dissemination, there would be no United States government — probably no free press either.

contact with the government to urge regular procedures to de-classify the material. None of them yielded to the pleadings of the federal government to stop publication. The material, for example, could readily have been paraphrased if principles of free press alone were the issue. Instead volumes of secret data were published verbatim — an act which could be of value to an enemy.

From *The San Diego Union*, June 23, 1971.

An Open Letter To U.S. Students From the YSA

On September 21, 1970, FBI Director J. Edgar Hoover issued a statement to the United Press International in the form of an "Open Letter to College Students." On the same day, Rep. Samuel L. Devine (Ohio Republican) read the text of Hoover's statement into the Congressional Record. More significantly, The New York Times reported on September 28, 1970, that President Nixon had sent the letter out with an accompanying cover-letter over his own signature to 900 college and university presidents. The text which appears below is taken from the text inserted into the September 21 Congressional Record by Rep. Devine.

OPEN LETTER TO COLLEGE STUDENTS
(By J. Edgar Hoover, Director,
Federal Bureau of Investigation)

(NOTE. — In the following Open Letter To College Students, FBI Director J. Edgar Hoover pinpoints eight ploys used by radical extremists in their efforts to steer justifiable campus protest into violent and destructive channels.)

As a 1970 college student, you belong to the best educated, most sophisticated, most poised generation in our history.

The vast majority of you, I am convinced, sincerely love America and want to make it a better country.

You do have ideas of your own — and that's good. You see things wrong in our society which we adults perhaps have minimized or overlooked. You are outspoken and frank and hate hypocrisy. That is good too.

There's nothing wrong with student dissent or student demands for changes in society or the display of student unhappiness over aspects of our national policy.

Based on our experience in the FBI, here are some of the ways in which extremists will try to lure you into their activities:

5. They'll encourage you to disrespect the law and hate the law enforcement officer. Most college students have good friends who are police officers. You know that when extremists call the police "pigs" they are wrong. The officer protects your rights, lives, and property. He is your friend and he needs your support.

6. They'll tell you that any action is honorable and right if it's "sincere" or "idealistic" in motivation. Here is one of the most seductive of New Left appeals — that if an arsonist's or anarchist's heart is in the right place, if he feels he is doing something for "humanity" or a "higher cause," then his act, even if illegal, is justifiable. Remember that acts have consequences. The alleged sincerity of the perpetrator does not absolve him from responsibility. His acts may affect the rights, lives, and property of others. Just being a student or being on campus does not automatically confer immunity or grant license to violate the law. Just because you don't like a law doesn't mean you can violate it with impunity.

The Young Socialist Alliance finds in this letter an outrageous twisting of the truth. It is a classic example of the kind of arguments used by the powerful when they perceive a challenge to their power to continue exploiting and oppressing people. These arguments have several features:

3. They try to make the victim into the criminal and the criminal into the victim. These men, who bear the responsibility for the deaths of hundreds of thousands of Vietnamese, tens of thousands of American GIs and countless others here at home and around the world, have the audacity to speak about violence as if it came from the students! As they prepare to interfere with the peaceful exercise of fundamental political and human rights by students — who are citizens like anyone else — they try to brand their victims as "extremists" and perpetrators of violence. These hypocritical accusations are designed to hide the truth about the real extremists — the mass executioners and exploiters who would rob those opposing them of their basic rights. Nixon and Hoover are the real extremists. The real source of violence is the cops and troops they maintain to guard private property and preserve the status quo around the world.

Above, courtesy of United Press International and Young Socialist Alliance.

Below, from *The New Republic*, April 10, 1971.

Under ordinary circumstances, a citizen's decision to withhold taxes could not be justified by a claim that he strongly disagrees with the way his taxes are spent. But the Indochina war is not an ordinary occurrence; it cannot be compared, say, with public school integration. Because the war makes moral culprits of us all, it brings into play the principles set forth by the US itself at Nuremberg. And while the Nuremberg tribunal did not go so far as to say that persons who willingly pay taxes or submit to conscription are guilty of complicity in crimes committed by their government, its judgments tend irresistibly in that direction. "Individuals have international duties which transcend the national obligations of obedience imposed by the individual state," the tribunal ruled. This admonition was addressed to past and future government leaders, but it is no less applicable to rank-and-file citizens.

The strongest argument against war tax withholding is that it might lead to further withholding, thereby undermining the government's ability to promote egalitarian goals, and ultimately to function at all. Three points deserve consideration here. One is that, given the enormous power of the state, the probability of an anarchic tax rebellion is, as a practical matter, slight. The second is that the obligation to support social order, while considerable, is not absolute; even soldiers, the Army reminds us at Lieutenant Calley's court-martial, should disobey some orders, whatever the consequences may be for military discipline. Third, there are times when it may be desirable to weaken a government's ability to function.∫

In Search of Law and Order II

It is impossible not to share President Nixon's conviction, expressed in a recent speech on reforming the judiciary, that "what is needed now is. . .the kind of change. . .that demands a focus on ultimate goals"—that will "reinstill a respect for law in all our people." Regrettably, however, the President's analysis bears little promise of moving the American judicial system toward "ultimate goals." *The* ultimate goal of any judicial system is, after all—justice.

Mr. Nixon said that "the nation has turned increasingly to the courts to cure deep-seated ills of our society—and the courts have responded. As a result, they have burdens unknown to the legal system a generation ago. In addition, the courts had to bear the brunt of the rise in crime—almost 150 per cent in one decade, an explosion unparalleled in our history." Then, just a few paragraphs later in the speech, this: "throughout a tumultuous generation, our system of justice has helped America improve herself."

How can the two observations be reconciled? Is it not clear that an unparalleled explosion of crime does not occur under an adequate system of justice?

Respect for law grows out of the justice of the law. Justice, in turn, grows not from a neat balance of society's rights with those of the individual, as the President suggested, but from the positive law's conformity with the law of God.

Three days after Mr. Nixon's address, a "clinic" opened in the capital city over which he presides, for the sole purpose of killing 900 unborn Americans per month. It opened on the presumption that American law sanctions that purpose. If the presumption is correct, American law cannot be respected—the distance between the system built around that law (and others like it), and the moral order inscribed in the very nature of human society, *objectively* precludes respect for the system. That distance is now measured by an expanding chaos of monstrous "rights," held in check only by a temporarily convenient and perpetually diminishing consensus. In such chaos, all respect for law must ultimately perish: when it is cut off from the moral order, law is only convenience, and men do not respect convenience.

If Mr. Nixon wishes his fellow citizens to respect the laws by which they are governed, he must tell us that, imperfect as human things are, the positive law exists solely to try to satisfy the justice of God. If he cannot tell us that, he cannot expect us to respect the law; the best he can hope for is that we will fear it. But of course, one hates what one fears.

In Defense of Dissent

The successful attempt by certain faculty members to keep Bill Shockley from speaking at Brooklyn Polytechnic Institute ("News in Brief," 24 May, p. 863) is a classic demonstration of the inability of many self-styled liberals to understand what free speech is all about. These unilateral liberals are willing to tolerate any dissent as long as it is not "wrong"; that is, in disagreement with or questioning the dogma currently held by themselves.

Dogma: "There are no racial differences in intelligence."

Shockley: "I dunno—let's find out."

Unilateral Liberals: "Racist! Nazi! We won't let you speak!"

Such an attitude, I submit, is less scientific or scholarly or liberal than it is dogmatically religious and is indistinguishable in kind from those of Adolph Hitler, both Joes (McCarthy and Stalin), the Birchers, and for that matter, Torquemada and the orthodox Marxists. . . . Free speech implies the toleration not only of "proper" but of "wrong" dissent—Voltaire, the Supreme Court, and the American Civil Liberties Union all seem to agree with me. And if any dogma is sacred and not to be questioned, the age of the Inquisition is on the way back. God preserve us from the man who knows that he is right!

JOHN D. CLARK

Green Pond Road, RD 2,
Newfoundland, New Jersey 07435

SCIENCE, VOL. 161

Left, from *Triumph*, a publication of the Society for the Christian Commonwealth, 278 Broadview Avenue, Warrenton, Virginia 22186. April 1971.
Above, letter to the editor of *Science* by John D. Clark, July 5, 1968.

Morality and Public Policy

The basic problem surrounding the issue of civil disobedience concerns whether or not the intentional breaking of a legal statute can be justified on moral grounds. A similar question arises at a more fundamental level in the legal system, where it is necessary to ask whether any moral considerations are relevant to the determination of what laws should be enacted in the first place. Just as it seems obvious to some people that certain laws are clearly immoral and thus ought not be obeyed (e.g., laws supporting slavery), it also appears to some that certain laws should not be passed in the first place because they are immoral. However it also is generally believed that we should not grant excessive license to legislators to use their personal moral beliefs to make these important decisions which affect the whole society.

The problems concerning the making of public policy are at least as complex as those of civil disobedience, and many of the same considerations are relevant to the two cases. It would be rash indeed to suggest some simple guide through these controversies. However we can outline several of the more common views about the role of moral deliberation in the making of public policy. At one extreme lies the view that public policy is essentially amoral, and that the only criteria relevant to such decisions are those of material cost, efficiency, political expediency, etc. In this view, no public policy can possibly be morally right, wrong, or neutral. At the opposite extreme is the view that all public policies are concerned with moral issues and thus require moral justification. In this view, even though it may be relevant to determine the cost in dollars, the efficiency, and the workability of a particular policy, it is also necessary to ascertain the moral rightness, wrongness, or neutrality of that policy. In judging whether either of these two extreme positions is correct, or whether some public policies are moral while others are amoral, we are in part concerned with the meta-ethical issue raised in the Introduction about distinguishing moral judgments from nonmoral ones. And we can only repeat our previous statement that this is not a simple question. We believe, however, that a careful analysis of the following concrete examples will be of some assistance in finding a reasonable answer.

Maybe the way to change the world is to join a large corporation.

We don't make a lot of noise, but this is where it's really happening. You see, a large corporation like Kodak has the resources and the skill to make this world a little more decent place to live. And we intend to do what we can to see that this is exactly what happens.

Take our home city, Rochester, New York for example. We cut water pollution in the Genesee River by using natural bacteria to dispose of unnatural wastes. We cut air pollution by using electrostatic precipitators in a new combustible waste disposal facility. We helped set up a black enterprise program in downtown Rochester, and we've been experimenting with film as a way to train both teachers and students—including some students who wouldn't respond to anything else.

And we didn't stop with Rochester. Kodak is involved in 47 countries all over the world. Actively involved.

Why? Because it's good business. Helping to clean the Genesee River not only benefits society... but helps protect another possible source for the clean water we need to make our film. Our combustible waste disposal facility not only reduces pollution... but just about pays for itself in heat and power production and silver recovery. Our black enterprise program not only provides an opportunity for the economically disadvantaged... but helps stabilize communities in which Kodak can operate and grow. And distributing cameras and film to teachers and students not only helps motivate the children... but helps create a whole new market.

In short, it's simply good business. And we're in business to make a profit. But in furthering our business interests, we also further society's interests.

And that's good. After all, our business depends on society. So we care what happens to it.

80

IS THE ABM MORAL?

An argument for the affirmative

EDWARD S. BOYLAN

Right, courtesy of Commonweal Publishing Company, Inc., June 11, 1971.
Below, from the *Daily World*, July 23, 1971.

Any amount is excess

With the due deliberation of an ox-hauled cart or court declaration on civil rights, the Army has completed tests on equipment to be used in disposing of 3,071 tons of mustard gas and will some day burn it.

The gas, stored since World War I, is being disposed of "because it is regarded as obsolete and excess material," we are told.

Not because it is an inhuman weapon, not because it has been outlawed — simply because it is "obsolete and excess"!

The world was horrified when mustard and other asphyxiating gases were used in World War I, and they were outlawed by the Geneva Protocol of 1925 which was signed by the United States but never ratified.

Born of the mad lust for conquest in a savage imperialist war for the redivision of the world, mustard and other gases and biological weapons bear the brand of imperialism and its lawless contempt for people and humanity.

While destroying mustard gas, imperialism holds tightly to even more deadly and evil weapons — nuclear instruments of annihilation, anti-personnel weapons, fragmentation bombs which have wreaked havoc on civilians in Indochina. Now is the time to demand the outlawing and destruction of these weapons also.

Does ABM make a nuclear war more likely? No definitive statement can be made but even the most optimistic estimate of the effectiveness of a large scale U.S. deployment of ABM (McNamara's Posture B) would see tens of millions of Americans die in a large-scale nuclear exchange. I do not see any American President blithely pressing buttons merely because ABM has been deployed. A nuclear war will come only as a reluctant, last alternative in some kind of desperate international crisis. ABM will not make such a war more likely, only more survivable.

Does ABM divert national resources from higher priority social problems? A good argument might be made that the Defense Department budget is too high, but why divert resources from ABM, which is at most 5 percent of the budget? Our country needs protection against nuclear crises and attacks of the type described above. Strangely, those who argue that the United States does not need any defense against nuclear attack do not support an inexpensive alternative to the deployment of Minuteman. If the United States and the Soviet Union were to agree to let each country deploy large nuclear mines under the other's large cities, then an expensive arsenal of nuclear missiles would not be needed for Assured Destruction. I doubt, though, whether the American people would agree to having Soviet mines under American cities. But without ABM, Soviet missiles are no more than long-range mines.

There are many arguments against ABM. Books have been written on the subject. If I have omitted any arguments it is not for lack of an answer, but for lack of space. I have tried to focus on the moral issues raised by opponents of ABM. To me, there is nothing immoral about supporting deployment of a system which could very well save millions of lives under a number of possible contingencies. There is nothing immoral about supporting deployment of a system which has shown its value in the search toward an arms limitation agreement between the United States and the Soviet Union. And finally, there is nothing immoral about supporting deployment of a system which provides the beginnings of an alternative to a policy which advocates the destruction of millions of innocent human beings.

First Decree for the Protection of Life

WHEREAS —

After thousands of years of slow and laborious development, mankind during the past few decades has rapidly come into possession of technological means which promise either unlimited opportunity and abundance or sudden and universal catastrophe.

The People of Earth are, in fact, confronted daily with the threat of instant extermination by the accidental or deliberate unleashing of nuclear weapons. This threat multiplies as more nations gain nuclear capability and install multiple warheads which defy inspection and control by treaty.

Even limited use of nuclear weapons and other weapons of mass destruction imperils civilian populations, towns, cities and country-sides, and can turn entire countries into ravaged battlefields.

The $200,000,000,000 being spent by the nations each year for military purposes, mainly for weapons of mass destruction and their deployment, is a criminal waste of resources and manpower which could otherwise be devoted to supplying the People of Earth with adequate food, shelter, clothing, education, health services and expanding opportunities in life.

So long as nations give priority to expenditures for military might, there is scant chance of applying the brain-power, manpower and resources needed to solve other rapidly mounting problems which threaten humanity with the breakdown of society, misery and death in multiple ways before the end of the century. These problems include environmental pollution, the gap between rich and poor, hunger and population, urban decay, technological cancers, social disorientations and other troubles.

Apart from dangers of universal ruin, the means of modern warfare comprise the tools of force by which stronger nations interfere in the affairs of weaker nations and enforce imperialistic and colonial policies.

Meanwhile, the civil and human rights of people in all countries are nullified when nations are permitted to keep large and heavily armed military forces, since it is with military force that dictatorships and tyrannies are enforced, movements for peaceful change crushed, and people kept subservient — making a mockery of the Charter of Human Rights adopted by the United Nations.

Despite the extreme dangers to all life on Earth, which are growing every day and year, the national governments not only fail to protect their citizens from these dangers, but on the contrary many national governments are actively increasing the hazards by continuing to install nuclear weapons and to devise other weapons with ever greater capacity for death and ruin.

During the next one to thirty years, in order to survive and prosper, the residents of Earth must overcome manifold problems and perils of planetary scope unknown in history. Yet at the world level, no agency exists which has the authority or competence to cope with the problems, and anarchy prevails.

THEREFORE —

When life is seriously endangered and existing governments are either unable or unwilling to remove the dangers and improve the conditions of life, then it becomes necessary for responsible citizens to proceed with remedies which seem appropriate.

Men and women acting under such circumstances may be described as Trustees acting for the common good, ultimately justified by whether their actions are endorsed by their fellow citizens.

In view of the increasing jeapordy to the lives and property of everyone on Earth, and in the absence of effective action by national governments and international agencies to protect life, we who are listed below, from many countries, have organized ourselves into an Emergency Council of World Trustees to take immediate action on behalf of humanity. Our purposes are to outlaw war and war preparations, to convene a Peoples World Parliament for continuous work, to prepare a Constitution for Federal World Government for submission to the Parliament, to appoint global legislative commissions to prepare legislation on urgent world problems for submission to the Parliament, and to take other appropriate action leading to the establishment of a Provisional World Government under democratic popular control.

As a first action to rescue Planet Earth and its inhabitants from destruction, and to provide a tangible rallying ground for people everywhere who want peace and human rights while moving towards the creation of a Provisional World Government, we do hereby issue this First Decree for the Protection of Life:

1. Upon the effective ratification of this decree, it shall be outlaw and forbidden everywhere on Earth to design, test, produce, transport, sell, buy, install, deploy or use nuclear weapons, chemical-biological weapons, or any weapons of mass destruction, including airplanes equipped for bombing, I.C.B.M.s and other delivery systems, battleships, tanks and all manner of bombs and newly devised weapons.

2. This decree shall go into effect as soon as it is ratified by groups of students and professors at 200 universities and colleges in at least 20 countries, or by the signatures of at least 10 million individuals in at least 20 countries, or any equivalent thereof.

3. Any and all executive, administrative and chief policy making officials in governments, the military forces, industry, scientific work education or labor who may be responsible for violation of this decree after effective ratification, shall be guilty of war crimes and crimes against humanity.

4. Those who sign or ratify this decree thereby pledge themselves personally to abide by the decree. Opportunity to ratify shall be continued beyond the minimum stated herein for the decree to go into effect.

5. Individuals found guilty of violation of this decree may be assigned to rehabilitation and reconstruction work in areas devastated by war, or to other work of service to humanity.

6. Procedures for enforcement of this decree shall be determined either by the Emergency Council of World Trustees upon effective ratification, or by the Peoples World Parliament or Provisional World Government as soon as the latter institutions are established.

PEOPLE OF EARTH, UNITE TO OBTAIN NEW PRIORITIES FOR LIFE, BY SIGNING OR RATIFYING THIS FIRST DECREE FOR THE PROTECTION OF LIFE!

This First Decree for the Protection of Life was issued at the inaugural meeting of the Emergency Council of World Trustees at Santa Barbara, California, Dec. 28, 1971, to Jan. 2, 1972. At time of issuance, the Decree carried the signatures of several hundred persons from all continents of Earth, more than half being presidents of university student unions and other student leaders.

ALL PERSONS WHO AGREE WITH THIS ACTION ARE URGED TO RATIFY THE DECREE AND SEND A CONTRIBUTION TO CARRY THE ACTION FORWARD!

Ratified by .... Native country ....

Print name .... Contribution $..........................

Address ....

Occupation or position ....

Please send me .... copies of the Decree to circulate for ratification, together with a list of the first signers. (Note: You can help the cause by printing the Decree at once and circulating it in your community or on your campus. Use this copy for offset printing.)

Return signed Decrees with contributions to the World Constitution and Parliament Association, Inc., Trustees Office, 1480 Hoyt St., Lakewood, Colorado 80215, USA.

Courtesy of the World Constitution and Parliament Association, Inc., and *The Humanist*, January-February 1972.

ECOCIDE AND THE GENEVA PROTOCOL

Ironically the United States first proposed the Geneva Protocol in 1925 and now stands as the only major nation which is not a party to it. The substantive provisions of the Protocol read as follows:

> Whereas the use in war of asphyxiating, poisonous or other gases, and of all analogous liquids, materials or devices, has been justly condemned by the general opinion of the civilised world; and
>
> Whereas the prohibition of such use has been declared in Treaties to which the majority of Powers of the world are Parties; and
>
> To the end that this prohibition shall be universally accepted as a part of International Law, binding alike conscience and the practice of nations;
>
> Declare:
>
> That the High Contracting Parties, so far as they are not already Parties to Treaties prohibiting such use, accept this prohibition, agree to extend this prohibition to the use of bacteriological methods of warfare and agree to be bound as between themselves according to the terms of this declaration.

The Protocol was submitted to the Senate for advice and consent in 1926. After extensive lobbying by the U.S. Army Chemical Service, chemical manufacturers and veterans' organizations and others, it was sidetracked and never brought to a vote. It was returned to the President as part of a housecleaning effort during the Truman Administration many years later. No further action was taken until it was resubmitted to the Senate by President Nixon.

Ethical arguments have been advanced on both sides of the Protocol issue. Proponents of the Administration's understanding have argued that tear gas is basically a humanitarian weapon which should not be prohibited for use in war. In most domestic cases tear gas is used by police because the offenses committed do not warrant the use of potentially lethal weapons. The Geneva Protocol by any interpretation would not limit the use of tear gas in normal police activities, even within a country at war. At the time of the policy debates on the tear gas issue, many felt that there were some unique humanitarian applications possible in war. It was argued that in cases where civilians were being used as a screen by the enemy, tear gas could incapacitate all parties involved, allowing time for separation and identification. In addition, it was felt that tear gas could be used to capture prisoners from tunnel complexes or caves. It was these humanitarian uses of tear gas which formed the most compelling arguments in the interagency debate in 1965, leading to Secretary Rusk's declaration that year.

The policies of 1965, however, have not proven realistic. Unfortunately, the use of tear gas in Vietnam has demonstrated conclusively that rather than being a humanitarian weapon of warfare, tear gas is most frequently used as a conventional military weapon to bring about indirect lethal effects. Since the Rusk statement in 1965 the use of tear gas in riot-control situations and in situations analogous to riot control has represented only a small fraction of the total use.

The use of herbicides to destroy crops also involves highly significant ethical considerations. In the course of investigations of the program in Saigon and in the provinces of Vietnam, I found that the program was having much more profound effects on civilian noncombatants than on the enemy. Evaluations sponsored by a number of official and unofficial agencies have all concluded that a very high percentage of all the food destroyed under the crop destruction program had been destined for civilian, not military, use. The program had its greatest effects on the enemy-controlled civilian populations of central and northern South Vietnam. In Vietnam the crop destruction program created widespread misery and many refugees.

It must be asked whether such a policy does not violate the nation's basic ethical standards. I believe it is a fair assumption that the national security is not only involved with physical security but also embraces the democratic and ethical concepts which form the basic raison d'être of the nation. It is important that the tactics used by the nation to preserve its security not come into conflict with the basic concepts which these tactics seek to secure. It is contrary to the broader meanings of the U.S. national purpose to perpetuate the use of tactics such as crop destruction in warfare.

It is important that the future of the Geneva Protocol not be solely dependent on the complex arguments relating to the immediate national interest. At this time, more so than at any other, the United States is in a position in which it can have a profound effect on the future of mankind. Historically, this era will be judged according to its ability to advance its technological capabilities for growth and development and to retard or restrict these same abilities for destruction. The Geneva Protocol of 1925 was a relatively small effort to achieve these objectives, but it was an important one. In this spirit the United States has recently taken the lead in efforts to prevent the proliferation of nuclear weapons, to propose negotiations which could lead to arms limitations, and to take a stand in opposition to the use of biological and lethal chemical weapons. It is in keeping with this historical trend that the present Administration must decide the fate of the Geneva Protocol. The alternatives facing the President are clear. If the current U.S. understanding is reversed or modified to include prohibitions against tear gas and herbicide use or if a concrete means can be presented to the Senate whereby the issue might be resolved among the parties, the Protocol would likely move to prompt Senate ratification. If not, there is little likelihood that the Protocol will be ratified during this session of the Congress. In making its decision the Administration must balance short-term military expediency against the long-term objective of prohibiting chemical and biological warfare.

In recognition of the dangerous consequences of eroding the meaning of the Protocol, and in recognition of the rapidly decreasing requirements for chemical herbicides and tear gas in South Vietnam, there is little question that the United States should now strive to obtain a unanimous interpretation of the Geneva Protocol to prohibit the use in war of all gases, bacteriological weapons and herbicides.

Reprinted by permission from *Foreign Affairs*, July 1971. Copyright 1971 by the Council on Foreign Relations, Inc., New York.

Thinking Out Loud

Permit me to debunk some of the favorite words and cliches of the liberals and left-wingers. One of these is the high-sounding phrase, "Academic Freedom."

Once it appeared to be a good word, when it seemed to give the teacher liberty to explore new horizons, and to teach within the limits of decency and respectability all available knowledge on any given subject, always careful to teach fact as fact, and theory as theory, and to point out and define the difference between the two.

"Academic freedom" was never intended to be divorced from moral responsibility; nor was it ever intended to challenge the existence of God Almighty, or His operations among the sons of men.

It was never intended to be an excuse for free thinkers to challenge the divine creation of man, nor to overthrow the law of God, nor to deny man's need of redemption, nor to teach infidelity.

"Academic freedom" is a misnomer if it seeks to operate outside of God's orbit, for man has no rights—not even the right to exist—outside the sovereign will of God.

But, alas, what has this so-called "academic freedom" come to mean in its present distortion? Never has a phrase been so corrupted or prostituted.

For many today who loudly demand the use of "academic freedom," mean, rather, "unrestrained license" to teach whatever they choose, with total disregard of the basic rights of those whom they teach, and regardless of the people who through their gifts, tax dollars, and sacrifices make possible the very existence of our schools and universities.

To them it means an unhindered, unrestrained, unsupervised license to teach, as they choose, infidelity, atheism, Communism, sex perversion, intemperance, anything — even the change of our form of government from a constitutional republic to a socialistic state.

Under the guise of this so-called "academic freedom" they presume to have the right to usurp the place of the parents, and teach doctrines and philosophies which will have the effect of completely changing the beliefs and the behaviour of our young people.

Under this damnable cloak of so-called "academic freedom" they presume to compel the society which supports them to completely refrain from interference with their program of humanism, and to arrogantly reach their slimy hands down your pockets for the funds necessary to subvert and corrupt your children. Not only so, but they are so lifted up with pride and vanity as to look with disdain upon any citizen who criticizes their licentious program.

If you dare to get in their way, they will brand you as a square, an ignoramous, an old fogey, a Puritan, a hater of arts and literature.

Although they boast of a supreme liberalism, when crowded into the corner they manifest the most pronounced spirit of bigotry. Their ideas, they think, represent the last word in intelligence; no other opinions, or philosophies, or religions are of any worth. All knowledge ends with them!

Well, I've got news for them. They are the biggest bunch of asinine parasites on the face of the earth. And so help me God, I shall continue to devote a good part of my life to exposing their hypocrisy. It is time that we begin to find out who the real phonies are in our society.

Dale Crowley in *The Capital Voice*, January 1, 1971.

WHAT IT'S LIKE TO BROADCAST NEWS

by WALTER CRONKITE

I don't think it is any of our business what the moral, political, social, or economic effect of our reporting is. I say let's get on with the job of reporting the news—and let the chips fall where they may. I suggest we concentrate on doing our job of telling it like it is and not be diverted from that exalted task by the apoplectic apostles of alliteration.

If it *happened*, the people are entitled to know. There is no condition that can be imposed on that dictum without placing a barrier (censorship) between the people and the truth—at once as fallible and corrupt as only self-serving men can make it. The barrier can be built by government—overtly by dictatorship or covertly by propaganda on the political stump, harassment by subpoena, or abuse of the licensing power. Or the barrier can be built by the news media themselves. If we permit our news judgment to be colored by godlike decisions as to what is good for our readers, listeners, or viewers, we are building a barrier—no matter how pure our motives.

Above, courtesy of Walter Cronkite and *Saturday Review*, December 12, 1970.

IT IS YOUR BUSINESS, MR. CRONKITE

by IRVING E. FANG

Walter Cronkite, in a recent article adapted from a speech to the Sigma Delta Chi national convention, stated, "I don't think it is any of our business what the moral, political, social, or economic effect of our reporting is" ["What It's Like to Broadcast the News," *SR*, Dec. 12].

I disagree with Mr. Cronkite. It *is* the journalist's concern to consider the consequences of his work, just as it is the physician's, the attorney's, the minister's, the professor's, and indeed every professional man's concern.

Of course, Cronkite is not heedless of public reaction. If an obscenity were part of an important news story (for example, what the Chicago Seven were really saying in court), he would not repeat it on the air. Nor would he repeat a blasphemy. Nor would he use pornography to illustrate a national concern. No responsible journalist does these things, whether or not they might be news.

The journalist operates as he does because society chooses that he do so. Our society, based on the libertarian ideals of a democracy, chooses wisely that journalists should, within certain bounds, "tell it like it is." Besides obscenity, blasphemy, and pornography, news that lies out of bounds includes certain military secrets, indefensible libels, matters of personal privacy, and unsubstantiated rumor. While broad, the rights of free speech and freedom of the press are not absolute.

To the left and to the right of our democracy lie the censored societies.

Franco's former foreign minister, Alberto Martin Artajo, stated:

There are certain substantive freedoms derived from natural law—man's freedom to worship his God, to found a home, to educate his children, to work, and to act with self-respect and independence. These freedoms [in Spain] once succumbed to the action of license, as a result of the excess of other freedoms, like freedom of the press, of party, of trade unions, of strikes, which are not of the same nature and degree, because they are, so to speak, secondary freedoms, "adjective" freedoms, of a lower order. That is why the [Franco] regime has in some way repressed these other political freedoms, which, because they are secondary, must be the safeguard of the previous ones.

Some Americans can always be found who would like more restrictions on what may now be broadcast or printed. I have even heard this from a few men who make their living in the news business. (I am reluctant to call them journalists.) Vice President Agnew's Des Moines speech has less significance than the apparent support it received across the land. Many, many Americans honestly believe that television network news isn't telling it as it is. I sometimes ask for a show of hands in a college classroom to learn how many students believe that television newscasts, network and local, report news in an unbiased manner, without fear or favor. The voting usually runs 4 to 1 against the newscasters. The reasons vary. Some students, supporting the Vice President, see a liberal bias. Some students see a conservative, Establishment bias. Some students are convinced that broadcast journalists do not report news harmful to advertisers. And so on.

If such an erosion of faith exists among university students, who are among the most libertarian members of our society, can the journalist argue that it is not his business what the effect of his reporting is?

Let us look beyond journalism for a moment. When a society feels itself sufficiently threatened, it reacts. Lenin and Franco felt sufficiently threatened by freedom of speech and freedom of the press to crush them. If those Americans who would restrict freedom of speech and freedom of the press take action, will the rest of America rise up in indignation or fury to stop them?

We hope so. We hope these freedoms matter to enough Americans. But should not the journalist be aware of the effect he is having? Should he not buttress his hope that most Americans value freedom of the press, even when the news is upsetting or grim or pleases their political opponents or undercuts their moral philosophy or appears to give aid and comfort to their nation's enemies? In short, news which shows us what we are, warts and all?

Mr. Cronkite may have expressed himself here more broadly than he intended. If he meant to argue that the journalist has a responsibility to report significant news, even if it upsets us, then he ought to have the support of all who regard the right to know as paramount.

The distinction between the journalist judging an individual story on its merits and the journalist ignoring the impact of news upon his audience is obviously far more than hairsplitting. To cite one example, riot news was once reported on television newscasts purely on its merits as news. But it soon became evident that the impact of riot news on television viewers—including the rioters themselves—was so great that television news departments trimmed their sails. Broadcast journalists had to make the effects of riot news their business. They did so voluntarily, behaving as responsible members of our society. To ignore the effects of this news would have been unacceptable, and everyone knew it.

In his article, Mr. Cronkite stated:

. . . I'm somewhat sick and mighty tired of broadcast journalism being constantly dragged into the operating room and dissected, probed, swabbed, and needled to see what makes it tick.

I'm tired of sociologists, psychologists, pathologists, educators, parents, bureaucrats, politicians, and other special interest groups presuming to tell us what is news or where our responsibilities lie.

He immediately qualified this by saying the researchers really have a right to research, "But we must not permit these matters to divert us from our task, or confuse us as to what that task is."

To his statement, I would say "Amen," if the journalists would undertake their own research instead. Who is better qualified to study journalism than the journalist? I don't mean every journalist should undertake a research project, any more than every lawyer does legal research and every physician does medical research. But some should, and others should support them. (To argue that journalism is merely a craft and not a profession is quibbling with definitions. Journalism is too powerful to ignore professional responsibilities.)

The networks and large television stations now have sales research departments. A few of the largest news departments also employ a "researcher" or two, usually a girl whose job it is to look things up and make telephone calls for information. That, plus some intelligently managed survey re-

85

search for network election coverage and some polling, is about it for news operations, so far as I know.

Networks and large stations ought to engage in basic and applied mass communications research, using university facilities where needed. And the results of their research should influence their work. Other professions benefit from their own research. Why not journalism?

For example, I should like to see research on the effect of visual images on auditory news information. When film of a farmyard is used to illustrate a story about farm legislation, it is possible that the picture of a cow munching hay overwhelms what the newscaster is reporting. I don't know that this is so, but I venture to guess that neither does the news director who ordered the film shot.

If this rustic example sounds simple, there is more complex and sensitive research to be done, not only by sociologists and psychologists who often don't know the territory, but by trained and concerned television journalists. How can film of a riot or a demonstration or strike violence best be put into perspective (the viewer's perspective, not the newscaster's) by words? How can war coverage be improved in the only way that really matters—the information being imparted?

The list is long, maybe endless, and the questions are not trifling. If electronic journalism is to have the future we hope for, continued growth in freedom, the men who practice it must make it their business to analyze the effects of what they do upon the tens of millions of Americans who watch television newscasts daily.

Above courtesy of Irving E. Fang and *Saturday Review*, January 9, 1971. Dr. Fang is an associate professor in the School of Journalism and Mass Communication at the University of Minnesota. A TV newsman for nine years, he is author of a textbook, *Television News*, published by Hastings House.

No forced sterilization

An ominous ploy used by many opponents of abortion--and unfortunately even by some supporters of abortion--is to link abortion with "population control." In Nixon's April 3 statement against abortion, for example, he termed abortion "an unacceptable form of population control." Politicians like Nixon refuse to recognize abortion as **a woman's right to choose** whether or not to have a child; they can only conceive of "controlling" women's lives--either by forcing them to be breeders through restrictive abortion laws, or by forcing them not to have children, through forced or pressured sterilization.

In the past several weeks, bills that would in effect prescribe forced sterilization for welfare mothers as a condition for continuing to receive welfare payments have been introduced into the Tennessee, Illinois and North Carolina legislatures. These bills, proposed as "population control" measures and also as a means of decreasing the welfare rolls, clearly illustrate how far these racist and class-prejudiced politicians will go in oppressing poor working-class women--Black, Chicano, Puerto Rican, Native American, and white--whom they consider less than human.

These diabolical attempts at manipulating women demonstrate that the demand of "No Forced Sterilization" is a crucial part of the struggle for legal abortions. The women's movement must make it absolutely clear that the movement for repeal of reactionary abortion laws supports the right of the woman-- and no one else--to control her own body.

ON THE RIGHT

William F. Buckley Jr.

*　　*　　*

WELFARE. Let's quit horsing around. The permanent denizens of the welfare rolls, as distinct from the handicapped and the helpless and the temporarily unfortunate, are moral criminals and should be treated as legal criminals too. If parents of a child born out of wedlock are unable or unwilling to care for the child, the parents should be jailed and the child should be put in an institution. For the second bastard, the parents should be sterilized. (Here I note parenthetically the distinction between punitive sterilization and eugenic sterilization. The latter is forbidden by the natural law, by the Catholic Church, and I trust by other churches. Not so the former—though I have no doubt the bleeding hearts would be aghast at the idea.)

Drastic, yes. But does anyone doubt that our present system calls for a drastic remedy? We should never forget that the cost of welfare is only secondarily financial. It breeds a growing underclass that saps the foundation of education, morals and patriotism, that assures an ever-growing criminal cadre. Welfare *attacks America*.

Above, © King Features Syndicate, Inc.

Top page, reprinted by permission of J. Michael Lux, copyright © 1971. May 14, 1971.

Text of Abortion-Bill Veto

Special to The New York Times

ALBANY, May 13 — Following is the text of Governor Rockefeller's message to the Legislature vetoing repeal of the state's liberalized abortion law:

The same strong reasons that led me to recommend abortion-law reform in my annual message . . . for 1968-69 and 1970 and to sign into law the reform that was ultimately adopted in 1970, now compel me to disapprove the bill just passed that would would repeal that reform.

The abortion-law reform of 1970 grew out of the recommendations of an outstanding select citizens committee, representative of all affected parties, that I appointed in 1968.

Under the distinguished leadership of retired Court of Appeals Judge Charles W. Froessel, the select committee found that the then-existing, 19th-century, near-total prohibition against abortion was fostering hundreds of thousands of illegal and dangerous abortions. It was discriminating against women of modest means who could not afford an abortion haven and the often frightened, unwed, confused young woman. It was promoting hypocrisy and, ultimately, human tragedy.

Connecticut Case Cited

I supported the majority recommendations of the Froessel committee through-out the public debate of this issue extending over three years, until the Legislature acted to reform the state's archaic abortion law. I can see no justification now for repealing this reform and thus condemning hundreds of thousands of women to the dark age once again.

There is, further, the recent Federal court decision invalidating the Connecticut abortion law, which is substantially the same as the pre-reform New York law. The law of that case, if upheld, would clearly invalidate the old New York law, as well, were the repeal of abortion reform allowed to stand. In such a circumstance, this state would be left with no law on the subject at all.

I fully respect the moral convictions of both sides in this painfully sensitive controversy. But the extremes of personal vilification and political coercion brought to bear on members of the Legislature raise serious doubts that the votes to repeal the reform has represented the will of a majority of the people of New York State.

Risk to Life Seen

The very intensity of this debate has generated an emotional climate in which the truth about abortions and about the present state abortion law have become distorted almost beyond recognition.

The truth is that this repeal of the 1970 reform would not end abortions. It would only end abortions under safe and supervised medical conditions.

The truth is that a safe abortion would remain the optional choice of the well-to-do woman, while the poor would again be seeking abortions at a grave risk to life in back-room abortion mills.

The truth is that, under the present law, no woman is compelled to undergo an abortion. Those whose personal and religious principles forbid abortion are in no way compelled against their convictions under the present law. Every woman has the right to make her own choice.

I do not believe it right for one group to impose its vision of morality on an entire society. Neither is it just or practical for the state to attempt to dictate the innermost personal beliefs and conduct of its citizens.

The bill is disapproved.

"Surely, The Unborn Have Rights . . ."

Following is the complete text of President Richard Nixon's statement against abortion which he issued on April 3rd to reverse an earlier decision by Defense Department officials approving permissive abortion in military hospitals.

~~~~~~~~~~

Historically, laws regulating abortion in the United States have been the province of States, not the Federal Government. That remains the situation today, as one State after another takes up this question, debates it and decides it. That is where the decisions should be made.

Partly, for that reason, I have directed that the policy on abortions at American military bases in the United States be made to correspond with the laws of the States where those bases are located. If the laws in a particular State restrict abortions, the rule at the military base hospitals are to correspond to that law.

The effect of this directive is to reverse service regulations issued last Summer, which had liberalized the rules on abortions at military hospitals. The new ruling supersedes this — and has been put into effect by the Secretary of Defense.

But while this matter is being debated in State capitals, and weighed by various courts, the Country has a right to know my personal views.

From personal and religious beliefs I consider abortions an unacceptable form of population control. Further, unrestricted abortion policies, or abortion on demand, I cannot square with my personal belief in the sanctity of human life — including the life of the yet unborn. For, surely, the unborn have rights also, recognized in law, recognized even in principles expounded by the United Nations.

Ours is a nation with a Judeo-Christian heritage. It is also a nation with serious social problems — problems of malnutrition, of broken homes, of poverty and of delinquency. But none of these problems justifies such a solution.

A good and generous people will not opt, in my view, for this kind of alternative to its social dilemmas. Rather, it will open its hearts and homes to the unwanted children of its own, as it has done for the unwanted millions of other lands.

Above, from *The New York Times*, May 13, 1971.
Right, from *The Wanderer*, April 22, 1971.

Spiro's Theory

"Sooner or later," said Spiro T. Agnew last month, extemporaneously, government must decide whether or not to let terminal patients die, deprive mothers of illegitimate babies of welfare payments and take children from unfit mothers. "I have a theory that these problems will never be subject to complete solution until somebody in public life is willing to take on the hard social judgments that, very frankly, no one I know in elective office is willing to even think about tackling" for fear of being "victimized by the demagogues."

In a newspaper column appearing at about the same time, the Vice President addressed himself to "one angle of the [welfare] problem that must have our best and most serious thinking." Since it is "ridiculous" to think of welfare mothers as capable of providing a "decent home environment," adoption laws must be liberalized to make it easier for couples "willing and able to give children the home they need." Mr. Agnew was not explicit about how the children were to get from their unqualified mothers into the hands of government-qualified parents (perhaps he did not want to dilute the effect of his next speech), but he did offer a clue as to what children he had in mind: children's problems are "far greater in the urban ghettos and it is here that we must begin."

A Republican-sponsored bill recently introduced in the Connecticut legislature proposes that welfare mothers with two or more illegitimate children be given $300 if they agree to undergo sterilization at state expense. Meanwhile the Supreme Court has ruled, in Justice Harry Blackmun's maiden opinion, that welfare recipients may not refuse, under the Fourth Amendment, to open their homes to "visits" by government social workers; to do so, in fact, should automatically disqualify them for further aid.

All rather surprising views to come from Republicans, from a "conservative" Supreme Court, from Spiro T. Agnew, no? No.

This Space Available

Broadcast cigarette ads have been banned. It won't end there—that's not the way of governments. Further federal interference was augured by the Surgeon General last month: "Nonsmokers have as much right to clean and wholesome air as smokers have to their so-called right to smoke, which I would redefine as a right to pollute." He specifically mentioned airplanes and restaurants (it won't end there) as public places where smoking should be banned.

Now, to our knowledge, everyone has the right *not* to smoke, whether subjected to an advertisement or not; nor is anyone denying nonsmokers the right to stay away from restaurants. Could it be, then, that the government is getting at the problem, not of "rights," but of pollution? Then why pick on cigarettes and not, say, airplanes or cars? If health is the issue, why not ban television (it causes scurvy of the mind), or saturated fats, or the Pill, or the Surgeon General?

The anti-tobacco evangelism is a neo-Puritan substitute for moral fervor: when no one any longer believes in sin, something new must be found to condemn. But morality, having connections with higher things, does not take kindly to such arbitrary treatment.

Moved by this higher morality, we repeat our willingness to run cigarette ads in our pages. And some of us, as Christians, will do penance for the sins of the state by not giving up smoking for Lent.

Top right, above, from *Triumph*, publication of the Society for the Christian Commonwealth, 278 Broadview Avenue, Warrenton, Virginia 22186, February 1971.

Right   from the booklet *The Sacredness of Life*, published by the Knights of Columbus, © 1966.

Sterilization

The position of the Catholic Church is therefore a condemnation of all forms of direct sterilization, whether compulsory or voluntary. Her condemnation is based on ethics which lay great emphasis on one's inalienable right to life and bodily integrity. The mentality of the contemporary social milieu cannot understand why God may permit suffering and other forms of societal problems to exist. Eugenists fail to see that happiness hereafter is purchasable by self-sacrificing care of the unfortunate. Divine Providence permits the unfortunate to be among us to give man an opportunity to exercise that charity which deserves the kingdom of heaven. They scarcely deserve that kingdom who would rid us of the inconvenient presence of unfortunates by violating nature's law. (See Higgins, S. J., op. cit., p. 214). If God allows misfortune and adversity to exist, He does so for a reason. Suffering may be the occasion for advancement in our spiritual life. Nothing takes place without a reason. God is the Creator of this universe, He is good, kind, just and all powerful. We must have faith in according Him the wisdom in knowing how to run this complex world in which we find ourselves.

Controlling your child's life

Bit by bit the advocates of social engineering in Washington are building the machinery required to convert America into a totalitarian society.

These are strong words but we use them with deliberation. It has become apparent in recent months that certain theoreticians and planners in the U.S. political community are out to achieve the most critical goal of every totalitarian regime — to impose the power of the state over that of the family, and to place the upbringing of children under the complete control of bureaucratic "experts." The stated object of this exercise is to use the power of government to create new types of human beings.

A major step toward this objective was taken in Congress Sept. 30 when the U.S. House of Representatives passed, as part of a bill for the Office of Economic Opportunity, a revolutionary "child development" proposal. The purpose of this legislation, which has also been adopted in the Senate, is to solicit massive patronage of a network of day-care centers across the nation, to establish federal child development programs and councils, and to set up "child advocacy projects" to snoop into family relationships.

Essential features of this legislation include the idea that day-care centers should be resorted to by all U.S. families, not just the "working poor," that child advocacy representatives should make it their business to inquire into and act upon the affairs of specific children and families, and that such programs should be "comprehensive" and available as "a matter of right," because they are "essential to the achievement of the full potential of the nation's children."

Emphasis is placed by child development advocates on getting children under such "expert" control at the earliest possible age.

The thinking behind all this, also manifest in controversies over busing and sex education, is that parents are too ignorant to be entrusted with shaping up their children's psyches, and that the job must be handled by the authorities of government.

We hope President Nixon will turn thumbs down on such alien notions and veto the bill in question.

Left, from *The Arizona Republic*, October 24, 1971

Between Her and Her Doctor

AS HAS happened in other states, a Michigan judge has held that the language of the Michigan statute on abortion is "vague and indefinite." District Judge Clarence Reid Jr. of Southfield says the law is a denial of due process as provided in the 14th Amendment of the Constitution.

The decision, which resulted in the dismissal of an abortion charge against a Pleasant Ridge doctor, certainly is within the bounds of reason. The Oakland County prosecutor's office will appeal it to the Michigan Supreme Court, however, and the wrangle will begin all over again.

Judge Reid argues that the state does not have a "compelling interest" in the sex lives of its citizens and that the original reason for passage of Michigan's abortion statute, to protect the life of the pregnant women, is no longer valid, with the improvements in technology.

The law, as it works out in modern practice, works in reverse. It drives women to kitchen-table surgery which places their lives in danger. It denies them sanitary facilities and competent surgery.

The move to strike the old restrictions against abortion and make such a process a matter which is strictly between a woman and her doctor is growing throughout the nation.

Prompt action by the Legislature on the Michigan problem will save us a lot of legalizing and is a far more direct and useful approach than complicated court arguing over what is really a pretty simple issue, a woman's right to make her own decision about something so personal and so much a matter of personal morality.

From the *Detroit Free Press*, April 1, 1970.

Was FDR Derelict in Not Visiting Hitler?

Nixon Ignores Moral Considerations in Planning China Trip

By WILLIAM F. BUCKLEY JR.

Concerning the evolving drama of Mr. Nixon's trip to China, a few observations:

If Mao Tse-tung had "free elections" in mainland China tomorrow, it is altogether possible that he would achieve 99 per cent of the vote even if immunity were granted to dissenters. The reason for this is apparent from the reports on China that have come flooding in since the authorities raised the curtain to a few athletes and journalists last spring. China seems to have killed or otherwise disposed of the incremental objector, so as to have achieved the society of the perfectly misled.

Even so, we are hardly absolved from the moral question. One could visit the slave markets of Charleston, South Carolina, in the early part of the 19th century, and find total docility, from which it did not follow that slavery was a happy estate. Terror in China, largely cloistered from public view, has produced Chinese Man: and it is before this audience that Richard Nixon proposes to exhibit himself.

One thinks of the forthcoming elections in South Vietnam, and of the critics of President Thieu who are already busy discounting those elections, insisting that they will not yield a government which is "responsive" to the will of the people. What is their quarrel with the government of Mao Tse-tung? Do they hope that Mr. Nixon will ask Mao to form a government responsive to people who have not been ground out by cookie cutters from his book of Thoughts? Will the Americans for Democratic Action ask Mr. Nixon to demand that China invite Chiang Kai-shek back from Taiwan, to form a coalition government?

NO, THE MORAL ARGUMENT is of course put permanently in abeyance. The critics of South Vietnam, which introduced rudimentary democracy 14 years ago, are like the concentration camp inmates, silent, and smiling, and unctuous, when they address Mao Tse-tung or Chou En-lai. Their sins are not only forgiven them, they are not remembered.

All the restraints one thinks of as decent against suddenly fraternizing with the killers are forgotten: and it becomes basely clear that what matters isn't so much whether a government is vile in its provenance, in its practices, in its ambitions, as whether it is powerful. If it is powerful enough, American liberals will preen like schoolboys before a headmaster. I am waiting for one of the progressive legislators who are congratulating Mr. Nixon to answer simply the question: was Franklin Roosevelt derelict for not traveling to Nazi Germany to be convivial with Adolph Hitler?

Why has Mr. Nixon neglected this dimension of the problem? Only a few months ago, asked by a reporter what excuse did we have left to continue to ostracize Fidel Castro, Mr. Nixon drew himself up and delivered some anti-Communist boiler plate on the evil behavior of Castro. The evil behavior of Castro! By Maoan standards, he is Florence Nightingale.

IN 1939, THE WORLD was stunned, as it was stunned last week, by the announcement of a Soviet-Hitler pact. The Soviets had been merchandising the Nazis as their principal enemies for six years, and vice versa. Suddenly, a pact.

One year and ten months after that pact, the two nations went to war, the reversal of feelings suiting the convenience of Hitler (and for that matter Stalin). But meanwhile, the two countries totally reversed themselves and accordingly even Stalin's fellow-travelers totally reversed themselves on the question whether the United States should go to the help of England.

The moral of this historical reminiscence is that Nazi-Soviet pacts are precisely possible between governments which are run by Nazis and Soviets. Free countries require preparation. Require, in this case, elaborate reasons and public discussion for suddenly turning as Mr. Nixon has done.

What makes him think that he can manipulate the nation, as Hitler and Stalin did? Because the public is hell bent on appeasement at this moment, he can probably get away with kissing the bull on the nose. But then when he gets around to making his move, and needs the strong military tools, the indomitable public mood, the tenacious public opinion, how is he going to come up with it? Who will believe him? Why should they believe him? Do you see what I mean?

The Great Trip-Wire Delusion

Courtesy of Alan Cranston, U.S. Senator from California and *Saturday Review*, July 19, 1971.

EDITOR'S NOTE: *The following guest editorial is by Alan Cranston, U.S. Senator from California, and longtime contributor to* SR.

The U.S. Senate recently voted down Majority Leader Mike Mansfield's attempt to compel a 50 per cent reduction in the number of American ground troops stationed in Europe.

In the Senate debate much attention was given to the need to scale down East-West tensions, to correct our adverse balance of payments, and to get our now quite prosperous allies to assume a larger share of the financial and military burdens of NATO. All good points. But I sensed a disturbing undercurrent.

There appears to be a tacit understanding on both sides of the Atlantic that a sizable number of American troops must be stationed on the Continent as a kind of human trip wire to assure our intervention in the event of a Soviet invasion of Western Europe.

The theory seems to be that thousands of Americans must be engaged in mortal combat in the first days of such an invasion, else we will not intercede. The belief is that the larger this human trip wire, and the more human flesh it contains, the more confident our friends and allies will feel, and the more hesitant the Russians will be.

I find this concept utterly repellent, and morally grotesque. I am appalled by the image of 300,000 Americans being offered up as sacrificial hostages in a new, perverted version of "earnest money" to reassure our friends that we will keep our pledge. I am shocked each time our foreign friends interpret any effort to reduce the number of hostages as hard evidence that we indeed intend to go back on our word.

What kind of friends are these anyway? What kind of opinion do they have of us to think that we do not value human lives unless they are American lives? To think that we would not consider the lives of other free men worthy of our concern in the event of Soviet aggression? And to think that only the on-the-spot slaughter of young Americans could provoke us to act in our own best interests?

Those who subscribe to the trip-wire strategy claim it offers us flexibility— a way to resist aggression without resorting to all-out nuclear retaliation. The fact is, however, that the great armies of NATO and the Warsaw Pact facing each other across an imaginary line in Central Europe are as dated as the cavalry that tried to stand up to the Nazi panzer divisions in Poland. Our troops in Europe are armed with tactical nuclear weapons as are, presumably, the Warsaw Pact forces.

The Davy Crockett, a cannon manned by a crew of five, has been called the "keystone of the Allied defense line." With an explosive force somewhat less than that of the Hiroshima bomb, it is our smallest tactical weapon, and we have others even more powerful.

In an East-West war in Europe, the side that is losing, or thinks it is losing, will without doubt resort to nuclear weapons to "save the day." Even the "winning" side would do so, if it thought the enemy was about to launch a strike. It is for just these eventualities that we have our tactical nuclear weapons positioned there. So our troops in Europe are targets for almost certain death or radiation poisoning in the event of war. They cannot win; they can only destroy and be destroyed.

We have been lucky so far, but the day must come soon—before this murderous insanity goes too much further —when we will have to reduce our NATO forces. We must recognize that there is no true security for us or for anyone else in a world in which nuclear weapons are on the loose. We must set about the task of providing leadership dedicated to achieving world peace through world law.

Do some of our leaders feel that they must use a trip-wire force to insure that we will keep our commitment to our NATO allies? Are we busily preparing for a day when we may be in the same position in Europe as we are now in in Southeast Asia? Will we someday be told that millions of Americans must die for those 300,000 American troops in Europe—just as we are being told now that still more Americans must die in Indochina so that the deaths of the 45,000 already killed there will, somehow, have been "worthwhile"?

If that is what some of our leaders think, if that is why they insist on maintaining 300,000 American troops on European soil, their perspective, in my judgment, is dangerously distorted. One such horror is more than enough in the lifetime of any nation.

The fact is that the whole structure of the trip-wire concept is built on false assumptions. The fact is that we do not need such an immoral mechanism forcibly to link Europe's destiny with ours. The fact is that we are inextricably linked with Europe—by past history and heritage, and by present politics and economics.

A free, independent Europe is vital to America's survival and to world peace; a free Europe and a free America stand or fall together.

That is why we are in the alliance, that is why we will unhesitatingly honor our commitment should we ever be called upon to do so—not to avenge the blood of American hostages, but to defend American freedom and the very concept of freedom.

Our European allies and those of our leaders who presume otherwise do the American people a grave injustice.

—ALAN CRANSTON.

SR/JUNE 19, 1971

A Matter of Judgment

Conservation controversies are disputes in viewpoint. Porter (Letters, 5 July), argues that the proposed mining in Glacier Bay National Monument is desirable because greater benefits would result than would by leaving the Monument inviolate. I would argue the opposite, but for exactly the same reason. The point of disagreement is not one which can be resolved by "objective analysis" of the "facts." These are differences in value and judgment. . . . Most resource allocation problems are not ones of "right" versus "wrong," of conservationists fighting greedy exploiters, but rather they are disputes over what constitutes the best kind of conservation. Certainly scientists can point out the danger of pesticides, but how can they decide the Glacier Bay mining dispute? Does the recent article on coast redwood ecology by Stone and Vasey (12 Jan., p. 157) resolve the Redwood National Park question? I think not.

Criteria for decision-making in conservation controversies (use versus preservation of landscapes) is needed. . . . The search for answers must start with defining the goals, values, and purposes of society. Science does not claim to answer questions of civil rights; is the problem of mining in Glacier Bay National Monument really any different?

TOM VALE

Department of Geography,
University of California, Berkeley

Above, letter to the editor of *Science* by Tom Vale, September 13, 1968.

ANATOLY AGRANOVSKY # Drafting New Laws:
Debate and Decision In the Supreme Soviet

In this article, Izvestia *Special Correspondent Anatoly Agranovsky, a leading writer on Soviet internal affairs, employs a breezy, informal style to capture on paper an aspect of the workings of Soviet democracy—the process of drafting new legislation. Rather than encumber Agranovsky's account with numerous completions and explanations, we have left it pretty much as written for Soviet readers.*

THE commissions of the Supreme Soviet, seventh convocation, had greatly stepped up their work in preparation for the elections held last summer. At that time I investigated the work of the commissions, to see how, and how well, they were working.

For example, the commission on health and social insurance is meeting (minutes of December 10, 1969). The chairman is N. N. Blokhin, 58, a prominent scientist and surgeon, no newcomer to the Supreme Soviet, he had been a deputy twice before.

As a rule, qualified deputies are elected to head the commissions. In addition to the deputies who make up the basic membership, economists, trade-union leaders, jurists, physicians, and other specialists are invited. They are volunteers, helping to work out the new legislation. The future law is probed line by line. Some corrections are of a purely editorial nature. It is suggested that the word "thus" precede the word "facilitating." Others are more essential: the word "towns" should be followed by "and other populated places." But, here is an essential matter: may a patient be operated on without his consent or that of his near relatives?

"How do you expect to get a patient's consent, if he is unconscious? And his relatives are in another city or no one knows where? Can the surgeon afford to waste time?"

"But I don't know of any law in any other country empowering a surgeon to operate at will."

"What about a suicide, when a person does not want to be saved?"

"You're wrong, they always want to be saved."

"And take perforation of an ulcer. The patient will give his consent when it is too late. In order to save lives the surgeon must be empowered . . ."

"I don't agree. During the war there were cases when patients refused to have amputations. And if not all, at least many of them recovered. How can I, without a person's consent, begin sawing his leg off?"

"There can be so many cases, it is impossible to foresee everything."

"It has to be legally provided for, otherwise the rendering of urgent aid will be impaired. When an operation is imperative, the surgeon cannot take time to search for relatives or conduct negotiations."

So it was written down: yes, the surgeon may and even must take the decision upon himself, but only in *exceptional cases,* when any delay *threatens the life of the patient,* when *it is impossible to obtain the consent of the above-mentioned people.* Subsequently, this wording became law.

Need I say that the lives of many people depend on each word? Debates are inevitable here.

From the quarterly magazine *New World Review,* Spring 1971.

Gigantic moral failure

The ordeal of Rabbi Tutnauer and his family (see above) makes it clear that the convergence theory—that notion, so popular in recent years, that Russia was evolving toward a democratic welfare state — remains a gigantic delusion. Russia's assault on human values remains as persistent as ever.

But those who advance the convergence theory, in defiance of every scrap of evidence, are unlikely to alter their opinion. If the Hungarian and Czechoslovakian invasions didn't alter their opinion, or the entire sordid record of the past 25 or 30 years didn't convince them, they aren't going to jettison their dogma because of intimidation and harassment against one U.S. family.

One of the lasting shames of our age is that decent Western liberals, otherwise so sensitive to assaults on human values, have failed to condemn Communist brutality and terror in other than pro forma phrases.

Instead, they have r e s e r v e d their obloquy for those who have perceived that communism is perhaps the most sordid d o c t r i n e ever to enslave the minds and bodies of masses of 20th century men. They have not been content to denounce merely the oversimplifiers among the anti-Communists; they have worked over virtually every public figure or scholar who has refused to genuflect before the belief that communism is merely another political system, worse than some and better than others.

Communism is not pernicious merely because it is atheistic, bureaucratic, and minatory. It is pernicious because it is a doctrine that transforms ordinary human beings into moral monsters, capable of even such heinous crimes as the wholesale slaughter and liquidation of its own people.

It is pernicious because it regards human beings as mere clay to be moulded and twisted according to official state doctrine. It is evil because, in every Communist nation on earth, it exacts obedience through fear, terror, and intimidation. It is, as Russian writer Valery Tarsis described it, a system of "police facism" on a scale unknown in history.

But leftists in the Western democracies, with only a handful of honorable exceptions, have regularly excused the crimes of communism and attacked its critics. Theirs is a moral failure without parallel in our century.

Russia remains what it has been — a vast prison run by guards driven by a brutal, debased ideology. And while we are appalled at the treatment given the Tutnauers during their visit, it is worthwhile to point out that they received red carpet treatment compared with the ordeal the average Russian citizen is subjected to throughout his lifetime.

Above, from *The Arizona Republic*, August 28, 1971.

Right, An ad for Doubleday & Company's *Americans and Chinese*: Purpose and Fulfillment in Great Civilizations by Francis L.K. Hsu.

Pot, Drugs, and Alcohol

That long-time favorite of commentators on the social and political scene, the "generation gap," is sometimes characterized today in terms of a conflict over each's respective "vices"—the "old folks" have their legalized vices (e.g., alcohol, cigarettes, and prescription tranquilizers), while the younger generation is deprived by the "establishment's" legal system of their vices (e.g., marijuana, LSD, and other "illicit" drugs). The query of the young people, "If you don't object to alcohol, why do you object to marijuana?" has a firm basis in ethical theory and much in common particularly with Immanuel Kant's dictum that morality requires consistency. In brief, this means that if someone believes that one thing (e.g., the use of marijuana) is morally right or wrong, then he must accept that all things similar to it with regard to relevant features are similarly right or wrong, or else his beliefs on these matters cannot be *moral* beliefs. Thus someone who objects to marijuana and not to alcohol, and who claims that his objections are moral ones—as opposed to prudential or legal ones—must be able to point to some relevant difference between the two. However if such a distinction cannot be drawn, if it is determined that there are no relevant differences between pot and alcohol, this would at most imply that their moral worth is similar. It still must be ascertained whether this moral value is positive or negative, whether they are both good or bad (or possibly neutral). Ultimately, another whole set of issues—that is, the problems of public policy and civil disobedience—must be faced concerning whether they ought to be legalized or prohibited, or whether one is justified in breaking already enacted laws involving the use of such items. And the consistency criterion is equally relevant in any discussion of these other issues.

Legalized Pot

HERE IS ONE small cheer for legalizing marijuana. Rah for *cannabis sativa*, pot, grass, Mary Jane.

Two rahs would be too many, because the principal reason for legalizing the happy-time weed is quite similar to the reason for repealing the prohibition against alcoholic beverages four decades ago. Both marijuana and alcohol seem to cause more trouble when they are illegal than when they become legal.

No one can argue compellingly that Americans become better persons by drinking Martinis, as President Nixon does, or by drawing pot smoke into their lungs, as many young and not-so-young people are doing in defiance of the law. Outside of occasional medicinal use—marijuana now is being tried as a relaxant for terminal cancer patients—there is no strong, positive reason for legalizing either drug.

But a positive reason is not really necessary. A strong negative reason against the grass ban will do. The argument for marijuana rests on such a negative reason and on one indisputable fact: Large numbers of human beings *will* use psychoactive drugs like pot and alcohol.

Today, marijuana is being smoked by great numbers of Americans. Most of them know, or at least guess, that grass is not as dangerous to them as alcohol is. As psychiatrist Lester Grinspoon of Harvard says in his new book, *Marihuana Reconsidered*, marijuana is "among the least dangerous of the psychoactive drugs." He points to the "curious fact" that Western society sanctions the use of tobacco and alcohol, though both cause tissue damage in humans. Marijuana does not. Nor does it lead to addiction. The question of whether pot leads to harder drugs is in dispute, but most authorities can find no real cause-and-effect relationship. President Nixon chose to ignore these findings last week when he said that legalizing marijuana would be "detrimental" to young people, because pot "is only a half-way house to something worse." Like Martinis?

Those who smoke grass also know they are violating the law, and are "criminals" subject to stiff jail sentences. This "punitive, repressive approach," argues Dr. Grinspoon, leads young pot smokers to view their society as hypocritical. A pot high is banned; an alcohol high is not, even though it is more dangerous.

That is the real problem of the legal ban against grass. As young people turn on with pot, they tend to turn off the society at large.

Dr. Grinspoon offers a reasonable solution: Legalize marijuana under controls similar to those for alcohol. No one under 18 could use it legally. Marijuana's potency would be strictly controlled to reduce the chance of a "bad trip." The quality would be guaranteed, so the smoker would know that his grass was not laced with other drugs.

Over all, this could be about as effective as present controls over alcohol—not perfect, but better than it was. There still would be abuse of pot smoking as there is of alcohol drinking. But no more criminal arrests for getting a simple pot high, as there are no arrests for drinking a Martini at the White House.

—*JAMES G. DRISCOLL*

From *The National Observer*, March 22, 1971.

Since marijuana is not a deterrent, no more than cigarettes, it seems inhumane that they *schlep* people and put them in jail with it.

"Well, maybe marijuana's not *bad* for you, but it's a stepping stone. It leads to heavier drugs—heroin, etc."

Well, that syllogism has to work out this way, though: The heroin addict, the bust-out junkie that started out smoking pot, says to his cell-mate:

"I'm a bust-out junkie. Started out smoking pot, look at me now. By the way, cell-mate, what happened to you? There's blood on your hands. How'd you get to murder those kids in that crap game? Where did it all start?"

"Started with bingo in the Catholic Church."

"I see."

Top left, from *The Essential Lenny Bruce.* Copyright 1967 Ballantine Books/A Product of Douglas Book Corporation.

Below, from *Psychology Today.*

Drug Abuse— Just What The Doctor Ordered

by J. Maurice Rogers

The image of the physician as expert and benign begins to evaporate when we see physicians pushing psychoactive pills whose consequences are not fully understood into patients whose problems require human, not chemical, solutions.

Ads. Doctors are strongly encouraged in their pill-for-every-problem syndrome by drug manufacturers who bombard them with advertisements in psychiatric and medical journals:

"WHAT MAKES A WOMAN CRY? *A man? Another woman? Three kids? No kids at all? Wrinkles? You name it . . . If she is depressed, consider Pertofane.*"

And:

"SCHOOL, THE DARK, SEPARATION, DENTAL VISITS, MONSTERS. THE EVERYDAY ANXIETY OF CHILDREN SOMETIMES GETS OUT OF HAND. *A child can usually deal with his anxieties. But sometimes the anxieties overpower the child. Then he needs your help. Your help may include Vistaril.*"

And this advertisement, which shows an attractive but worried-looking young woman with an armful of books, and describes the problems that face a new college student:

"*Exposure to new friends and other influences may force her to re-evaluate herself and her goals . . . Her newly stimulated intellectual curiosity may make her more sensitive to and apprehensive about national and world conditions.*" The headline reads: "TO HELP FREE HER OF EXCESSIVE ANXIETY . . . LIBRIUM."

Such advertisements redefine normal problems of living as medical problems to be solved by drugs. Most small children, of course, are at some time afraid of the dark or anxious about school. A person may become depressed after personal loss, upon facing a new job, having to adjust to new conditions, or upon experiencing impotence in the face of increasing social turmoil. But the advocacy of drugs for such problems is socially irresponsible.

One Wrong To Justify Another

Greenberg's excellent article on the marijuana raid at Stony Brook (9 Feb., p. 607) is a perfect exposition of the older generation's apparent helplessness when confronted with adolescent stupidity. The misguided young pot smokers attempt to justify their behavior on the grounds that other things (tobacco and alcohol, used to excess) are known to be bad but are not prohibited; therefore marijuana (the extent of whose deleterious effects are not known with scientific precision) must also be permitted. To generalize, we must not proscribe any evil as long as we allow some other evils to exist.

It seems to me that this rationalization is being used in all kinds of situations by those who would defy any form of authority. In matters of religion we are told that because there are some hypocrites in the congregation (which is true) all pronouncements of churchmen are without standing. In matters of morals, the fact that certain deviations are tolerated or poorly enforced is held to negate all moral authority. The fact that some adults are Babbitts or "squares" is considered ample justification for spurning the advice of all adults. The fact that we don't allow the police to break people's doors down to check up on what they are reading in bed is supposed to make it all right to peddle semipornographic trash in bookstores and theaters. The fact that some white people are prejudiced is given as reason enough to "burn Whitey," and because some Negroes riot there are those who would put "the Negro" back in his place. In every instance, one wrong is being used to justify another.

There is no reason to be surprised that such childish reasoning is used by immature people—this has been going on since time immemorial. What is so discouraging is that supposedly intelligent people, including a fairly strong and vociferous segment of our educators and scientists, are not only unable to cope with such arguments on the part of adolescent students, but actually side with the students in their blind rebellion against any standards of conduct.

JOHN D. ALDEN
98 Sunnyside Avenue,
Pleasantville, New York 10570

Above, letter to the editor of *Science* by John D. Alden, May 10, 1968.

Deterioration of the Human

All that sets man apart from lower forms of animal life, all that makes human life truly human, in some way depends on man's cerebral cortex. So far as we know, that bit of gray protein is the pinnacle of God's creation. It is the growing edge of evolution. Therein lies the seat of rational thought, of moral judgment, of self-awareness, of qualitative distinction, of meaning-perception. To the degree that the cerebral cortex is temporarily numbed, the human is temporarily de-graded back toward the animal. This is precisely what happens when psychotropic drugs are ingested. The brain still works, but it is impaired — reduced to lower than its natural level. It responds not to changes in its real environment, nor to the real needs of the self nor to the Spirit of God, but to toxic substances introduced into its blood supply. Such a condition may be pleasurable — indeed, that is precisely why it is sought. But in such a condition a man is less than fully himself, though he may feel ten feet tall. It is, then, the use of psychotropic drugs, not their misuse, that is the moral issue. It is precisely their intended effect, not just their side effects, that we must ponder.

Better the Ambiguities

It might seem to be a cruel asceticism for a man to deny himself short holidays from his woes, even though our contemporary happiness drugs are faulty and fiendishly risky. But in the long run it is even more cruel to the best that is within us to take trips from which we must return with neither ourselves nor our environment changed for the better, and with some past accounts long overdue to boot. Better the ambiguities and tensions experienced by a real man interacting with other real men and the real God of the real world than the euphoria of chemically induced sensation of escape that does not really let us escape from anything at all, and that frequently forges some very strong chains of its own.

Mark tells us that just before Jesus was nailed to his cross he was offered as an anodyne "wine mingled with myrrh, but he did not take it." Few of Jesus' modern disciples begrudge themselves an anesthetic under any physical suffering whatsoever, be it so slight a thing as a headache. But for the figurative headaches which are so plentiful in our modern lives a damn is still better than a gram. Then when the euphoric moments come they will be genuine.

Thinking Out Loud

Our national leaders must further demonstrate that they are interested in the preservation of human lives.

If only a small percentage of the time and effort that is expended to stop the slaughter of Americans in Vietnam could be exerted against the greatest killer of all — the monstrous liquor traffic, much progress could be made.

This publication has been against the illegal and immoral war in Vietnam from the very start. It has also been overwhelmingly demonstrated by the politicians who launched it that it was to be a "no win war".

And now at this late date, after sacrificing 45,000 young men, and suffering over 300,000 casualties, any effort to reverse the trend and launch a crusade to win the war has about as much chance as a snowball in hell — and those who are pursuing this ill-fated course are well aware of this fact.

It would doubtless be far less appealing to those who demand "victory in Vietnam", waving flags and marching under banners, if they should be required to shoulder arms and lead in such a crusade in the marshy swamps of Indochina. But knowing that they shall not be called upon to make such a sacrifice they can go right on demanding that more thousands of young Americans must be slaughtered. And for what purpose?

But the subject of this editorial is not Vietnam but the Number One Killer—the abominable liquor traffic. Why can't we work up some steam against this horrible destroyer of human life? How long since we have heard of a politician in Congress — of any stature — getting up on the floor and making a speech — a two-fisted, knockout blow — against the liquor traffic?

Let us take a look at this problem specifically as it is known to be the Number One killer on the highways — to say nothing for the moment of its terrible drain on the national economy, its unspeakable immorality, its conscienceless wrecking of homes and its titanic waste of human bodies through alcoholism. Just think particularly of what it does on the highways:

30,000 lives were snuffed out last year from drinking drivers! This means that in only one and one-half years the liquor traffic claims as many casualties as we have lost in Vietnam in the entire duration of the war. Also, last year alone more than 800,000 accidents in traffic were attributal to beverage alcohol!

And, if we could became interested in comparative statistics on crime, we should be jolted by the fact that twice as many Americans died last year in automobile wrecks in which alcohol was involved as were murdered.

Consider also that twice as many innocent bystanders were killed by drunken drivers as were killed by robbers, rapists, arsonists and thieves combined!

More adults were convicted of drunken driving than of murder, robbery, assault, rape and burglaries combined!

Property destroyed in accidents involving alcohol was six times greater than that of property stolen in all robberies, larsonies, and burglaries in this nation.

The Department of Transportation reports that roughly 2 per cent of the drivers on the highways have enough alcohol in their systems to be legally drunk — but that these two percent are involved in more than 50 per cent of all fatal accidents.

This means that one in every 50 drivers on your highways today is a potential killer. WATCH OUT FOR YOUR LIFE!

And remember, the social drinkers are the greatest offenders! According to Raymond K. Berg, Chief Judge of the Chicago traffic court, a recent study shows that in that city only 20 per cent of those convicted of drunken driving were chronic alcoholics. This means that EIGHTY PER CENT WERE SOCIAL DRINKERS!

The liquor that is consumed at a private social gathering, even at a wedding, will kill on the highways, just the same as if it were consumed at some filthy bar, tavern, or saloon!

In the name of all that is high and holy and respectable and decent; in the name of precious human lives, when will some men in public life, and in national leadership, get up and speak out against this damnable killer — beverage alcohol?

"Wine is a mocker; strong drink is raging: and whosoever is deceived thereby is not wise," Prov. 20:1.

Dale Crowley in *The Capital Voice*, October 1, 1970.

MY LETTER TO THE PRESIDENT

December 8, 1970

The Honorable Richard M. Nixon,
President of the United States,
The White House, Washington, D. C.

Dear Mr. President:

In your office as Commander-In-Chief of the Armed Forces, I direct these urgent words to you. I fully believe that you are concerned about the morals, as well as the morale, of our enlisted men; and I do not believe that you will be indifferent to certain actions of our defense leaders which will inevitably demoralize our service men and impair the health of many of them. I refer to actions taken both by Army Chief of Staff, General Westmoreland, and Chief of Naval Operations, Admiral Elmo R. Zumwalt.

Recently, I was shocked and bewildered by the announcement that Admiral Zumwalt would sanction beer vending machines for the barracks of enlisted men. Now, on the heels of this, comes the astonishing announcement from General Westmoreland that beer will not only be made available on the army posts through the vending devices but also will be served with the evening meals in the mess halls!

In the name of high heaven, what do our military leaders mean by such a deplorable lowering of the standards. We all realize that alcoholism is one of the top problems of our nation today. Why should our defense establishment contribute further to the weakening of the morals and the destruction of the health of our fine young men upon which we so much depend at this critical time?

Many of these young men were reared by parents who have long regarded alcoholic beverage as the Number One curse on our society. Is it fair to these parents who turn their sons over to the defense establishment which will through such insane policies make alcoholics out of them? Mr. President, it is easy to see that our nation is losing vital ground through such outrageous practices. Will you not take immediate steps to override those decisions of our military leaders? Millions of citizens will thank you for reversing this demoralizing policy.

Thank you for your consideration of this matter.

Yours very sincerely,

From *The Capital Voice*, December 8, 1970.   (Signed) Dale Crowley

SECTION X

Crime and Punishment

The connection between crime and punishment is more complex than it may at first appear. The concepts of crime and punishment are not entirely free of ambiguity and vagueness, a fact which becomes particularly apparent when questions such as the following are asked: "Is it a crime to privately indulge a whim or fancy which hurts no one except (possibly) the agent?" (i.e., are "victimless crimes" really *crimes*?), "Is it punishment to put someone in jail who *wants* to go there?" "Is there 'good' (as opposed to 'cruel and unusual') punishment?" and "Is 'crime' identical to 'law-breaking'?" (if so, what are we to make of talk about "crimes against humanity," many of which break no legal statutes?). Such questions should be sufficient to put the reader on guard against naïvely assuming that these concepts are perfectly clear; the arguments in this section will illustrate the point even further.

In many states, jails and prisons are referred to as "correctional institutions"; others call them "penal institutions." This reflects a widely held assumption that "punishment" and "rehabilitation" refer to opposing philosophies. "Punishment" is thought to reflect a vengeful attitude toward criminals: an eye for an eye, a tooth for a tooth. "Rehabilitation" is supposed to reflect a desire to educate, or, in the terminology of certain psychologists, to modify behavior. The retributionist seeks to harm the criminal, the rehabilitationist seeks to help him. But we often find the two groups utilizing the same means to achieve their divergent ends, particularly incarceration. Beginning with the basic principle that causing suffering is morally wrong, the retributionist asserts that justice demands that those who cause suffering or death must themselves suffer or die. But others who share this same basic principle argue that if it is wrong for one person to harm another, then harming a criminal is just as wrong as the criminal's own act. (This disagreement is similar to that between the pacifist and the person who believes that some wars are morally justifiable.) On the other hand, the retributionist asserts that causing suffering is not wrong in itself and that causing a criminal to suffer is justifiable if that is the most efficient means for preventing further suffering. All of these viewpoints are so forcefully presented in the following selections that it will be difficult for the reader not to be partly sympathetic to each, and *that* is a genuine moral quandary.

Underlying this general problem are the more fundamental problems of freedom of the will and moral responsibility. In brief, if a person is theoretically *never* able to choose freely how he will act, then it is difficult to justify blaming him and punishing him for any of his actions. But the problems concerning freedom and responsibility are far more extensive than those surrounding the topic of punishment, and thus cannot be discussed further here.

Feiffer

LAWS ARE DESIGNED TO PROTECT SOCIETY.

WHEN CRIMINALS BREAK THE LAW AND GET AWAY WITH IT—

THE RESULT IS RISING VIOLENCE, CRIME IN THE STREETS, ANARCHY.

WHEN BIG CORPORATIONS BREAK THE LAW AND **DON'T** GET AWAY WITH IT—

THE RESULT IS FALLING STOCKS, RISING UNEMPLOY-MENT, CRIME IN THE STREETS, ANARCHY.

SO PROSECUTE CRIMINALS!

AND SUPPORT CORPORATE CRIME!

KEEP AMERICA STRONG!

Dist. Publishers-Hall Syndicate

4-16   © 1972 JULES FEIFFER

Above, © 1972 Jules Feiffer.

The efficacy of imprisonment

Americans who wear their social conscience on their sleeve have staked out compassion for prisoners and justice for consumers as two special concerns.

Often they say that the convicted criminal's crime is actually morally neutral: There are so many relative factors involved, and he suffered so much deprivation, that an unjust society is really to blame.

Furthermore, they add, imprisonment is useless because it only amounts to vindictiveness, society's way of shunning its obligation to rehabilitate the individual.

On the consumer front, however, moral relativity suddenly vanishes. The dishonest businessman is not the mere victim of his environment and all the intermeshed social forces. He is not simply caught up in a great tragedy. He is a conscious shyster or polluter who must pay the price of wrongdoing.

This doublethink r e a c h e d its apex — or perhaps its nadir — when a California sociologist at a recent conference on "corporate accountability" said: "The most effective deterrent for corporate c r i m i n a l s is the imposition of criminal penalties on executives who have knowingly committed outlawed acts of a serious nature."

He said a jail sentence, or even the threat of one, would encourage such executives to mend their ways. Corporate f r a u d s and fakers should be brought to account, no less than other offenders. Still, it is paradoxical that the efficacy of jail sentences is only now being recognized, and only for corporate malfactors rather than for the worst category of criminals, those who commit crimes of violence.

Above, from *The Arizona Republic*, November 5, 1971.

Violent Us

The Burgesses Would Turn Prisons Into Torture Chambers

By a PRISON GOVERNOR

LONDON—If criminals are to be punished even more severely (be it hanged or beaten or flogged or psychologically assaulted, humiliated, degraded, or broken as human beings) who is supposed to do the punishing?

Where will the wild men who advocate such punishment recruit those who will punish other men as their daily contribution to the health of society?

There are, of course, in every society, sick and perverted men and women who would gladly spend their lives as professional punishers, degraders, humiliators, hurters, torturers and killers of their fellow men—people who are fulfilled by psychological and physical violence against others. They exist in every society. But when any society legitimizes their perversion by employing them in numbers to degrade and punish and destroy, that society itself is sick unto death.

We know about the Gestapo, the SS and the concentration camps and the gas chambers. In our own time we see around us in this stricken world the same phenomena. God forbid that our society, sick though it is, should decide to employ professional punishers. When we do, if we do, civilization has gone ultimately from our society. These are not times in which we can afford to stand lightly by such matters.

The task of the Prison Service in our country is to ameliorate, as best it can, the appalling effects of imprisonment.

Prison staff are not employed to punish or to degrade. The only punishment the courts deal out in this respect is loss of liberty. Prison governors are instructed to hold in custody, not to *punish* prisoners. Loss of liberty is terrible enough for most men to bear without additional punishment.

Imprisonment — especially in the quite appalling conditions of overcrowding which exist today and which will continue to exist for as long as can be reasonably anticipated — can degrade and dehumanize both prisoners and staff alike unless there is constant moral vigilance and an unremitting conviction that human beings, even in captivity, must be treated with respect as persons and accorded the highest degree of dignity possible in their circumstances.

Only such an attitude, and the behavior appropriate to it within the penal system, can preserve the fabric of civilized society. Civilization is a tenuous concept even in Britain today. If the present staff of prisons are forced to become, or are replaced by, professional punishers and degraders, society will not be helped

I, for one, would want no part in a society which employed men for such a task and which legitimized violence of such a kind.

I am more afraid—and all of us should be more afraid—of the violence of those respectable burgesses who cry for death and blood and pain and degradation for criminals, than I am of criminals themselves—and I have known thousands of criminals. The violence of the frightened burgess is the most terrifying of all, and the most destructive of all.

What we need to recognize more than anything else in our disintegrating world is that violence is not a problem only of the criminal.

The concept of responsibility is particularly weak when we trace behavior to genetic determiners. Individuals presumably differ, as species differ, in the extent to which they engage in sexual behavior or are affected by sexual reinforcement. Are they, therefore, equally responsible for controlling their sexual behavior and is it fair to punish them to the same extent? If we do not punish a person for a clubfoot, should we punish him for being highly susceptible to sexual reinforcement? We cannot change genetic defects by punishment. What we must change is not the responsibility of autonomous man but the conditions, environmental or genetic, of which a person's behavior is a function.

Out. Although people object when a scientific analysis traces their behavior to external conditions and thus deprives them of credit and the chance to be admired, they seldom object when the same analysis absolves them of blame. The alcoholic is the first to claim that he is ill; if he is not responsible, he cannot be justly punished.

Above, from *The New York Times*. This letter is excerpted from *The Guardian* of London. The author, who asked that his name be withheld, is governor of an English prison.

Left, from *Beyond Freedom and Dignity* by B. F. Skinner.

A 'Plea' for Prisoners

By AL CAPP

The Reverend Utter Chaos had one experience with crime in all his long and gentle lifetime. That was in 1926, when he was compelled to rebuke a certain Boston caterer (of the lower classes) for having padded the cookie bill for one of his Ladies Aid Society teas.

Since then, he has given the subject of crime a great deal of thought and, finally, this week he called a press conference to announce the Utter Chaos Plan for Criminal Rehabilitation.

"Some criminals," he told the assembled reporters, "leave jail more unfriendly to society than when they were put in."

"Didn't I read something like that," asked a reporter, "in Ramsey Clark's book?"

"You did," beamed the reverend, "and so did I. In fact, I was inspired by Ramsey Clark."

"So was your fellow-authority on crime, J. Edgar Hoover," said another reporter. "He was inspired to call Ramsey Clark a 'jellyfish'."

"Someone," sighed the chubby, white-haired old man, "should have a discreet word with Mr. Hoover about his language. Although I *do* understand the coarsening influence that his years of associating with criminals must have had on him.

"**Fortunately, Mr. Clark and I have had practically no personal contact with criminals, and that is why we can approach their problems in a . . . well . . . *nicer* way.**

"The difference between us is that Mr. Hoover merely wants to remove murderers, muggers and child molesters from society. All *he* worries about is the future of society."

"Mr. Clark and I have a broader, finer vision. *We* are worried about the future of our murderers, muggers and molesters.

"Mr. Clark has two theories I firmly believe in. One is that convicted criminals are really decent chaps at heart, and all their murdering, mugging and molesting are really symptoms of their deep discontent in the society *we* have created. And so it is *us* who are guilty of their crimes . . . not them.

"Mr. Clark's other theory that I firmly believe in is that when those really decent chaps get together in jail, it makes them even *more* maniacal murderers, muggers and molesters.

"The solution, of course, is to provide each convicted criminal with an *individual* residence. Something nice and cozy and cheerful and no two of them within communicating distance. That would mean substituting two or three thousand of these residences for every jail. It will be expensive, of course, but it will eliminate jails—even the word itself.

"Think of how much more *friendly* convicted criminals would be to a society which sentences them to 10 to 20 years in their own cozy, cheerful individual residences instead of 10 to 20 years in jail.

"From the moment they are convicted and sentenced, we will begin to win their affection.

"But that's not all. If we must deprive our convicted criminals of the pleasure of the company of other convicted criminals, we must realize that they need some sort of social life, same as any other group of normal Americans. And so we must provide them with company—but only of the highest type. Several evenings a week."

"How will you manage that?" asked a reporter.

"Ask for volunteers," replied the bright-eyed old clergyman.

"Suppose not enough brain surgeons, Nobel Prize-winning novelists and astronauts volunteer to spend their evenings with convicted murderers, muggers and molesters?"

"**In that case,**" replied the author of the Utter Chaos Plan sternly, "**we must bus them.**"

"And I, for one," he continued, "am not going to sweep the issue of sex under the sofa. Do you realize that in this land of plenty, tens of thousands of unfortunate Americans in such areas as Dannemora, San Quentin, Sing Sing and Raiford are sex-starved? How can Hugh Hefner go to bed at night, knowing that?" he shook his head, sorrowfully.

"Under the Utter Chaos Plan, however, all convicted criminals will be provided with girl friends. But strictly of the nicest types. And my study of the Charles Manson case, gentlemen, leads me to believe there will be no shortage of volunteers."

WHEN PUNISHMENT IS A CRIME

article **BY RAMSEY CLARK**

the former attorney general indicts america's medieval prison system for corrupting and dehumanizing rather than rehabilitating those behind bars

The goal of modern correction must be not revenge, not penance, not punishment, but rehabilitation. The theory of rehabilitation is based on the belief that healthy, rational people will not injure others. Rehabilitated, an individual will not have the capacity—will not be able to bring himself—to injure another nor to take or destroy property. Rehabilitation is individual salvation. What achievement can give society greater satisfaction than to afford the offender the chance, once lost, to live at peace, to fulfill himself and to help others? Rehabilitation is also the one clear way that the criminal justice system can significantly reduce crime. We know who the most frequent offenders are; there is no surprise when they strike again. Even if nothing but selfish interest impelled us, rehabilitation would be worth the effort. When it works, it reduces crime, reduces the cost of handling prisoners, reduces the cost of the criminal justice system and even relieves pressure to provide the basic and massive reforms that are necessary to affect the underlying causes of crime.

Fred Hampton lies in an uneasy grave yet the Grand Jury report marches on. Rap Brown is underground yet the courts go thru their dance of death, grinding out some form of legitimization of his outlawry. Throughout this country courts grind out every day the most horrible pound of flesh — against those who speak out. Sometimes it is done with 30 years for the possession of one joint, as with Lee Otis Johnson in Houston, Texas, or 10 years for John Sinclair in Michigan . . . and everyone says, well, that's due process of law . . . he broke the law, he had a marijuana cigarette in his possession, and no-one begins to wonder why its life imprisonment in Texas for that crime and a max. of 10 days in Washington D.C. And how could you reconcile those two punishments with the identical crime? Because Lee Otis Johnson was a member of SNCC, 30 years for his joint; because John Sinclair was a leader of the White Panthers in Mich., its ten years, and the court applies the rationale that the sentence was within the permissible limits.

Above, from *Outlaws of Amerikkka* in *Nola Express*, as reprinted in the *Underground Press Digest*, January 1971.

By W.G. ROGERS
Saturday Review

CRIME IN AMERICA: Observations on its Nature, Causes, Prevention and Control. By Ramsey Clark. Simon & Schuster. 346 pp. $6.95.

SINCE I HAVE TO STOP somewhere, just one more: noting that Spiro Agnew in the 1968 campaign advocated the shooting of looters, Clark writes: "Persons under the influence of alcohol killed 25,000 Americans in automobile accidents in 1967. Fewer than 250 people died in all the riots of the 1960's. Looters, as such, killed no one. Why not shoot drunken drivers?"

Top page, from *Playboy Magazine*; © 1970 by Playboy, November 1970.

Right, reprinted from *Saturday Review* by the *Albany Times-Union*, November 22, 1970.

Witness Admits She Killed Heiress At Tate Mansion

LOS ANGELES (AP) — Patricia Krenwinkel calmly confessed on the witness stand Thursday that she ran down and killed coffee heiress Abigail Folger at Sharon Tate's home and the next night stabbed to death the wife of a wealthy market owner.

She said she and other members of the two killer parties were stoned on LSD. She said she felt "nothing."

The 23-year-old member of Charles Manson's hippie style clan—second of two women defendants to admit slayings at the Tate murder trial—also said she carved "WAR" in the chest of victim Leno LaBianca, the market owner, and stuck a fork in his stomach.

And asked if Manson "had any connection with you in these homicides you are on trial for," Miss Krenwinkel replied: "None whatsoever."

Attorney Objected

Miss Krenwinkel, soft-spoken and articulate, testified despite an objection from her attorney that she might incriminate herself and a warning from the judge that she might talk herself into a death penalty.

She described her life with Manson's nomadic family, and said she deemed him "perfection" personified. Then, she told of the night of August 1969 when Miss Tate and four visitors to the Tate home were shot and stabbed to death.

She said, referring to Miss Folger, 26: "I had a knife in my hand and she ran out a back door ... I chased her through the door and onto the lawn and I stabbed her and I kept stabbing her and I looked up and there was blackness and that was all."

Because of the LSD, she said, she remembers little: "It was like all reaction ... It's all a picture of motion and reaction. I can't remember details. There was some man I was tying up. I can remember looking up and Sadie was fighting with two women. I remember I just got up and went over and I was fighting."

Sadie is the nickname of defendant Susan Atkins, who admitted killing Miss Tate.

What did she feel, her attorney asked. "I guess complete paranoia ... Nothing. It was just there, and like it was all right."

No Remorse

On cross examination Miss Krenwinkel was asked by Deputy Dist. Atty. Vincent Bugulosi why she stabbed Miss Folger.

"It was just there to do," she replied.

Bugulosi continued:

'Q: Do you have any remorse?

A: I don't even know what that word means.

Q: Do you have any sorrow?

A: No ... it was right then, yes.

Q: Do you still feel it was right?

A: Yes.

Q. Did the thought enter your mind that Abigail Folger wanted to live as much as you did?

A: No. Because I am willing to give up my life.

She said there was no reason for the stabbing and she doesn't know why she did it.

"I don't judge it. All I know is what happened and it was right because it happened. I don't try to figure it out."

On March 29 Charles Manson was sentenced to death. On the very same day Lt. William Calley was found guilty of murdering 22 Vietnamese civilians. The reaction was swift: silent approval for the death sentence for Manson and loud protests against the guilty verdict for Calley. While the comparison may seem unfair, it nevertheless makes one ask why people would approve one verdict and protest another—both having been given by the same system. Is the system bad or are people simply letting their prejudices take the better of themselves?

Shall we be consistent in our system of justice? Or shall we take the easy way out—disregard the facts and follow public opinion?

ADELA SANTOS
Los Angeles, Calif.

'To Be Truly Just'

You define crime in the sense of street crime and discuss justice only in relation to street crime. Your article (SPECIAL REPORT, March 8) conveys the impression that justice would become a reality if only the police, courts and prisons dealt more efficiently with street criminals.

Would not justice also be served if our legal system aimed a few of its big guns at white-collar crime? Price fixing, tax evasion, swindling and consumer fraud are just a few examples of serious crimes that your report completely ignored. America overlooks the rich man's crime because it is not as visible as that of the poor man. In order to be truly just, a legal system must cope with both.

Pfc. GARY MISSEL
241st Military Police Detachment
Denver, Colo.

Left, courtesy of Associated Press Newsfeatures.
Top page, letter to the editor of *Newsweek* by Adela Santos, April 25, 1971.
Above, letter to the editor of *Newsweek* by Gary Missel, April 12, 1971.

Capital Punishment Protects Civilization

By THOMAS A. LANE

WASHINGTON — In our city, we learn all too frequently of some young policemen being gunned down by criminals. A wife and children are bereaved. Good men are murdered; evil men survive. Justice is mocked.

In Britain, the killing of a policeman is so horrendous a

Thomas

A.

Lane

crime that even the criminals outlaw it. In the rare cases when a policeman is killed, criminals cooperate with police in identifying and exposing the murderer. He is the common enemy of all mankind, straight and crooked.

But in our society, the killing of a policeman is condoned by the silence of people and officials. In our city, criminals are executed only by policemen defending themselves or by storekeepers defending their property. The processes of justice are so attenuated by a sickly sentimentality as to be an obstacle to law enforcement. Through flagrant abuse of judicial discretion, in a perversion of philosophy and purpose, the courts have become instruments to protect the criminal from the community.

Some States are considering the abolition of capital punishment. Various arguments are advanced to support the proposed legislation: that society should not set an example of killing; that society should reclaim errant citizens, not destroy them; that society may err and execute an innocent man; that the death sentence is not a deterrent.

These arguments are a retreat from truth and rationality. They illustrate the difficulty which the human mind sometimes encounters in distinguishing between fantasy and reality. They repudiate the great truths about man which philosophy has taught us.

To assert that capital punishment is not a deterrent to murder is to deny reason. We know that criminals act out of conceptions of their own self-interest. If British criminals do not condone police killing, that is because British society did not condone police killing. British criminals foreswore a course which would have been against their self-interest.

If an American robber cold-bloodedly murders a gas-station attendant to prevent future witness to his crime, he does so because he believes it is to his advantage to kill. Pity the society which encourages such a judgment. If murder is to be outlawed from our society, murder must never be advantageous to the potential killer.

The question of deterrence is obscured by the records of jurisdictions in which capital punishment is prescribed but not assessed. Criminals deal in reality, as they see it. If the law is a dead letter, indeed it does not deter them. Where the law in enforced, it does deter murder.

If the law is not enforced, the cure is enforcement, not repeal. We must elect officials who will perform their duties, not abet their malfeasance by repealing the law.

The greatest reclaimer of errant citizens is justice, pure and swift. It operates to prevent crime by making it clear to all that crime does not pay. When the penalties of the law are suspended in misguided charity, offenders are encouraged to err again.

The execution of murderers is an imperative of justice. If you believe that the cold-blooded killing of a law-abiding citizen is an intolerable crime, you must believe that the only just punishment is the forfeiture of the murderer's own life. No other punishment is adequate. This is the law of Moses.

If you do not exact that just punishment, you create a society in which wanton killing is encouraged. This is the condition of our society today.

There is a terrible consistency of decadence in a society which executes its unborn children but will not execute its murderers. Both errors illustrate the rejection of philosophy which influences our law-givers. Decadence contrives its own justification.

Courtesy of Thomas A. Lane and *The Wanderer*, April 15, 1971.

Shapp on Capital Punishment

ON MARCH 23, nine years ago, the late Gov. David Lawrence announced in Harrisburg a freeze on capital punishment until the Legislature resolved the issue of whether to execute or not to execute. Later that year the General Assembly voted to retain the death penalty.

The freeze was lifted. But, except for 1962, the following years saw no human beings die in the electric chair in this state.

With Gov.-elect Shapp's weekend statement of total opposition to capital punishment, the freeze is back on. It will be up to the General Assembly to do what it failed to do under previous governors, from Shafer (who, as Lieutenant Governor, favored the death penalty), through Scranton (who doubted its efficacy) to Lawrence (who opposed it outright).

It will be up to the General Assembly to legislate us out of this vestige of tribal barbarism by replacing capital punishment with life imprisonment. In this predominantly Christian nation, we understand the moral rule to be one which prohibits the taking of human life except in self-defense and, by extension, in war—although we like to think that that tribal form of aggression will soon be conquered, too.

In any case, neither the state nor

Right, from *The Pittsburgh Post-Gazette*, December 30, 1970.

its citizens can know absolute truth, which is solely for the gods to ponder. Yet unerring, perfect truth is the assumption on which sentencing and executing a person is based. The state's killing a convicted killer is the final, absolute act.

Scientifically, we know just enough about psychology and about brain circuitry and its malfunctions to know how little we do know, far from enough to "know" who is really guilty enough to deserve death. That, again, is for the gods to ponder.

Under Mr. Shapp's moral impetus, we suspect the Legislature will find it difficult to duck this issue which has hung fire so long. We hope, however, that the people's representatives in Harrisburg will have the wisdom to eliminate the death penalty completely, rather than keeping it for some classes of crimes—like the killing of an on-duty police officer, an exception which some legislators favor. There is no moral or logical reason to place higher value on a policeman's life than on any other human being's. Either capital punishment is an effective deterrent or it isn't. Crime figures over the years do not support its efficacy. Logic and morality do not support it at all.

Let us have done with it.

Below, from *The Times Record*, January 19, 1971.

How About The Victim?

All sorts of legal semantics are involved when there is argument over the death penalty as has just taken place before the U.S. Supreme Court. But it comes down to a simple moral issue.

All along the line from the less severe crimes right up to murder, the victim is increasingly becoming the forgotten man.

But to nail the issue right on the head let us confine the discussion to murder and to be more specific let it be a typical case of murder committed during a holdup.

A housewife, walking home to her husband and children is assaulted and robbed. When she resists she is shot and killed, the assailant is later caught, tried and convicted. The opponents of capital punishment would say that to electrocute this man would be cruel and unusual punishment and that the death penalty has been "repudiated by the conscience of contemporary society."

Now this matter of conscience: Where does proper concern comes in? A family is left motherless. The focus of the opponents of capital punishment is centered not on the victim but on the killer who has contributed nothing to society and in fact is a proven enemy of society. If he had not been apprehended he would likely have committed more crimes.

Yet the concern is that capital punishment would be a cruel penalty for him. We feel that the surviving husband and children of the dead woman know more about cruelty than the attorneys who would strike down the death penalty.

What Does the Bible Say About the Death Penalty?

By Carl McIntire; distributed by 20th Century Reformation Hour, Collingswood, N.J.

3. Modern Humanism

It is the social gospel, which is nothing more than a pious expression of humanism, that is being used to attack the death penalty in the various state legislatures. The liberals and leftists in ecclesiastical circles come in the name of an appreciation of human life and of doing good, and without the knowledge and the standards of God's Word many are misled in this field. The truth is that such propagandists have a very low view of human life and its importance. Their humanistic philosophy is built upon a thoroughly anti-Christian and unbiblical concept of the universal brotherhood of man and the universal Fatherhood of God.

According to this erronnous and apostate line, the world indeed is not under the curse and the wrath of God, and all men are His children. The Scriptures say: "The wrath of God is revealed from heaven," "Cursed is the ground for thy sake," "The wages of sin is death," "Sin is the transgression of the law," and the penalty pronounced by God is death. Only when men repent of their sin and look to Jesus Christ by God's grace and in faith can they become the children of God. "Ye are all the children of God by faith in Christ Jesus" (Gal. 3:26). Surely our Saviour knew what He was talking about when He said to the religious leaders of His day: "If God were your Father, ye would love me. . . . Ye are of your father the devil, and the lusts of your father ye will do. He was a murderer from the beginning. . . . He is a liar, and the father of it" (John 8:42-44). These humanists completely ignore the exceeding sinfulness of the heart of man and the depravity of the race.

It is the Bible that tells us the consequences of man's sin—the physical evil, the pains and miseries of life which have come upon the race, and finally the separation of man from God in hell itself. The death penalty for the capital crime is divinely decreed in keeping with the judgment and the justice of God pronounced against sin in all of its heinous offense against God. Humanism offers no saviour. Humanism anticipates no judgment. Humanism offers man no future and no hope.

4. The Current Arguments

The arguments of those who want to abolish the death penalty are humanistic and based upon the pride and the lusts of man and an inversion of what might be called the moral force.

The majority of the New York State Penal Law Revision Commission favoring abolition of capital punishment wrote, "The execution of the penalty of death calls inescapably on the agents of the state to perpetrate an act of supreme violence under circumstances of the greatest cruelty to the individual involved. . . ." At this point the majority has departed completely from any concept of moral judgment and punishment deserved, as pronounced by a righteous God.

The next statement of the majority also involves the same level of thinking, ". . . the social need for the grievous condemnation of the gravest crimes can be met, as it is met in abolition states, without resort to the barbarism of this kind." The reflection is primarily against God, for a God who would require capital punishment would Himself be a barbarian. The fact is that the humanists have an entirely different god. Man is their god, not the God of divine revelation, whose penalty for the breaking of law when it comes to murder is the forfeiture of the life of the murderer.

The next argument partakes of the same emotionalism, "The very fact that life is at stake (in a capital crime trial) introduces a morbid and sensational factor in the trial of the accused and increases the danger that public sympathy will be aroused for the defendant." The conscience of the public should be so attuned to the demands of God —and it would if the Word of God were being preached from the pulpits of the country—that public sentiment would approve of the justice of the conviction just as it did in the United States, for instance, in the famous Lindbergh case where the child was first kidnaped, then murdered, and the murderer paid for his crime.

Those who defended the death penalty on New York's Commission made an appeal to morality:

"Because wanton murder is so extremely wrong, morally wrong, the punishment therefore must remain proportionally extremely severe to emphasize to other would-be murderers the high outrage that society feels against the commission of such crimes.

". . . were there to be no room in our system for sentences any more severe than the presently understood 'life sentence' even for the most bizarre and outrageously heinous crimes of murder, there would in time be further erosion of the concept of the dignity of human life and a corresponding weakening of faith in, and respect for the law on the part of a preponderant majority of law-abiding citizens. Human nature, being what it is, must be understood to demand, on occasion, a reversion to earlier penal concepts of retaliation, vengeance, and the placation of an outraged community."

The statement further said:

"There is more crime in the State of New York than anywhere else in the world. The historical reasons and justifications that have kept the death penalty for certain crimes in this state to the present time, should not be suddenly and summarily invalidated or nullified by untested and unproven claims of the humanitarianism of other methods of punishment or the ineffectiveness of the old one."

5. The General Moral Breakdown

The campaign to have the death penalty removed in the various states of the United States is simply a reflection of the general moral breakdown and debauchery that is multiplying in the United States. Four of the major commandments dealing with man's relationship to man as presented in the Bible are: (1) "Thou shalt not kill" —this protects and honors human life. (2) "Thou shalt not commit adultery"—this protects the purity of life and makes possible the honor of the family. (3) "Thou shalt not steal"—this protects the property to which a man is divinely entitled. (4) "Thou shalt not bear false witness"—this protects the truth and the good name of the individual against slander and false accusation.

In Our Opinion

On death row

One of the most barbaric decisions made by the U.S. Supreme Court in recent months was its May 3 ruling that juries have the power to impose a sentence of death in the 38 states where the death penalty is still on the books. The court also upheld the common practice by which juries decide guilt and then immediately determine whether the death penalty will be imposed, without hearing further evidence.

The court, however, has yet to rule on the challenge to capital punishment as a violation of the Constitution's Eighth Amendment prohibiting "cruel and unusual punishment."

Since 1967, officials have been awaiting the Supreme Court ruling on these issues and no executions have taken place in any state. As a result, there are now 648 men and women on death row, the largest number at one time in the history of the country.

It is not certain what will happen to these prisoners in light of the high court's ruling, but indications are that there will be further appeals, and most states will probably await a decision of the Eighth Amendment cases.

Why did the high court of capitalist "justice" make such a barbaric ruling? Why, in fact, do 38 states still have the death penalty?

The answer can be found in the statistics of who is sentenced to die.

Most notable is the disproportionate number of Black Americans who are executed. Of the 3,827 men and 32 women executed since 1930, 53 percent were Black. Of the 648 persons now on death row, 52 percent are Black. Almost without exception, those given capital punishment are poor — men and women from the working class. Of 18 death row prisoners interviewed by the **Washington Post** in Maryland's prisons in March 1971, none of them had attended college, many of them had not attended high school, and all of them were from the working class.

It can almost be laid down as a law of American capitalist society that rich people are not sentenced to death. In a Jan. 11, 1971, **Newsweek** article, Boston University President Dr. John Silber is quoted as saying, "I don't think you can find a single person who was represented by counsel and who had plenty of money to develop his defense who received the death penalty."

There are two standards of justice in this country. One for the rich and one for the working class and oppressed nationalities. This holds true, not only for the application of the death penalty, but for all forms of "social punishment" in the United States.

The apologists for capital punishment contend that it is a deterrent to crime. But the statistics alone belie this claim. For example, since 1930, Georgia has executed more prisoners than any other state in the country. It has also had the highest number of murders.

When these apologists argue that it is a "deterrent," what they actually mean is that they hope it will serve as a means of terrorizing and intimidating the most oppressed sectors of society to respect capitalist property rights and capitalist "law and order."

The thousands of working men and women — Black, Chicano, Puerto Rican, Native American, and white — who fill America's jails are the victims of this rotten capitalist system. This society — through all forms of class and racial oppression — pushes people down into poverty and insecurity, forces them into degrading and dehumanizing social relations, and brutalizes them through many kinds of harassment and inequity.

The tiny ruling class, with the blood of countless Southeast Asians on its hands, says: "It is unlawful to kill." From the working majority, they steal billions of dollars in profits, taxes and graft and then say: "It is unlawful to steal."

The biggest criminals go free while the prisons and death chambers are reserved for the victims of capitalist society.

The death penalty must be abolished!

What Death Row Has Taught Me About Living

By Leaman R. Smith

After what seemed an interminable pause, the bailiff's dull, flat voice intoned: "We, the jury, having found the defendant, Leaman Russell Smith, guilty of murder in the first degree, fix the penalty as death."

What had begun as a bad-check spree had ended with my killing two policemen and receiving the death decree. Society demands my life, and I will no doubt pay in full. In the interim, I have existed for nearly seven and a half years on San Quentin's overcrowded death row, apprehensively waiting for someone to push the button that will end my existence.

Although I have offended society and must pay for it, you and I may have more in common than you suspect. I have read where 91 percent of people questioned admitted they have committed acts for which they might have received prison sentences. Ninety-one percent!

And may I be forgiven for asking: What good does my punishment really do? □

Capital Punishment—For What?

By DAVID BRUDNOY

Shortly before the election, in what could probably be seen as his gesture to the friends of "law and order," Massachusetts Gov. Francis W. Sargent gave a tough little speech in which he urged the imposition of compulsory capital punishment on anyone convicted of killing a police officer or bombing a building in which someone was killed.

The governor's talk seemed to evoke little comment in the press, although, coming from a liberal like Sargent, the position should have been more widely remarked. His position—death for two types of killers, and two only—raises several questions and leads at least to a few tentative answers.

Those favoring capital punishment have long contended that the ultimate penalty deters would-be criminals from committing their crimes and/or is morally right, in that our respect for the lives of innocents is shown by demanding death for those who kill.

Anti-capital punishment people rebut, saying the death penalty does not deter crime and/or that the morally correct response to a heinous crime is compassion, not the further taking of a life.

As stated, these two positions have the virtue of internal consistency, whatever one might think of that view with which one disagrees.

The argument as to morality also admits of no final proof. No one can "prove" the existence of God scientifically, nor disprove His existence; no one can prove what "morality" is by reference to objective criteria, but only by reference to man-made systems of ethics, which may or may not derive from divine inspiration—which gets it all back again to the non-provability of God's existence by scientifically verifiable criteria.

Thus we can assert until kingdom come that capital punishment is moral or immoral, and be "right" by our own lights, but dismally wrong according to other, perhaps just as thoughtful, observers.

Why, then, capital punishment for cop-killers and bombers who kill while bombing? If Gov. Sargent thinks capital punishment is such cases will be a deterrent, then surely we might demand that he press for capital punishment for all killers, in the hopes that such punishment will deter their crimes as well. If the governor believes it is morally right to kill killers under cover of law, then are we to believe that he thinks the lives of policemen are worth more than the lives of others, or that those killed by a bomb are any the less dead, or of more worth, than those killed by a knife, gun, pipe, rope, razor, what have you?

Perhaps the governor has arrived at his conclusion because he thinks the two types of crimes which he has named are so dreadful that they exceed in wickedness all other types of crime; that is, the Eichmann analogy. May others not feel just as strongly that some other form of killing—such as the bashing in of a skull of some defenseless old person, by a brutal attacker—is even more reprehensible, or at the very least, equally as reprehensible?

Gov. Sargent's proposal seems short of the mark, according to those who favor capital punishment for whichever or both of the reasons I've suggested and it seems to be excessive to those who are against capital punishment.

Suspicion as to the governor's motivation for his proposal continues to bother one. Is Mr. Sargent trying to steer a careful course between the "get-tough" types and the "go-soft" sorts? Because of the current wave of bombings and cop-killings? If not, why? If so, what of other terrible types of killing?

My own view, for what it's worth, is that whether capital punishment is a deterrent or not—and my hunch is that it is, although as mentioned above I cannot so prove—it is morally right for society to avenge the death of innocents by demanding the death of the killer, after a fair trial, according to scrupulous due process, and with access to appeals procedures.

There, too, my "morally right" position is based on faith, not on proof. But my position is only one man's and need not cloud the major point I wish to make which is this: The governor's position lacks internal consistency and hints at expediency.

Both the governor of Massachusetts and the rest of us should examine the matter seriously, right now, and bring the issue to the point of active intellectual controversy. Perhaps we can arrive at a statewide consensus which could help guide the General Court in its next session.

Reprinted with permission from the July 5, 1971, issue of *Human Events*, 422 First St., S.E., Washington, D.C. 20003.

Why Punishment Must

By THEODORE L. SENDAK

(Following is the text of a speech made by Mr. Sendak, who is the Attorney General of the state of Indiana, before the Law Enforcement Luncheon Meeting of Officials of Northern Indiana at Wabash, Ind., May 12, 1971.)

The purpose of our system of criminal law is to minimize the quantity of human suffering by maintaining a framework of order and peace. The primary object of the law in this area is to forestall acts of violence or other aggression by which one person inflicts harm on another. To the extent that government fails to do this, the primary function of the state is neglected, and individual suffering is increased.

The question we must ask ourselves about the death penalty is: which of several possible courses of action will serve the true humanitarian purposes of the criminal law? We must weigh the execution of the convicted murderer against the loss of life of his victims and of the possible victims of other potential murderers.

Many factors enter into the perpetration of crime, some of which are obviously beyond the bounds of social control. And it is true that some murders occur under circumstances which no system of penalties can prevent. Yet the objective, statistical evidence available to all indicates one major factor in the commission of crime is the relative probability of punishment *or* escape. If punishment is certain, the impulse to crime is to some extent checked. If escape seems probable, the criminal impulse has freer reign.

The propaganda drive to abolish capital punishment appears to be a geared part of a general drive toward leniency in the treatment of criminals in our society. Such leniency has had in my opinion, undeniable psychological impact on potential murderers, and has contributed to the upward spiral of the crime rate. There is a striking over-all correlation between the recent decline in the use of the death penalty and the rise in violent crime. Such crime has increased by geometric proportions.

In the first three years of the last decade, the number of executions in the United States was by present standards relatively high. Fifty-six persons were executed in 1960; 42 in 1961; and 47 in 1962. During these same three years the number of people who died violently at the hands of criminals actually declined and the murder rate per 100,000 of population also declined.

Beginning in 1963, however, there was a drop in the number of legal executions, and the graph line of violent crime simultaneously began moving up instead of down. In the following years the number of legal executions has decreased dramatically from one year to the next, until in 1968 there was none at all. But each of these years has seen murders increase sharply both in absolute numbers and as a percentage of population.

In 1964, for example, the number of legal executions dropped to 15. Yet the number of violent deaths moved up from 8,500 to 9,250, and the murder rate per 100,000 went up from 4.5 to 4.8. In 1965 the number of legal executions

---

The Pay-Back Crime Code

By JENKIN LLOYD JONES

Senator Mike Mansfield and Rep. William Green of Pennsylvania have introduced bills in Congress that would appropriate federal money for the relief of the victims of criminals.

The proposed legislation would not only provide funds to victims of crimes under federal jurisdiction, but it would supplement payments which the legislatures of six states have now authorized for the victims of state law infractions.

Crime compensation at taxpayer expense is getting popular. Britain, New Zealand, Sweden and seven Canadian provinces have now enacted such laws.

There is, indeed, little logic in freely spending public money to enable the criminal to perfect his defense, while leaving the bleeding victim to borrow money to overcome his lost earnings and the cost of doctors and hospitals.

But the idea can be improved. It can be improved by going back to the first principle of ancient law—the principle that it is the perpetrator of the crime who has the primary obligation to the victim.

In ancient days the idea of paying damages was not limited to civil law. Hammurabi and Draco understood that a criminal was not merely the enemy of the people as a whole, but was a particular debtor to his victim. Draco provided for fines in oxen, not to be paid to the state, but to the aggrieved party.

A couple of weeks ago Dr. John Kielbauch, prison psychologist, resigned from the Oklahoma Department of Corrections to take a position in the federal penal system. And in departing, he made a few radical suggestions:

It is time, he said, that the man who robs or injures makes direct restitution. To this end, he proposed that the courts determine proper compensation and that the state set up elaborate training programs and prison industries which would enable the prisoner to earn real money in behalf of those he had wronged.

Dr. Kielbauch suggests indeterminate sentences, the duration of which would largely depend on the efforts the prisoner would make toward full restitution. He adds that if a prisoner is released or paroled before this restitution is completed, a portion of his outside wages could be deducted.

The trouble with most prison job-training programs, according to Dr. Kielbauch, is that many prisoners associate the training with their punishment. This gives them a negative attitude toward useful work. They develop skills reluctantly and slowly and often turn

Fit the Crime

dropped to seven, while the number of violent deaths increased to 9,850, and the murder rate went to 5.1. Similar decreases in legal executions have occurred in the following years, accompanied by similar increases in the murder rate.

In 1968, with no legal executions at all, the total number who died through criminal violence reached 13,650, while the murder rate climbed to 6.8 per 100,000.

The movement in these figures, with murders increasing as the deterrence of the death penalty diminished, confirms the verdict of ordinary logic: That a relaxation in the severity and certainty of punishment leads only to an increase in crime.

These remarks concern the deterrent effect of the death penalty on those who might commit murder but do not. That is a negative phenomenon which can be inferred both from the record and the assessment of common sense. The repeal of the death penalty would not repeal human nature. To these truisms we may add the fact that there are numerous cases on record in which criminals have escaped the capital penalty for previous murders and gone on to commit others.

Likewise there are numerous cases of prison inmates who have killed guards and other inmates, knowing that the worst punishment they could get would be continued tenancy in the same institution. Opponents of the death penalty usually resist even life sentences without parole, and the deterrent function of that would be even less effective than capital punishment.

The general growth of violent crime in the past decade is the outcropping of the attitude of permissiveness and leniency going hand in hand with an increase in the rate of victimization. As more and more loopholes have been devised for defendants, the crime rate has increased steeply.

Between 1960 and 1968, the over-all **crime rate in America increased 11 times as fast as the rate of population growth —plainly meaning that more and more people are being subjected every day of every year to major personal crimes—** murder, rape, assault, kidnapping, armed robbery, etc.

Is a course of action humanitarian which actually encourages a vast and, continuing increase in the number of people killed and maimed and otherwise brutalized?

There have been many sentimental journeys into the psychological realm of the criminals who are to be executed; I think there should be more sympathetic concern expressed for the thousands of innocent victims of those criminals.

Opponents of the death penalty may rejoice that in 1968 there were 47 fewer murderers executed in this country than was the case in 1962. But do they say anything of the fact that some 5,250 more innocent persons died by criminal violence in 1968 than was the case in 1962?

In the question of human suffering, this is a staggering loss of more than 5,000 individual innocent lives. What about the human rights and civil rights of the individual victim? Are not those 5,000 persons entitled to the dignity and sacredness of life? Is that a result of which humanitarians can be proud? I think not.

Only misguided emotionalism, and not facts, disputes the truth that the death penalty is a deterrent of capital crime.

Individuals must be held responsible for their individual actions if a free society is to endure.

---

their backs on them when they hit the streets.

If, on the other hand, hard work and the acquisition of marketable trades became their keys to freedom, this might put shop training in a different light.

If a court can decide that the man who suffers a broken arm has $1,000 coming to him from the non-criminal who hit him with his car, why shouldn't the criminal who breaks an arm in a brutal assault also owe the victim $1,000?

And there have been too many cases where robbers who have made big scores have sat out their prison years in the smug confidence that the caches will be waiting for them when they emerge. If full restitution is insisted upon the profit vanishes.

Since a law was passed in Michigan making parents financially liable for the depredations of their minor children the incidence of juvenile vandalism in Detroit has turned down remarkably. Parents who were quite casual about scolding in juvenile court began to take a lively interest in the behavior of their young as soon as they received bills from the school board for wrecked classrooms.

Money may be the root of all evil, but the possibilities of using money as a means of discouraging evil have been underexplored in America. The trouble with the bills proposed by Sen. Mansfield and Rep. Green is that they would load upon the blameless taxpayer the indemnity for the victims of crime.

What's wrong with charging the criminal?

"Paying one's debt to society" would then take on a new and more practical meaning.

And it's about time.

Top, reprinted with permission from the January 2, 1971, issue of *Human Events*, 422 First St., S.E., Washington, D.C. 20003.

Left, copyright 1971 General Features Corporation; reprinted with permission.

SECTION XI

The Right to Life–and Death?

⸙

Advances in medical technology, changes in social structure, concern about overpopulation, and other factors have recently pushed certain questions of life and death—abortion and euthanasia ("mercy-killing") in particular—into the center of the arena of moral debate. Discussions concerning the problems of abortion—especially regarding the desirability, feasibility, utility, justifiability, and/or morality of legalizing it—have frequently involved some of the most passionate and eloquent pleas on behalf of the fetus, the mother, God, or "morality" in general. Some of the examples in this section will provide the student with first-hand evidence of the difficulty of extracting the essence of a moral argument from beneath rhetorical window dressing. Once the rhetoric is eliminated, numerous thorny problems still remain, not the least of which being those of defining "life" and "human being." If a fetus is a human being, then abortion might well be considered a form of murder; but *is* a fetus a human being? This is not a moral question in itself, but it is not clear whether it is a medical, legal, theological, or some other kind of question. Other difficult nonmoral questions which also appear to be relevant to the problems of abortion concern the determination of whether a particular fetus may be deformed or whether its birth would endanger the health of the mother, the possible consequences of allowing unwanted children to be born into society, and so on. When one has worked through all of these problems to his own satisfaction, he is confronted with not one, but many moral questions.

In addition to the always necessary meta-ethical considerations, one often finds it necessary to consider the rights and responsibilities of a number of parties, including the fetus, the mother, the father, the doctor, and society as a whole. These and other points are illustrated and elaborated upon in the arguments comprising this section, and the connections between the abortion arguments and those concerning euthanasia and suicide should be easily recognized. We suggest that additional insights may be gained by considering these problems in the light of some of the arguments included in other sections of this volume, especially the following:

Crime and Punishment and *War and Peace.* (If the taking of an adult human life is sometimes justified, then it is more likely that the taking of the life of a fetus might be morally justifiable.)

Civil Disobedience. (When, if at all, is one morally justified in violating legal statutes against abortion?)

Morality and Public Policy. (Should abortion be legalized?)

Do Animals Have Rights? (Even if the fetus is not a human being, might it not be a living thing with all the rights pertaining thereto?)

Science, Technology, and Ethics. (Even if abortion is legal, does a doctor have a moral obligation to perform an abortion on anyone who asks for it, even if the doctor believes it is morally wrong?)

Sex and Sin. (Is birth control less evil than abortion?)

Atrocities, War Crimes, and the Calley Case. (Does abortion involve the murder of a defenseless, innocent child?)

"Why shouldn't I kill myself if I want to?" he demanded.

She replied to that quite seriously.

"Because it's wrong."

"Why is it wrong?"

She looked at him doubtfully. She was not disturbed in her own belief, but she was much too inarticulate to explain her reaction.

"Well—I mean—it's wicked to kill yourself. You've got to go on living whether you like it or not."

"Why have you?"

"Well, there are other people to consider, aren't there?"

"Not in my case. There's not a soul in the world who'd be the worse for my passing on."

All the more he felt determined to force an admission from her on the ethical side.

"At any rate I've got a right to do what I like with my own life."

"No—no, you haven't."

"But why not, my dear girl, why?"

She flushed. She said, her fingers playing with the little gold cross that hung round her neck.

"You don't understand. God may need you."

He stared—taken aback. He did not want to upset her childlike faith. He said mockingly:

"I suppose that one day I may stop a runaway horse and save a golden haired child from death—eh? Is that it?"

She shook her head. She said with vehemence and trying to express what was so vivid in her mind and so halting on her tongue.

"It may be just by *being* somewhere—not doing anything—just by being at a certain place at a certain time —oh, I can't say what I mean, but you might just—just walk along a street someday and just by doing that accomplish something terribly important—perhaps without even knowing what it was."

From *Towards Zero*, © 1944 by Agatha Christie, published by Dodd, Mead and Company, Inc.

THE CHURCH'S VIEWPOINT

Suicide as we mentioned signifies any act whereby a man deliberately chooses to end his life on his own authority. According to Catholic teaching suicide is a grave sin whose malice consists in an invasion of the supreme and total dominion of God over human life. Suicide is essentially immoral. We have heard many times where a man may expose himself to certain death in order to save the life of another person, but this is not suicide; it does not mean killing oneself, but accepting death for another. Suicide is the deliberate taking away of one's own life, and no matter what the motive, this is never allowed.

Man is but a steward of his corporeal life and of all his faculties, he is not the owner of his life in the sense that he owns a car, a boat or a summer home. When he deliberately takes his own life he exercises a sort of ownership which does not belong to him. "The intrinsic evil of suicide is clear also from a consideration of the truth, that, since God is the Maker and Last End of man, man belongs totally and essentially to God, he is the property and servant of God" (T. Higgins, S. J., *Man as Man*, p. 202).

Man was created to love, honor, serve and obey God here on earth and to be happy with Him forever in Heaven. By suicide man is rejecting his status of servitude; he is invading God's exclusive right and by taking his life, he assumes the role of God. The suicide puts an end to the potentiality of further service to society and of his own moral growth and perfection. It is a deliberate challenge to the moral law and an act of rebellion against God.

The first and foremost inalienable right is that of life and physical existence. This primary right flows from the concept of person and the nature of man. Since all human persons have this right, the right is possessed from the moment of conception. The right to life and especially to bodily integrity is possessed regardless of physical or mental condition. (See Pius XI, Encyclical on *Christian Marriage*). The only exception to the right of life is the case of one who is being deprived of his life in just punishment for crime. The criminal can forfeit his right to life, as the common good takes precedence over individual good, and it may become necessary that certain crimes be punished by deprivation of life in order that the rights of one's fellowmen are safe and secure.

The state, however, is no more the supreme owner of life than is the individual. It cannot order the individual to kill himself. "Suicide cannot be exercised by appeals to honor nor hallowed by reasons of state. To make an exception in the name of patriotism is to deny that there is any essential morality in suicide at all; it is to leave all moral absolutes at the mercy of the 'situation ethics' which says that nothing's right or wrong but thinking makes it so" (*America*, June 18, 1960).

According to Christian teaching the individual possesses certain fundamental rights which the state must protect and respect. The right to life is one of these. The totalitarian state grants or limits at will the rights of men, even the right to life. The life of every citizen is at the mercy of the political clique or the state. According to totalitarian thinking, the individual exists in order to serve the state. This is contrary to the Christian thought that man is not a pawn of the state and cannot be ordered to the utility of society. Man is not a mere instrument or cog in the machinery of the state. The state has no right to encourage or command suicide. To accord the state this right would not only be contrary to Christian teaching but it would open the door against all other things we consider sacred.

From the booklet *The Sacredness of Life*, published by the Knights of Columbus, © 1966.
Right, courtesy of United Press International, July 2, 1971.

Dying Woman Wins Court Plea to Stop Terminal Surgery

MIAMI, July 2 (UPI) — A daughter, appointed guardian of her mother by a judge, accepted today her pleas against the "torture" of more surgery, although it is all that can save her.

Dr. Orlando Lopez told Judge David Popper in Circuit Court that if treatments were stopped, Mrs. Carmen Martinez, 72-year-old Cuban exile, would die.

Dr. Lopez brought the case into court because he feared he could be charged with aiding the woman's suicide if he granted her request to stop treatments.

Judge Popper, noting that the cure appeared almost as bad as the disease, ruled that because of her weakened condition Mrs. Martinez was not competent to decide her fate. He appointed her eldest daughter, Mrs. Margarita Gottlieb, as guardian and gave her power to make the decision.

Suffers From Anemia

Dr. Lopez said his patient suffered from hemolytic anemia, a disease that destroys the red blood cells. He said she required either surgical removal of her spleen, or continued blood transfusions involving "cut downs" — surgical opening of her veins to facilitate transfer of blood.

"I am not able to state precisely that Mrs. Martinez will live if she is given the transfusions, but if she is not given the transfusions, then she will die," the doctor said.

"No more cut downs, no more cut downs," the daughter cried. Mrs. Gottlieb told the judge her mother had been "begging, 'Please don't torture me any more.'"

The judge said a person "has the right not to be tortured." But he said his ruling did not mean Mrs. Martinez had the right to commit suicide by refusing treatment.

He ruled that Mrs. Martinez could be given any treatment so long as it does not give her pain.

117

HB 3184

By Representative Sackett

Prefiled October, 1969

1
2
3   A bill to be entitled
4   AN ACT relating to the right to die
5   with dignity; providing an effective
6   date.

7   Be It Enacted by the Legislature of the State of
8   Florida:

9   Section 1. All natural persons are equal be-
10 fore the law and have inalienable rights, among them
11 the right to enjoy and defend life and liberty, to
12 be permitted to die with dignity, to pursue happiness,
13 to be rewarded for industry, and to acquire, possess,
14 and protect property. No person shall be deprived of
15 any right because of race, religion, or national
16 origin.

17   Section 2. Any person, with the same
18 formalities as required by law for the execution of
19 a last will and testament, may execute a document
20 directing that he shall have the right to death with
21 dignity, and that his life shall not be prolonged
22 beyond the point of a meaningful existence.

23   Section 3. In the event any person is unable
24 to make such a decision because of mental or physical
25 incapacity, a spouse or person or persons of first
26 degree kinship shall be allowed to make such a
27 decision, provided written consent is obtained from:

28   (1) The spouse or person of first degree
29 kinship, or
30
31

1   (2) In the event of two (2) persons of first
2   degree kinship, both such persons, or

3   (3) In the event of three (3) or more persons
4   of first degree kinship, the majority of those persons.

5   Section 4. If any person is disabled and there
6   is no kinship as provided in section 3, death with
7   dignity shall be granted any person if in the opinion
8   of three (3) physicians the prolongation of life is
9   meaningless and if such opinion is stated before and
10 approved by a circuit judge.

11   Section 5. Any document executed hereunder
12 must be recorded with the clerk of the circuit court
13 in order to be effective.

14   Section 6. This act shall take effect upon
15 becoming law.

House Bill 3184 introduced and rejected in
the 1970 session of the Florida State Legislature. Courtesy of Citizens' Action Committee, Santa Ana, Calif.

'Dad Asked Me If the Doctor Would... Put Him to Sleep'

HELENA, Mont. (AP) — Poignantly tracing the lingering death of her 85-year-old father, a housewife pleaded with a committee to provide in a new state constitution the right to die.

"I maintain that to give to people facing certain death . . . the right to die quickly, easily and in peace when they want to do so, is being compassionate, intelligent and humane," Joyce M. Franks of Alberton told a hushed audience Thursday in the Senate chambers. "And I affirm that it is an act that God, who gave us all life. would approve of."

Mrs. Franks, the mother of two children, described her father's suffering to the Bill of Rights Committee at the Montana Constitutional Convention.

After her father broke a hip, his doctor described the necessary operation, she said.

"Dad asked me if the doctor would please give him something to put him to sleep right then," Mrs. Franks said, but she did not ask the doctor to do so.

As his health deteriorated, she related, her father made the request again.

"My father had been a farmer, and he had given merciful death to animals who had been pets and companions," Mrs. Franks said, sobbing. "He could not stand to see them suffer prolonged and agonizing death when they were severely mutilated or dying of illness.

"He was compassionate and merciful. He asked for the same mercy for himself."

"For eight weeks he died, little by little minute by minute, day by day," Mrs. Franks said.

"He was just denied a release from the suffering and torture which he knew, and we knew, and the doctor knew he faced."

He died in December.

"Have you wiped the eyes that will not close and that look as though they had never closed in over 85 years since they opened on the world?" Mrs. Franks asked.

"Have you struggled with your own breathing, trying unconsciously to help his labored gasps which came nearly as fast as your own pulse beats?

"Have you wiped the thick, choking mucus out of the mouth that filled again nearly as fast as you cleansed it?. . .

"And have you, then, rebelled at a system where this barbaric suffering was called necessary because unfeeling and unimaginative men declare that God willed it?"

Mrs. Franks said it was inconsistent to call it merciful to kill mortally wounded animals but not humans.

"Do you call veterinarians murders?" she asked.

Mrs. Franks proposed constitutional language saying, that "every citizen be allowed to choose the manner in which he dies."

The legislature would have to outline specific detail, if the proposal were adopted, Mrs. Franks said.

She advocated a proposal that would guarantee an individual's right to determine the manner of his death, barring accidents. Moreover, it should be legal for a person to receive a quick medicated death if he desires, she said.

Mrs. Franks has written letters to delegates and editors of Montana newspapers, polled doctors and spearheaded a move for the right to die with dignity.

Above, courtesy of Associated Press News-features.

Euthanasia

BY EUTHANASIA OR MERCY KILLING is meant the slaying of helpless invalids and of people in incurable pain. It is called mercy killing because it is prompted by the motive of relieving a person from suffering. No doubt, freedom from pain in dying is most desirable and that was the original meaning of euthanasia (eu — well, thanatos — death). It had reference to the work of a physician when death seemed imminent and his accepted role was to alleviate as far as possible, through his medical knowledge, the suffering of death whenever it occurred.

The word today has taken a new connotation and implies the bringing about of death itself — accelerating death, not easing it. The practice of medicine in such situations is a premeditation to kill and end the suffering of an individual. Mercy killing is merely a euphemistic term; easy death by lethal doses of drugs or other means to hasten the end of life is murder and against the Fifth Commandment, which states, "Thou shalt not kill." If legalized, it will be but legal murder. Mercy killing is contrary to the natural law because it is against human nature and, consequently, against the duties of reason.

Euthanasia is detrimental to the welfare of society because it destroys man's idea of sacrifice, loyalty, and courage in bearing pain. "If some dying persons accept their suffering as a means of expiration and a source of merits in order to go forward in the love of God and in abandonment to His will, do not force anesthetics on them. They should rather be aided to follow their own way" (Pope Pius XII, op. cit.). The Catholic Church adheres to the principle that drugs which have the unintended effect of shortening life may be given to relieve pain. The patient must consent and there must be no intention on the part of the doctor to kill the patient.

Above, from the booklet, *The Sacredness of Life*, published by the Knights of Columbus, © 1966.
Below, from the *Atlantic Monthly*, April 1968.

The notion that life is sacrosanct is actually a Hindu idea, although Hindus practice things like suttee. It is not Christian or biblical. If it were, all heroism and martyrdom would be wrong, to say nothing of carnivorous diet, capital punishment, and warfare. The sanctity (what makes it precious) is not in life itself, intrinsically; it is only extrinsic and *bonum per accidens, ex casu* — according to the situation. Compared to some things, the taking of life is a small evil, and compared to some things, the loss of life is a small evil. Death is not always an enemy: it can sometimes be a friend and servant.

Life is sometimes good, and death is sometimes good. Life is no more a good in itself than any other value is. It is good, when and if it is good, because of circumstances, because of the context. When it is not good, it deserves neither protection nor preservation. Our present laws about "elective death" are not civilized. It is high time we had some constructive guidance, perhaps from a model code committee of the American Law Institute. Let the law favor living, not mere life.

— *Joseph Fletcher*

Right, reprinted by permission of the Chicago Tribune-New York News Syndicate, Inc.
Below, from the *Detroit Free Press*, May 9, 1970.

DEAR ABBY: The headline over your column read, "Is there mercy in killing?" My answer to that question is, "Definitely, yes!"

My mother in law watched her handsome, 6-foot, 200-pound husband dwindle down to 87 pounds when he finally died, and that took four years.

I lost a daughter a year ago. She was 12 years old. For two years she laid there like a rag doll. I saw her go from a beautiful, active 10-year-old girl to a nothing of a 12-year-old vegetable; and all this because of an inoperable tumor, the size of a pea in her brain. She didn't know me or anyone else. Her heart was beating — that was all. They said they couldn't do anything so "inhumane" as to deliberately let her die. You call this living?

The hospital bill alone was $15,000. And after that, the "convalescent" home was $600 a month. A fortune to us which we would have gladly paid to save her life, but it was hopeless and everyone knew it.

Yes, sometimes it is merciful to let a person die. I've seen others suffer and linger this way, and if it ever happens to me, I will kill myself.

A MOTHER

A Woman's Decision

THE STATE Senate's vote against abortion reform springs primarily from the deeply felt moral conviction of many senators and their constituents that abortion is simply wrong.

We respect that moral conviction, but we would ask them to search their consciences about another aspect of the issue: Is it right for them to impose on the general populace a moral position that is so widely disputed?

That, we believe, is an ethical question too. The attempt to equate an abortion early in pregnancy with murder imposes on many people a view of life that they do not accept. The attempt to suggest that the next step is euthanasia ignores the difference between the undeveloped fetus and the fully developed person.

In an area where agreement as to right and wrong has so completely broken down, is it not wrong for the state to dictate, with criminal penalties, what private behavior shall be? The use of the law may provide a shortcut to imposing what some individuals and some churches see as moral behavior, but it can do so only at the expense of others' freedom.

Many of us think it more immoral to bring an unwanted child into an overpopulated world than to abort a pregnancy. We think the state should provide the freedom for us to follow that moral code.

Thus, when the Senate reconsiders the abortion bill next week, we would hope that the senators will take this other consideration into account. Perhaps a few more senators can be reassured by changes in the language and not the substance of the bill.

To do otherwise is to condemn many panicky women to the tender mercies of the illegal abortionist and many children to birth in a world without love. The humane, the decent thing to do in our judgment is to change this statute and give the person most affected—the woman in whose body the fetus is carried—the right to decide whether she shall go through with the process of giving birth.

Abortion and the Church

In particular cases the decision to abort may be completely justified.
Legalization itself, however, does not make all abortion wise or right.

JOHN MOORE and JOHN PAMPERIN

When Is Human Life Human?

To return to the question basic to this entire problem of abortion: When is human life human? At conception? After three months? At birth? An old, old question. Embryo, fetus, infancy, childhood, youth, old age — all are stages of human development, all are full of possibilities.

Some believe that to call the life of a human embryo "human life" and to legalize its destruction would clear the way for sanctioning infanticide. Our argument runs exactly counter to theirs. Granted, whenever any form of human life is cheapened, all human life is endangered. In Hitler's Germany abortion was legalized early, then, in succession, euthanasia, experimentation on unwilling human beings, aggression throughout Europe, death camps. Gas chambers do not inevitably follow the legalization of abortion, but in a climate where human life at any stage of growth is denied to be human, it is easier to belittle human life at other stages of growth. For instance, proposals for euthanasia are frequently made. Some medical scientists have suggested that retarded human beings be treated as suppliers of organ transplants — that, as one man put it, hospitals for these brothers of ours become "organ farms." Again, military training and, even more, actual combat turn the enemy into "gooks," "ginks," "slopes." Every way of depersonalizing human life in our society cheapens all of life. And casualness toward abortion contributes to a climate that robs human life of value. Granted. Granted, too, that this year the graduates of Harvard medical school affirmed the Declaration of Geneva, which includes the statement: "I will maintain the utmost respect for human life from the time of conception: even under threat, I will not use my medical knowledge contrary to the laws of humanity."

But what is the meaning of affirming "respect for human life from the time of conception" — or at the time when one who has life longs for release from it? The affirmation must be made, but it puts us in a dilemma. Our heritage says "Yes!" to the reality of death, but it has always said "Yes!" to the affirmation of life. Crucifixion is swallowed up in resurrection. Paul wrote: "If we live, we live for the Lord; and if we die, we die for the Lord, so that alive or dead we belong to the Lord." We look for meaning in life and in death and we view both in relation to God.

"For everything there is a season . . . a time to be born, and a time to die; . . . a time to kill, and a time to heal" — so Ecclesiastes wrote. He went beyond merely observing that men do kill to affirm that there is a time for killing. When we say "Yes" to abortion we are saying, "This is a time to end life." The question of abortion for those who affirm life must be: Is this one of those times? Throughout its history, the church has sanctioned taking human life in particular circumstances. We should be uneasy when church or state sanctions killing. But the price of denying what we do is far higher.

The Significance of Sacrifice

What then, specifically, can the church do as regards abortion? Is this one of the human experiences it should ritualize, as it has long since ritualized life and death? Such a rite would have rich resources to draw on. Presumably it would be private, involving only those invited to participate. It might include an act of confession, an affirmation of the preciousness of life, and an acknowledgment that it is human life which has been or is to be ended.

Above all, a pre- or post-abortion rite should stress our faith's understanding of sacrifice. By sacrifice, we mean giving up something or someone for what is more valuable. A person's choice to limit his family means giving up the possibility of other unique, lovable children. A society's choice *not* to limit population may mean starvation and the destruction of all human life. In relation to abortion, then, we must ask: For what is this life being sacrificed, and what does my decision to sacrifice another human life mean to me? For the church must affirm human life *within* a living environment.

There are, then, good ways and destructive ways for individuals and communities to deal with abortion. But today there seems to be little realization of this fact. Surely the church has a word that desperately needs to be heard here! With its understanding of life and death and sacrifice, the church can help both individuals and society to face abortion. But if it is to do so, it must re-examine its own life, its ways of counseling, its pronouncements and its liturgy.

A Grave Distortion Of The Abortion Issue

By REV. FRANCIS PIRO, S.T.L.

BY
WILLIAM B. OBER, M.D.

WE SHOULD LEGALIZE ABORTION

The question posed by such cases is to what extent society should subordinate individual human values to the codes it has inherited from generations with somewhat different values, different goals, and certainly a different role assigned to women. State and church use "moral" objections to prevent abortions, and yet permit some abortions. I submit that there is no moral difference among abortions, whether the fetus is the result of rape, incest or rich conjugal love. By what right does state or church claim a jurisdiction superior to that of the woman involved in pregnancy? I believe that every woman should be able to have an unwanted pregnancy aborted at her own request, subject only to the consent of her husband and the advice of her physician.

In the May 13th issue of **The Philadelphia Inquirer**, an article by a Dr. Wood read in big headlines: "Religious Freedom, Majority Rule Are The Real Abortion Issues."

The article represented a grave distortion of the concept of freedom and a flagrant assault on the basic right to life by someone who is particularly duty-bound and foster that very right. A few observations may help Dr. Wood and those who agree with his views understand the real issue of abortion:

1) The alleged encroachment of religion on the rights of people disregards the fact that abortion is fundamentally a human problem and, as such, it should be the concern of any human being regardless of his religion.

2) We ought to distinguish between physical freedom and moral freedom. A person physically free to kill, steal, etc., is not morally free to do so. In fact, any such violation carries penalties in the framework of civil and penal laws.

3) The right to life applies to any human being as such — independently of its "environmental" condition. Whether a human being be born or unborn is not essential to the fruition of that right. Furthermore, the more incapable a being is of its own defense, the more strictly the respect of its right to life should be enforced. For this very reason the American law protects animals from being cruelly treated.

4) From a scientific viewpoint, it is almost universally accepted that the fetus is a human being. Any doubt, however, could not change its condition of inviolability. Dr. Wood should remember that no law would ever condemn a person unless his guilt is proven beyond doubt. Should not this principle apply to a fetus as well? The slightest presumption as to its human condition would make a direct destruction of a fetus by abortion a crime of **murder**.

5) If the alleged "burden" of the unborn, rather than objective moral standards, is the criterion of human behavior, by the same token and logic society should rid itself of the aged, the handicapped, the retarded, etc. These people, too, are a "social liability." Millions of Jews murdered under Hitler were a liability in the Nazi doctrine.

6) The alleged violation of the rights of the majority, as claimed by Dr. Wood, is based on the false assumption that people are the source of morality. No majority could ever change certain objective moral principles as the criterion of normal human conduct. No referendum could ever change the fact that murder, for example, is a grave crime.

I trust that Dr. Wood and all those who favor a permissive abortion policy will find inspirational a passage from the Hippocratic Oath: "I will give not deadly medicine to anyone if asked, nor suggest any such counsel. Furthermore, I will not give to a woman an instrument to produce an abortion."

SOME POPULATION FACTS - Nobody can predict the population of the United States in years to come. The best is only an educated guess. THE BIRTH RATE has fallen from 25 per thousand to a current 18 per thousand population, a figure that only has to reach about 15 to give us population stability over an extensive time. To put things in the right perspective, we have to look at the DEATH RATE, that is less than 10 per thousand population. (These figures give us an average lifespan of over a hundred years) It is a figure that is sure to rise eventually to about 15 per thousand population. We are faced with great health care needs in our society as the average age of our people rises toward the end of this century. WHERE will the young be to take care of those in need? A BIRTH RATE OF 10 PER THOUSAND POPULATION WOULD BRING ON THE EVENTUAL EXTINCTION OF THE HUMAN RACE.

Top left, from *The Saturday Evening Post*, October 8, 1966.
Above right, from *The Wanderer*, copyright 1971.
Above, courtesy of the Non-Sectarian Committee for Life, October 1971.

Bishop's Office
465 State Street
Albany, New York

MAILING ADDRESS
P. O. BOX 6045 · QUAIL STATION
ALBANY, NEW YORK 12206

THE CATHOLIC BISHOPS OF NEW YORK STATE

Dear Friends in Christ:

We find ourselves once more in the season of Advent, looking forward to Christmas and the coming of the Christ child. As we prepare our minds and hearts to welcome Him, we cannot fail to wonder at the glory of new life. For every child is fashioned in God's image, and as Christians we believe that he is destined to be a son of God.

Tragically, our age has seen the growth of a movement that belittles human life and urges the destruction of unborn children. This ruthless assault on human beings in the first stages of life has now been written into the law of New York State.

The appeals that we have made in behalf of unborn babies year after year and especially last Spring, went unheeded by a majority of our lawmakers this year. In April a law was enacted which now makes it legal, at any time from conception to six months later, to destroy the baby cradled in his mother's womb.

Once this law was passed the abortionists lost no time in plying their death-dealing trade. Each day they grow wealthier from the killing of unborn children -- some of whom have been heard to cry as they were dropped into surgical trash cans. They even advertise their monstrous commerce beyond the confines of the State, thus making New York the abortion capitol of America.

Once more we denounce this outrage against humanity. Together with all the Bishops of the world we hold and teach that "abortion is an unspeakable crime". We urge you, our fellow Catholics -- and through you all men of good will -- not to be deceived because a civil law permits abortion. God's law comes first, and God's law says: "Thou shalt not kill". No civil law can ever displace God's Commandment.

Indeed we remind you that lawmakers of another generation and in another land once claimed the right to decree the extinction of innocent human beings for so-called social and eugenic reasons. It happened under the Nazi regime; who is to say it cannot happen here?

We plead with you to recognize the terrible consequences of legalized abortion. Once innocent life at any stage is placed at the mercy of others, a vicious principle has been legalized. Thereafter, a simple majority may decide that life is to be denied the defective, the aged, the incorrigible, and granted only to the strong, the beautiful and the intelligent. The day may come when lawmakers could set standards which people must meet if they are to remain alive. Already one standard has been set; who can say what others will come next? For, once respect for human life has been undermined, the murderous possibilities are limitless.

We urge you, as strongly as we can, to oppose and reject abortion. Lest anyone take our words lightly, we must also remind you that the Church invokes a severe sanction against any Catholic who raises his unfeeling hand to destroy this most defenseless of all human beings -- the unborn baby. The Church disowns by immediate excommunication any Catholic who deliberately procures an abortion or helps someone else to do so.

It is our prayer and hope that, with God's help, the people of our day will come to a true understanding of the sacredness of each human life.

Faithfully yours in Christ,

⚜ Edwin B. Broderick
Bishop of Albany
and the Catholic Bishops of New York State

December 2, 1970

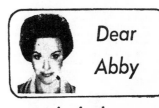

DEAR ABBY: In regard to abortion: Women must learn to say NO to their husbands more often. In fact, everyone must say no to evil. We are now living in a warring, whoring, boring world because we have forgotten God's word. Jesus told us that if a family cannot afford more children they should quit having sex.

I have never married or had sex even though I have been asked. If a person can say no to evil once, it is a lot easier the next time.

Jesus also said, "Love the sinner, but hate the sin." People today have it turned around. They love sin and hate the sinner. If I sound holier than thou it is because Christ has made me holy.

"A SAVED WOMAN"

DEAR "SAVED:" You insist upon equating sex with sin, and feel that the absence of sex has made you somewhat "holy." Theologians (and indeed Christ Himself) would disagree with you.

Left, open letter of Edwin B. Broderick, Bishop of Albany, and the Catholic Bishops of New York State, December 2, 1970. Above, reprinted by permission of the Chicago Tribune-New York News Syndicate, Inc.

The Catholic Viewpoint On Murder Of Infants Is Ours

SOME TRUTHS ABOUT ABORTION

By Walter W. Krebs
Editor of Johnstown Tribune-Democat

(Editor's Note: The author of today's column is Charles E. Kane, president of Johnstown Curia of the Legion of Mary. In this article, he presents arguments against the spreading permissiveness in regard to abortions.)

If you should walk into a public building, and there confront a distinguished-looking man with a knife poised to stab a young chld, and he should turn to you and say, "I have decided the life of this child must be ended; do not interfere with my freedom to do as I see fit," would you agree? Or would you try to stop him?

This act is being performed in many places. The child is 2 . . . 4 . . . 6 . . . 8 . . . months old. The only difference from the above scene is that the child is still in the mother's womb.

Ever since Vatican Council II, Catholics have become very self-conscious about imposing our will on those of other faiths. Meanwhile the forces of existentialism have not been reticent about imposing their will on us. The time has come to cut through the web of permissive mumbojumbo and look at a few objective truths.

Life begins at conception. For support of this position we go back to 400 B.C. to the age of Hippocrates. For those few doctors who may have forgotten, this is the oath they pledged: "I will not give to a woman an instrument to produce abortion."

Common law for centuries has recognized the rights of the fetus. It is a very recent development (I say "development" advisedly) that the desire of the mother not to have a baby has been imposed over the right of the child to be born.

Turn to the Bible and read the account of the Annunciation wherein Jesus Christ is conceived. Then read on to the account of the Visitation a few weeks later.

The God-Embryo sanctified John the Baptist while both were in their mothers' wombs.. Yet it is young souls like this from which some would snatch the right to life, without even offering the sanctifying waters of baptism so that the infant soul could be saved. If Jesus Christ were conceived today under the laws of some of our states, the pregnancy would probably be aborted.

Those who are obsessed with the idea that the murder of unborn infants should be made legal, moral, even desirable, will not settle for half-way measures. They began by advocating abortion of pregnancies resulting from such despicable acts as rape or incest. But this has proved a wedge to abortion on demand. The question in my mind is: At whose demand?

One proponent of abortion labeled it "the ultimate method of birth control." Another advocated on TV that abortion should be imposed on all mothers after the third pregnancy? Still another says the state should allow only two children per couple.

Yet another confused young girl declared to the nation that she will never permit any children to be born because it contributes to pollution. (I suppose she and her husband will invest the money they save by not having children in another expensive sports car or a motor boat.)

If we accept the validity of such argument, where will it stop? Shall we "put to sleep" a child which we discover to be retarded or deformed after birth? If we can kill at 6 . . . 7 . . . 8 months after conception, why not 9 . . . 10 . . . 11 . . . months?

It is obvious the stop will not be called until we give in to those who would supplant God's function of giving life with a committee to decide which children would be born; where and when they would be born; what sex, race and intelligence they would be born with.

Another argument of the abortionists is that legalizing abortion would eliminate illegal abortions. Ridiculous! As a corollary we might say, "We can eliminate speeding on the highways by eliminating speed limits." To carry the argument to the extreme, we could eliminate all crime by eliminating all laws.

A similar argument is made for the legalization of marijuana - by many of the same people. I cannot understand how someone can be so disturbed by the deaths of children in Asia and Africa—unfortunate though they be - but at the same time advocate smashing the life from millions of our own children.

But whatever changes we make in the laws of man, there still remain the laws of God. "Thou shall not kill." The abortionists are asking us to say murder is not murder when the victim is still in the mother's womb.

The dehumanization of our society has been noted by many prominent philosophers. This has led us to our current problems, including pornography, sexual deviations, abuse of drugs. The beginning of the decline of respect for human life led us to advocation of artificial birth control. The advocation of abortion for "medical reasons" was only a logical extension of this. This, in turn, has expanded to abortion on demand.

The next "logical" step will be euthanasia. Why not? With millions of abortions - legal and illegal - every year in this country, it is already tantamount to genocide.

I do not call upon my fellow Catholics to impose their beliefs on those of other faiths. But I do call upon all men of good will to recognize an objective moral evil and to speak out while time remains to protect the value of human life.

Right, from *The Wanderer*, March 11, 1971.
Top page, from *The Capital Voice*, March 1, 1971.

In Our Opinion

Abortion on demand

In the past few weeks, several important victories have been won in the continuing struggle to eliminate all legal restrictions on the right of women to abortion. On May 18, the New York Supreme Court ruled unconstitutional an order by Governor Rockefeller to deny state payments for abortions requested by women who currently receive medicaid assistance. In another court victory, a New York Supreme Court justice ruled unconstitutional an attempt by the Town Council of Orangetown, N.Y., to declare abortions done in doctors' offices illegal. Still another concession won was the decision of the California Supreme Court on May 20 that a pregnant minor does not need her parents' consent to have a therapeutic abortion (California law permits only "therapeutic" abortions, which are abortions performed to preserve the physical or mental health of the woman).

Rockefeller's attempt to deny medicaid for abortions was a concession to reactionary antiabortion forces in a crass deal to get support for his budget. If this directive had been upheld, it would have created tremendous suffering for thousands of women. From last July to March of this year, medicaid paid for 10,008 of the 23,530 abortions performed in New York's municipal hospitals. The fact that Rockefeller would so cynically bargain with the lives of thousands of women to further his won political career exposes his disgusting contempt for the human rights of these women.

The ruling that abortions done in doctors' offices in Orangetown, N.Y., are legal will help many women for whom a hospital abortion is too expensive. Abortion is now one of the safest operations, if done in the early stages of pregnancy. It is safer, for example, than dental surgery, which is done in doctors' offices. The attempt to limit abortions to hospitals only has the effect of increasing the cost and preventing the building of safe, inexpensive abortion clinics.

The California decision eliminating the need for parental consent for an abortion requested by a minor is an important precedent for other states. All females, no matter how young, should be able to decide for themselves whether or not they want to have children.

These victories, although modest, are a reflection of the widespread public support for the right of women to abortion. They show that the women's movement can win gains through a consistent struggle to mobilize masses of women and win public opinion for the repeal of all antiabortion laws.

The mobilization of women to fight for this right is crucial in view of the counter-mobilization of reactionary forces who oppose the right to abortion. As the New York medicaid case showed, the women's movement can prevent concessions to the antiabortion movement that would reverse gains already won. By mobilizing the mass power of women, we can wipe all barbaric antiabortion laws off the books.

A successful campaign to repeal the reactionary laws against abortion, involving hundreds of thousands of women, is needed to create the united strength and confidence to continue the fight for making abortions free on demand. This is the only way that all women will have control over their own bodies regardless of their financial status.

Reprinted by permission of J. Michael Lux from *The Militant.* Copyright © 1971, June 4, 1971.

Do Animals Have Rights?

This book's introduction began with a discussion of some of the problems with which one finds one's self confronted when trying to provide a set of general criteria for distinguishing moral arguments and judgments from nonmoral ones. It was stated that a frequently suggested element of such a set of criteria is that moral judgments can only be made about actions of human beings which affect other human beings. Some of the arguments in this section offer a direct challenge to such a restriction, and suggest that the scope of morality extends to actions affecting any sentient being. The Hindu culture represents one extreme on this issue with its belief that every sentient creature has equal rights (e.g., to life, liberty, the pursuit of happiness, freedom from suffering, etc.). Certain elements of the Western Christian culture tend toward the opposite extreme—that nonhuman beings have no rights whatsoever, and that humans can treat nonhumans in any manner they desire without violating any moral principles. (An even more radical view was presented in several arguments in the previous section, where it was asserted that some *humans* do not even have some of these basic rights.) Once again many of the main points of disagreement involve nonmoral facts (e.g., "Do animals have feelings?" "Would wild animals suffer more if their numbers were not reduced by hunters?"). But even when these questions have been resolved, disagreements over basic moral values can still arise, as in the case where causing suffering on the part of several thousand experimental animals might prevent suffering on the part of an equal number of humans. The real questions thus concern the extent to which we consider ourselves to be more valuable than other animal species, and the extent to which such beliefs can be justified.

Monterey County Calif. S.P.C.A.

There is no such thing as
A TENDER TRAP

Consider the raccoon — one of the earth's friendliest, most lovable creatures. He is part of the woodland lore and wonder of nature. Favorite children's stories endow him with almost human qualities along with the otter, the fox, the beaver, the muskrat and other forest dwellers.

Trapping animals like the raccoon is neither a friendly nor lovable occupation. Forty million leg-hold traps are set out continuously in the United States and Canada alone. The cruel, jagged-toothed traps can crunch an animal's leg, leaving him to bleed, suffer and starve for days before the trapper comes to deal the final death blow. The animals are so agonized that they often chew off their own feet.

It takes forty raccoons to make one coat for a human. Yet hundreds of defenseless animals may die before those forty pelts are collected. The traps snap at anything — turtles, eagles, groundhogs, porcupines, dogs and cats. A trap doesn't have any feeling about that . . . and neither does a trapper.

You, too, can help in the crusade to stop the vicious killing of animals that keep our environment alive and give joy to our children. You can refuse to wear the skins of animals for prestige or pleasure. You can speak out against these ungodly trapping practices in the name of the animals that still survive. And you can make a TAX DEDUCTIBLE CONTRIBUTION to Friends of Animals which is doing something constructive about this wanton destruction. DO IT NOW and feel better immediately — in the knowledge that you are helping to preserve our natural wildlife heritage — for your children and their children.

Courtesy Friends of Animals, Inc.

It's Open Season On Hunters

By JERRY KENNEY
Outdoor Editor of THE NEWS

HUNTERS this weekend are quietly moving through the painted autumn uplands of New York, stalking the lordly whitetail deer and the elusive black bear that for a short season are legal targets.

And stalking the hunters, but not quietly, are the seasonal crowd of ecologists, conservationists and other cause collectors to whom hunting is a bloody atrocity.

In New York alone, a half-million hunters will be on "binges of mayhem and murder," to hear the anti-hunting zealots tell it.

"Miserable cowards with a lust to kill," is how one so-called animal-lover described hunters on a radio program. Then she was permitted to express her wish that all of them be shot, too.

This bitter critic of hunting represents just one of several organizations that are determined to put an end to all game shooting.

They aren't opposed to killing steers, pigs, sheep, turkeys and other critters that are lured to the block by a man in a white, blood-spattered apron and an ax or hammer. And they aren't particularly upset that mink, beavers, raccoons and all those cuddly creatures have to be dispatched unceremoniously to provide warmth for some soft, pink bosom.

But the 17 million men and women who hunt for sport in this country have to go. This anti-hunting movement continues to grow even though its supporters have no concept of game management or what the ultimate outcome will be if they accomplish their goal.

It's easy to understand how the anti-hunters arouse the greatest amount of sympathy from the Bambi-lovers. Innocent, lovable, limpid-eyed creatures are pictured being slaughtered by ruthless hunters who will shoot anything that moves.

Unfortunately, there are a few creeps around the woods who fit this description. They take their share of horses, cows, dogs and chickens and they pepper farm houses, roadsigns and automobile tires. And every time one does, this transgression is blown all out of proportion and held to be typical of the hunting breed. But this charge is as unjust as tabbing every New York City cop a bribe taker.

The sport hunter does his damnedest to keep these characters out of circulation because they are his biggest threat. They keep the anti-hunting forces supplied with ammunition. But it's the only valid charge they have. Once they switch to the "hunters - exterminate - game - charge," they don't have a leg to stand on.

Game management professionals don't even like to use the term "hunting." It is hunting to us who tramp the woods and mountains. But, to them, killing animals is considered a harvest. Like any growing crop, game must be harvested or it will choke itself out of existence.

If deer and other game animals kept within the bounds of their habitats and obtained sufficient sustenance within that area, there would be no hunting. But there are no birth control pills out there, and doing what comes naturally can send any population completely out of control.

As the population increases, the habitat shrinks and the winter food supply disappears. The result is starvation and sick, weak deer. Additional starvation is likely in subsequent winters because the food supply is not replenished in one season, but may take from three to 10 years.

An unchecked game population is doomed, and this would have happened to the deer if sound game management hadn't been practiced long ago. The excess population must be harvested, and it's the hunter who harvests it. Hunters have taken over a million deer in New York in the last decade, but for every deer a hunter kills, there is still one that starves or dies a "natural" death.

Those who insist we should let nature take its course have never seen a deer starving, a doe trampling her fawn to get browse on a tree or dogs tearing at deer until their guts are dragging on the ground as they run.

Cars and trucks alone kill about 20,000 deer every year in New York. Predators—wolves, wildcats and such—no longer are a threat to deer. But domestic dogs, the collies, poodles, beagles and mutts that are allowed to roam untended, are becoming one of the most serious threats to deer in the Northeast. It's so serious that game protectors shoot any dogs they find in the woods from October through April.

The dogs don't eat the deer. They just kill them, thus wasting a link in the food chain. Man is also a predator, and has been since the beginning of time. Most men do not have to hunt to eat today, but if they eat meat, someone has to kill it for them. So, when a hunter kills swiftly with an accurate, high-powered bullet, and makes good use of the meat, why should he be condemned?

Every hunter aims for a clean kill. Anything short of that lessens his chance of taking his prize. Everyone can't be a marksman, but with the quality of firearms and optics available today, hunters rarely wound animals and lose them.

A hunter's bullet is at least as humane as a slaughter house worker's ax, hammer or knife, and probably more so, but even the most dedicated of conservationists is seldom moved to tears by the sight of a succulent steak on his plate.

From *The New York Daily News*, November 21, 1971.

HUNTERS *Make it "Dear"...*
not "Deer"
will you...won't you...can't you?

friends of animals, inc.   11 West 60th Street, New York, N.Y. 10023   Circle 7-8120

Rod Hunter, "Sports" Columnist
Echoes Sentinel
Stirling, New Jersey

Dear Mr. Hunter,

You suggest that hunters have a "reverance" for life. Is it then something akin to the reverence the Marquis de Sade had for women? We never thought of it that way but it seems to make sense.

To your astute observation that nature is "no Disneyland" may we add: nor is it a boudoir. We're not turned on by a show of masculinity which takes place in the forests through maiming or occasionally killing helpless animals. We like guys whose virility holds on better proving grounds.

But, credit where credit is due: You hunters certainly are potent with the politicians. Now you may enter a sanctuary and blast off. On December 19, the New Jersey Great Swamp National Wildlife Refuge will throng with 150 of you lucky lottery-winners, tested for sharp-shooting by your ability to pay $7.15 for a license to murder.

Please spare our minds as you spare our bodies and don't try to ennoble your psychotic behavior by claiming you are trimming the herd for the benefit of the herd (which you say consists of 400 deer). We've read your magazines where you admit to each other that it's fun... fun...fun...to kill...kill...kill.

The only herd that needs trimming is the herd of hunters. So please garb yourselves, you brave 150, in fawn color on December 19, and double your thrill... thrill...thrill.

Sincerely yours, For the Girls:

GRETCHEN WYLER

LAUREN BACALL   GLORIA DE HAVEN

ALI MacGRAW   JUNE HAVOC   PATRICE MUNSEL

SHEILA MacRAE   BETSY PALMER   JOANNE WOODWARD

Can You be Indifferent?

In January of 1970 the President of the United States promised the people "peace with nature." Yet, in the summer of 1970, men were sent forth to murder 60,000 sentient animals: 9,000 for Japan, 9,000 for Canada—and 42,000 ostensibly for the people of the United States.

As president of Friends of Animals, I, Alice Herrington, spent ten days on the Pribilof Islands, our Federal public territory, to observe and report on this massacre of seals. Hour after hour I watched helpless animals being driven inland a mile or more, until their lungs were bursting; watched the clubs being raised over and over as the seals were battered into insensibility. As my eyes watched, my mind recalled the litany of the bureaucrats, remembered their statements that this is mercy killing, done to save the seals from starvation and disease. And then I moved closer to the seals as they grouped together in terror. The men were killing only the healthy seals whose coats would gleam on fashion row. The seal with fish net imbedded in its fur was ignored after only one bash of the club—a bash which removed an eye. And I remembered these same bureaucrats' statement that only 15 out of every 100 seals born survives the first three years. And there they were, the 15 three-year-old seals nature wanted to survive, being crushed at that very moment by employees of the United States Government.

That individual man often engages his lust to kill is apparent. That our society, our government, condones murder for profit is abominable. And then the profit is only for the Fouke Fur Company which holds a monopoly contract with the government; the whole barbaric "program" is subsidized by the tax dollar of the American people.

If you are one who feels, one who recognizes that all life is bound together on this earth, won't you join and ask Congress to pass this law:

A. To permit the Aleut native on the Pribilofs to kill, for their own commercial profit, 18,000 seals per year; the sealskins—not the American dollars—to be delivered to Japan and Canada ...until 1975 when the current agreement to kill for those countries runs out.

B. To ban the import into the United States of all products, raw or finished, from marine mammals (seals, whales, walrus, polar bear, otters, etc.)

C. To direct the administration to initiate a truly international agreement to protect marine mammals.

As the prime consumer of the world's resources, we owe it to the world and the coming generations of all species not to abuse the world. Please join and write your representatives in the Congress today, asking them to sponsor this measure.

An advertisement in *The New York Times*, courtesy of Humane Legislation, Inc.

Sixty years ago Congress passed a law to save the Alaska fur seal.
This year they're considering a law that could destroy it.

In 1911, a four-nation treaty was signed to save the Alaska fur seal from indiscriminate slaughter on the open sea, a method that had reduced the fur seal population to near extinction.

Alaska Fur Seals Increased 1,000%

As a result of the treaty, and with the careful guidance of the U.S. government, the Alaska fur seal population has grown from approximately 120,000 to 1½ million — an increase of over 1,000%.

In March, a Bill was introduced into Congress that would end the treaty, leave the Aleut natives, who are dependent on the harvests, jobless and with no practical alternative, and eventually return the Alaska fur seal to open sea killing — a method that is sure to complete the job it didn't sixty years ago.

What Is The Issue?

Why, you might ask, has such a Bill been proposed?

Because certain "conservation" organizations have succeeded in misleading many people into believing that what has been going on in the Pribilof Islands for the last sixty years is nothing but some kind of inhuman carnage.

Have all the knowledgeable conservationists and scientists involved in establishing and administering this fur seal program since 1911 been wrong?

Has it been wrong to have administered the fur seal program in such a way that the herd has grown from near extinction to 1½ million?

Has it been wrong that a four-nation treaty dependent on international cooperation has permitted this phenomenal growth?

Is it wrong to harvest animals surplus to the needs of the herd so that disease and starvation are minimized for the benefit of the great majority of the animals?

Is it wrong that man, through sound principles and programs, manages nature, to the benefit of man and nature?

Emotion Vs. Conservation

Because these organizations cannot attack the fur seal program on its record of successful wildlife management, they have resorted to innuendo and exploitation of emotions. How? By clouding the major issue of conservation with the issue of the harvesting method. Yes. The seals are clubbed. Because scientists have as yet found no other method that is more humane, quicker, or more efficient.

The $1,000 Misunderstanding

Which seals are taken? Mostly three- and four-year-old bachelor males. No baby seals are killed; no animals are ever skinned alive. And if anybody can produce an authentic photograph of a baby fur seal being killed on the Pribilof Islands as part of the annual U.S. commercial harvest, The Fouke Company will pay them $1,000.

Consider The Consequences

If this Bill is passed, the consequences will be disastrous.

The Aleuts, who have been dependent on the seal harvests for generations, will be without their livelihood and left with an alternative that is neither practical nor satisfactory to the Aleuts. Many others' jobs will be threatened, or eliminated. (Yes, the fur seal program is also a business — a business that supports a conservation program at no cost to the taxpayers. The United States receives a share, as do Japan and Canada. The state of Alaska gets 70% of the net proceeds from the Pribilof harvests, and the balance goes into a general treasury fund).

The greatest consequence, however, is for the seals. Most of their time is spent in international waters—and they can be preyed upon by any nation, using any method they care to use. Don't mislead yourself into believing others will practice good will if the treaty is ended. They won't. Many countries have commercial fishing industries — and the fewer seals around, the more fish.

Banning the importation of Alaska fur pelts into the U.S. will have little, or no, effect on world seal harvests. The majority of Alaska fur sealskins are sold to Europe, and they can just as easily buy from any of a number of other countries, or individuals, who would now be able to get into the act.

There is little doubt that the Alaska fur seal cannot survive a return to open sea sealing.

We Need Your Help

Think about it. And think about the long-range consequences of this Bill. Don't delude yourself into believing it's for a good cause, because its end is an evil one. And if it goes through, it's only the beginning. (We kill domestic animals and use their products in our daily lives—is that not also "immoral?")

If you're on our side, and the side of conservation and the Alaska fur seal, please write to your senators and representatives in Congress and protest the enactment of S.1315 and H.R.6554.

The Fouke Company, Route 1, Box 168, Greenville, S. C. 29611

An advertisement in *The New York Times*, courtesy of The Fouke Company.

Weep Not for the Lamb?

OH, PITY the poor, defenseless little baby seals! Block the heartless hunters from bludgeoning them brutally and mercilessly to death for mere profit and fashion! Stop the threat to still another irreplaceable species! Shouldn't we all shed tears for the poor baby seals?

I won't.

Not until it becomes more fashionable to bewail a far bloodier, far greater slaughter of the innocents than hardly anyone—not even the tenderest heart—speaks much of.

I speak of the lambs and calves who perish by the millions every year for you and me for our breakfast, lunch, and dinner.

I speak of the 500,000 sound, healthy adult animals—sheep, cattle, hogs—that suffer terror and death daily under the packing-house captive-bolt device that supposedly stuns, the electric prod that supposedly stupifies without burning. And there are the billions of chickens that die for you and for me every year by the implacable finger knife.

It would be nice to think that these animals and birds don't know what is happening. But their terrified squealing and bellowing in the slaughter pens engraves the memory.

And it would be nice, too, to think that their deaths are instantaneous and painless. But no one can be sure, despite Federal and state humane-slaughter laws, that the methods prescribed and in widespread use are in fact humane. Packers themselves acknowledge that the act of slaying meat animals is a problem that continues to defy resolution.

The fact is, almost all meat animals are stunned one way or another before they are killed. Baby seals are clubbed, as prescribed by law, because that's the most humane way anybody has so far devised—better than former practice, which included kicking, shooting, gaffing, and ripping open their bellies.

If clubbing seals is inhumane and should be stopped, so also should killing meat animals the way we do. And if no better way can be found, we should all embrace vegetarianism.

But it is safe to say that hardly any hogs, sheep, or cattle will be spared if our palates must suffer.

—JOE WESTERN

I believe I have omitted mentioning that in my first voyage from Boston to Philadelphia, being becalmed off Block Island, our crew employed themselves catching cod and hauled up a great number. 'Till then I had stuck to my resolution to eat nothing that had had life; and on this occasion I considered, according to my Master Tryon, the taking every fish as a kind of unprovoked murder, since none of them had or ever could do us any injury that might justify this massacre. All this seemed very reasonable. But I had formerly been a great lover of fish, and when this came hot out of the frying pan, it smelled admirably well. I balanced some time between principle and inclination till I recollected that when the fish were opened, I saw smaller fish taken out of their stomachs. "Then," thought I, "if you eat one another, I don't see why we mayn't eat you." So I dined upon cod very heartily and have since continued to eat as other people, returning only now and then occasionally to a vegetable diet. So convenient a thing it is to be a *reasonable creature*, since it enables one to find or make a reason for everything one has a mind to do.

Above, from the *Autobiography of Benjamin Franklin.*

☆ ☆ ☆

Seals and Lambs

Editor, The National Observer:

In regard to Mr. Western's editorial "Weep Not for the Lamb?" [Observations, March 29], there is a difference in lambs and calves we eat for food and sealskins we wear to keep up with fashion.

JOAN MOONEY

Washington, D. C.

☆ ☆ ☆

Call for Realism

Editor, The National Observer:

At last someone spoke out expressing my sentiments about the killing of baby seals.

I've had some experience with the economic side of this, so it doesn't seem like wanton killing of a defenseless baby. The parent seals are at sea—the baby is at hand. In most cases, subsistence and even existence of the hunter and his family are involved.

Having spent over a year in a coastal Eskimo village on the Seward peninsula, I've seen what takes place. The hunter takes the sealskin to the trading post, and usually before the actual cash involved leaves the area it has gone through four or five transactions. For these skins he gets food, clothing, fuel, lumber, shells, and other things necessary for his family.

Right, wrong, cruel — who is to say? Clubbing baby seals to death in order to eat, clothe, and keep warm is still a far cry above trophy killing by sportsmen or hunting deer by car lights or crocodile killing at night or the killing of great numbers of seals by early fur-company ship's crews.

Let us be realistic about this and not pick just one isolated group without knowing anything about the circumstances behind the slaughter.

As Joe Western wrote, "We might all embrace vegetarianism." But what about the theory that plants grow better if one speaks kindly of them? Surely this means they, too, have feelings which hurt when we pull up, pare, boil, fry, or chew them.

MALINDA CARROLL

Hyannis, Mass.

☆ ☆ ☆

Top left, from *The National Observer*, March 29, 1971.

Top right, letter to the editor of *The National Observer* by Joan Mooney, April 12, 1971.

Above right, letter to the editor of *The National Observer* by Malinda Carroll, April 12, 1971.

They're as much of concern to us as anyone.

The fate of the world's starving may seem very much outside the RSPCA's province.

The truth of the matter is quite the reverse.

Of course humanity must be fed.

And animals must be exploited in vast numbers if Man is to survive.

It's a fact that modern methods of intensive farming have done much to increase production.

Yet in facing up to a vital human right, we feel another is being denied.

The animals'.

As often as not, we make them into machines.

Piglets are frequently kept in total darkness.

Pigs can spend the whole of their productive lives confined in restrictive stalls.

Hens are crammed into battery systems.

Five-day old calves are kept in boxes for fourteen weeks, then taken out and slaughtered.

We believe there simply have to be alternatives.

Economically viable. So the hungry can be fed.

Yet humane.

It's a big job. And in our fight to help solve these problems, we need your support.

To help us find alternative methods of farming. Through our own contribution to research.

And to help us make more people aware. So we gain even more support.

Today tens of thousands of people will die in misery.

Today tens of thousands of animals will die in misery.

In overcoming one problem, we believe there's no reason for turning a blind eye to the other.

Hence this advertisement. But such advertisements are far from cheap.

Won't you help us by sending a donation?

Write to us here at the RSPCA, so we can continue to plead the animals' case.

In return we'll send you a leaflet detailing precisely what you can do to help animals.

Including those you wouldn't normally see.

RSPCA

Be human.
Show animals a little humanity. *Too!*

RSPCA (SE-S-1), 105 Jermyn Street, London SW1Y 6EG.

SECTION XIII

Are Some People
More Equal than Others?

Although most of the selections in this section are concerned in varying degrees with current racial issues in the United States, the basic moral issues with which they deal are not really related to questions of race at all. Problems similar to those discussed in this section appear in many contexts, such as the Israeli–Arab situation in the Middle East, or the conflict between the Punjabi in West Pakistan and the Bengalis in Bangladesh, where there are *no* racial differences. (If one disagrees with this assertion, one will find one's self involved in a debate over the concept of "race," thus raising another complete set of interesting but extremely complex questions which can't be answered here.) These problems are not necessarily problems of minority groups either, for they exist in situations where the oppressed groups comprise a significant majority as in Rhodesia and South Africa.

We suggest that the basic moral issue in all discussions of discrimination against racial, ethnic, or minority groups is that of consistency—an issue discussed in several previous passages. If we accept the principle that we should treat similar cases similarly, then we must treat *all* human beings the same way in particular situations, unless we can specify some morally relevant and significant difference between two or more individuals. This can certainly be done in many everyday situations; for example, in normal circumstances we have no obligation to help most people cross a street at an intersection where there is a traffic signal, but we do have such a responsibility to an individual who happens to be blind and is using a cane rather than a seeing-eye dog. This is essentially the same kind of situation as that in which an individual is deprived of certain political or economic privileges because (and only because) he is a black Rhodesian or a Catholic in Northern Ireland, the one difference being that these latter cases are clearly morally unjustifiable. It would certainly be difficult (if not impossible) to provide any argument that the color of a person's skin (and nothing else) is relevant to the possession of basic economic or political rights.

Most attempts to justify such discrimination in the past have not been based merely on skin color, but also on the basis of certain biological or theological theories relating skin color to other characteristics such as intellectual capacities or "moral fiber." None of these theories has been able to withstand careful scrutiny and testing, and thus there does not seem to be any valid justification for relating these characteristics. And even if some correlation could be established between skin color and intelligence, it would still be necessary to demonstrate that a moral justification can be provided for determining an individual's political and economic rights on the basis of intelligence, rather than eye color, hat size, or the number of letters in his last name. In considering such questions, we must always keep in mind that criteria of discrimination work both ways, and that they can be used for discriminating *against* a special group as well as in favor of that group.

"You have blue eyes. You are inferior."

In Riceville, Iowa, a teacher named Jane Elliott taught her all-white class the meaning of an ugly word.

The blue-eyed Mrs. Elliott told her third graders that brown-eyed people are superior.

The blue eyes had to sit in the back of the class. They drank from paper cups, not the fountain. They were refused second helpings at lunch. And they received five minutes less recess.

Soon, the blue eyes were acting like inferior people. They did their lessons poorly. And the brown-eyed children behaved as though they were really superior.

The next Monday, Mrs. Elliott reversed the roles. And suddenly, the brown-eyed children were behaving like inferior pupils.

Mrs. Elliott's pupils know the meaning of discrimination and prejudice. They have experienced it.

Every American child should have a gifted teacher like Jane Elliott. For education to match the challenge of our times calls for more than money. It calls for the imagination of our brightest people.

Yet, a Mrs. Elliott is the exception, not the rule. And will be, until we again give priority to the education of our children.

Our most precious resource is not the plants that dot our land, the cities that house our people, the fields that grow our crops, or the wealth that pays for bittersweet affluence.

Our most precious resource is the child who becomes the man or woman who will inherit this nation.

We cannot fail to give our first priority to the development of that resource.

Unless we are content to become an inferior nation.

Courtesy Addressograph Multigraph Corporation

MY ANSWER TO GENOCIDE

Bitter comic prescribes big families as effective black protest

BY DICK GREGORY

LETTERS

BLACK/WHITE DATING

Sirs: In "Black/White Dating" (May 28), Joan Downs asks the question: "How, in a time of deeply troubled black/white relations, does one reconcile group loyalty with friendship —even love—across the color line?" The answer is clear: by recognizing that one's group is, in reality, the whole human race.

CHARLES F. GOLDBERG
Spring Valley, N.Y.

Above, letter to the editor of *Life*, June 18, 1971.

MY ANSWER to genocide, quite simply, is eight black kids—and another baby on the way.

I guess it is just that "slave master" complex white folks have. For years they told us where to sit, where to eat, and where to live. Now they want to dictate our bedroom habits. First the white man tells me to sit in the back of the bus. Now it looks like he wants me to sleep under the bed. Back in the days of slavery, black folks couldn't grow kids fast enough for white folks to harvest. Now that we've got a little taste of power, white folks want us to call a moratorium on having babies.

Of course, I could never participate in birth control, because I'm against doing anything that goes against Nature. That's why I've changed my eating habits so drastically over the years and have become a vegetarian. And birth control is definitely against Nature. Can you believe that human beings are the only creatures who would ever consider developing birth control pills? You mention contraception to a gorilla and he will tear your head off.

Above, *Ebony*, October 1971.

I read Dick Gregory's October 1971 EBONY article twice. The first reading made me angry, which I suppose was Gregory's intended effect on white readers. The second reading made me feel sorry for his eight beautiful black kids. They are being raised not for their own individual worths but as a protest against imaginary genocide. After Mr. Gregory is dead and gone, they may have to live in a world made unbearably overcrowded by just such uninformed bigotry.

If birth control is a plot by whites to eliminate blacks then why do white women form the majority of pill users? And why have so many young whites decided to forego having children even though they want them? If Dick Gregory wants to raise a mob of children according to his beliefs, why does he and his wife not adopt some of the black babies who are being emotionally crippled in institutions?

He uses the rationale that he does not believe in unnatural practices, but his oldest daughter wears glasses. I believe the reason he hides behind the "natural way" is that he is too selfish to care about his children's future and too unsure of his manhood to give his wife a respite from being a baby machine.

Dick Gregory's children will have to associate with whites eventually, because we are not going to stop having babies either. If Mr. Gregory is as concerned for his race as he claims to be, let him teach his kids to love their fellow man regardless of his color. Having children to spite your neighbors is foolish.

MRS. MARY SHAW
San Antonio, Tex.

Never before have I read an article that stated so many of the things I would like to say myself. The article I'm referring to is "My Answer to Genocide," by Dick Gregory (October 1971). I am from a large family of 12 children —seven girls and five boys—and I am the oldest.

Mr. Gregory is one black man I truly respect because he speaks his mind and shows the world that he is the head of his house and that no one can tell him what must go on in his bedroom.

"The Lord giveth and the Lord taketh away." Don't play around with the babies yet to be born. Let nature take its course. Don't let man take the place of our Master. Only He knows how far to let you go. The Lord looks out for all of us, and there is a justifiable reason for everything He has anything to do with. God never makes a mistake, so why should man try to change things?

During the time of slavery, the blacks could not have babies fast enough for their master. Look at the change now that we have a little power.

MISS CAROLYN A. DONNELLY
Mullins, S. C.

Left, letter to the editor of *Ebony* by Mrs. Mary Shaw, December 1971

Above, letter to the editor of *Ebony* by Carolyn H. Donnelly, December 1971.

If Mr. Richard Gregory is really interested in having the black population rise, why, oh why, doesn't he adopt black children that are for various reasons parentless? These kids get tossed from foster home to foster home. Some never acclimate and spend their entire lives in institutions.

If Mr. Gregory really feels that genocide is being subtly pushed, he should further the cause of blacks adopting blacks. I believe that if he inquired of the authorities in Chicago alone he would find there are many black children needing strong permanent homes.

Come on, Dick, lead the way. Get the blacks to adopt the black—otherwise, they'll be adopted by whites and eventually true integration will take place and then there will be no need for genocide of any sort. We will all really be brothers—both under and outside the skin.

JOSETTE H. MARTINS
Eau Claire, Wisc.

As a black, professional woman, and mother of two, I found the article by Mr. Gregory and his insane reasoning appalling and beyond belief.

The fact that this man wants X amount of children is not my point. The fact that he and his wife share a common desire to have a large family is such an intimate, personal matter, that a comment here would be out of order. But to openly admit that he is capitalizing on the fertility of his wife and himself to strike a blow at the white population of this nation is, in my humble but sincere opinion, bordering on lunacy.

He is using the body of his wife as a weapon, reducing her to the level of a cow, and she apparently accepts her lot as inevitable. It is significant to recall that he did not once mention an offspring as an individual unique personality, did not once speak of a child as a child for his or her own sake, but rather as some wild, distorted joke on the plans and schemes of the white man. Herein lies the crux of my confusion.

I would implore Mr. Gregory to fight his war and his bitterness as a man, and thus allow his wife to become a person, his children to become people in their own right, and not tools for his use, or outlets for his frustrations. As brother James Brown might say, "Check yourself."

MRS. SHIRLEY NALLEY
Roosevelt, L. I., N. Y.

Dick Gregory states, "All birth control is definitely against nature. Can you believe that human beings are the only creatures who would ever consider developing birth control pills? You mention contraception to a gorilla. . . ."

Indeed a gorilla does not need birth control because he has no power of death control. The present population explosion is a human problem; most animal species are stable or declining. Within the human species, however, the problem exists in varying degrees for all races. The cause is in part due to great improvements in medical knowledge and resultant reduction in death rates. "Natural" is a high infant mortality; "natural" is a high death rate for women in childbirth and "natural" is a short life expectancy!

Maybe Mr. Gregory will feel better if he reads that the annual rate of population growth in Africa is 2.7 per cent compared to a meager 1.1 per cent in the U. S. But, alas, who is going to catch up with Asia with 2.1 billion people. . . ?

MARINA B. BROWN
Loudonville, N. Y.

Above, letter to the editor of *Ebony* by Marina B. Brown, December 1971.

One may agree or differ with Dick Gregory's opinion on genocide, but when he gets off his subject and states what animals do "naturally," he has entered a field where even his opinions cannot change the facts.

You see, some animals practice infanticide to keep their population down. Other species have smaller litters in times when food is scarce. Still others will *not even* mate if they are unable to provide adequate shelter for their offspring.

Even man, namely the African Bushman, practiced birth control 50,000 years before Dick Gregory was born—but then they didn't know it wasn't natural to do it.

HOWARD FIGOWITT
Harrisburg, Pa

Top left, letter to the editor of *Ebony* by Josette H. Martins, December 1971.

Left, letter to the editor of *Ebony* by Mrs. Shirley Nalley, Roosevelt, Long Island, December 1971.

Congratulations to EBONY for printing Dick Gregory's excellent article, "My Answer To Genocide." I strongly agree with Gregory's intellectual and moral stand on birth control. It is good to hear his voice loud and clear on this vital issue. I believe firmly that artificial contraceptive birth control is against nature. It is beautiful to hear a strong black voice calling our attention to this simple fact of life.

BROTHER DON FLEISCHHACKER, C.S.C.

St. Edward's University
Austin, Texas

It is really discouraging to hear that Dick Gregory is preaching against one kind of genocide while at the same time he and his wife are practicing another kind. When our population gets bigger than our farmland can support, people will die, and there is no ethnic magic that will keep the same thing from happening to the black brothers and sisters that will happen to the whites.

RUTH B. BALL

Portland. Ore.

Above, letter to the editor of *Ebony* by Ruth B. Ball, December 1971.

Top right, letter to the editor of *Ebony* by Brother Don Fleischhacker, C. S. C., December 1971.

Left, letter to the editor of *Ebony* by Howard Figowitt, December 1971.

Hypocrisy laid bare

The full-scale row which always looked likely to break over the all-white South African cricket tour of Australia is on. Sensing a good issue to snipe at the new McMahon Administration, the Opposition leader, Mr Whitlam, has now called for cancellation, and thus joined the slowly swelling anti-apartheid movement in Australia. The particular cause of Mr Whitlam's wrath is the blunt rejection by the Vorster regime of the mild Springbok request that two non-whites should join the touring side. Mr Vorster's Minister of Sport, Mr Frank Waring, has challenged the South African Cricket Association to open their doors to non-whites at all levels. Let them use the white's clubs. Let them play in the whites' league.

In logic Mr Waring's position cannot be faulted, even though he knows that if the white cricketers agreed the Government would not sanction it. But he has effectively called their bluff. The selection of two non-whites was window-dressing and a relatively painless attempt to allay international opinion. If you want non-whites on your tour, have them with you at home, too, the Minister is saying. To which the cricketers could retort (although they will not): "If the Government wants its own form of window-dressing by talking of a dialogue with black Africa, why not be logical and have a dialogue with black South Africans? Why allow a black Malawi ambassador to use white hotels, but not allow the same right to a black South African?"

The episode only shows that there is ultimately no logic in South Africa's system of white supremacy. The argument is between hard-line pragmatists like Mr Vorster's Government and slightly less hard-line pragmatists like the United Party. The most interesting current development is that the Nationalist Government has moved in the past two months back towards its old "verkrampte" position. The cricket decision is the latest in a series of tougher moves. It seems that Mr Vorster has interpreted his recent slight electoral losses to the United Party as a signal that he must move back to the Right. His Labour Minister Mr Viljoen, recently confirmed that there is to be no slackening in job reservation. Indeed, it is to be tightened. There has been the campaign against the Church and the detention or expulsion of Churchmen who have spoken out. And in the face of the worsening economic situation, the Government is looking for a harsh deflationary cure by putting up the sales taxes. The poor will suffer most, and that, of course, means Africans.

Top page, from *The Guardian*, April 10, 1971.

Sirs: I am black. Recently I took a white girl to a show. Therefore, your article was remarkably timely for me.

The idea that interracial dating and marriage will be accepted more readily in 20 years is a lot of nonsense. It is in keeping with that old American pastime, passing the buck. The people who tell you "in 20 years" are too stubborn or too foolish to bend a little in their narrow-minded views. They are the ones who probably figure on not being alive then—so that anything that happens is simply not their problem. Talk about escapists!

These people bring up their children with the same numskull ideas. So how in hell are things going to be different for the next generation? The change in people's minds about this topic and others is going to have to take place now—not 20 years from now.

DAVID E. FREEMAN
New York, N.Y.

Sirs: It seems that the whole "problem" is brought about by people of all races who hold opinions about things that are none of their business and do not affect their own lives personally. This includes my opinion, too.

M. E. GWYNNE
Alamo, Calif.

Above, letter to the editor of *Life* by M. E. Gwynne, June 18, 1971.

Left, letter to the editor of *Life* by David E. Freeman, June 18, 1971.

Below and right, from *The Guardian Weekly*.

MANCHESTER:

Rest in Peace

NEGRO HUMOR is in rather short supply in the United States, but I would like to tell you a story I heard in South Carolina a couple of weeks ago.

It's about an African who was resting under a coconut tree when he was addressed by a passing Englishman. "What," asked the Englishman, "are you doing for yourself, just idly sitting there? Why don't you get busy and develop your fields, those mines, and build cities?"

"What for?" the African asked.

"To establish commerce," the Englishman replied.

"Commerce for what?"

"So you can make lots of money."

"What good is money?"

"Money will bring you leisure."

"What will I do with leisure?"

"Then you can rest."

"But why do all that," asked the African, "when I'm resting now?"

—*The Guardian Weekly*.

138

Sex and Sin

The selections in this section reflect sharply differing moral attitudes toward sexual behavior. It is tempting to trace these variations to differing factual and religious beliefs, but they are only part of the story. In reading these selections one senses a chasm between the disputants so deep that their differences seem irreconcilable. We suggest that many of the authors here exemplify different *metaphysical* stances, and that their disagreements over moral, factual, and religious matters is a symptom of fundamentally different ways of seeing man and his place in the universe.

Some people see the world in terms of a grand dichotomy between mind and matter; mind is identified with good, matter with evil. Accordingly, they believe that the mental ought to reign over the material body. In specific terms, this very general way of seeing the world manifests itself in rigid codes of sexual morality. These codes embody the metaphysical belief that the resistance of bodily desires is the resistance of the evil, the material.

Needless to say, many people do not share this world view, and they often see sexual desires as neutral or even good. Such people have little sympathy or use for strict codes of sexual morality. The two sides of the controversy can neither communicate easily nor fruitfully argue the moral issues until they bridge the deep *metaphysical* gulf that separates them. Different metaphysical beliefs are contributing factors to other moral disputes as well. The question raised in discussions of abortion—"When does the fertilized egg become a living human being?"—is interpreted by many as a metaphysical question. The belief that nonhuman as well as human life should be preserved is also traceable to very general beliefs about the universe, to metaphysics. Thus we see that metaphysical beliefs can manifest themselves in morally significant ways. This makes it imperative that we understand these various beliefs, including those to which we are committed, and try to evaluate them. For, by and large, choosing a metaphysics is a big step toward choosing a moral code. It cannot be taken lightly.

Learn All About Sex

By Terence Shea
FROM BOSTON

The slides showed masterpieces of erotic art, and dark-shadowed photographs of embracing couples in positions of love-making. But to the church-school boys and girls who previewed the visuals as part of a new curriculum about sex, the material didn't show much more than they already knew.

The students generally felt that the loving couple in Rodin's *The Kiss* might proclaim the French sculptor's artistic genius but chiseled figures can't teach teen-agers much about intercourse. The way to show love-making, they said, is with brightly lighted close-ups of couples making love.

The authors of the course agreed. The slides were replaced with a color filmstrip of three separate couples having intercourse. And the filmstrip became just one more teaching tool in what already was the most comprehensive, explicit, and possibly controversial set of materials ever assembled for use in a classroom.

Cautious Introduction

The course is called "About Your Sexuality." It was formulated by educators here in the national offices of the Unitarian Universalist Association mainly for junior-high-school students in Unitarian churches' weekly religion classes. It is expected to be used also with older teen-agers and with adults. The course is being released this month by Beacon Press, the Unitarians' publishing arm. And it is being provided to Unitarian groups through the most cautious and exacting introduction strategy ever devised for a course of its type.

Voluntary for Students

The prospect of imminent classroom use could stir some concern among Unitarian parents, although no student can take the course if he or his parents object. Church leaders expect little internal or external criticism of their use of the course, but it may not escape allegations that it is psychologically too much too soon for adolescents.

That is a major argument of many who oppose increasingly explicit classroom sex education. Many say that such education should be thorough, but it should be at home, or in the privacy of a school psychologist's office. Dr. James M. Parsons, a Melbourne, Fla., psychiatrist who

is national president of the Scientific Information and Education Council of Physicians, contends that most explicit material "is suggestive, and it produces obsessive thinking about human sexuality when [the students] are least able to repress it."

The curriculum covers topics such as anatomy, masturbation, intercourse, contraception, homosexuality, petting, slang, and deviations. The topics are treated in both printed materials and in visuals such as the filmstrip on love-making and others on anatomy, birth control, conception, childbirth, masturbation, and same-sex behavior. In addition, the course includes recordings of young people describing their first heterosexual intercourse

No Single Set of Values

The curriculum's makers contend that it dictates no single set of values. It is built on the principle that each situation affects the ethics of a person's actions, says Mr. Hollerorth. He offers the example of what happens in the course when "a student asks, 'Is it okay for junior-high kids to have intercourse?'

"We tell teachers that you don't say yes and you don't say no. That's not an effort to cop out. You don't say yes because what about the kid who isn't having intercourse? You don't say no, because what about the kid who is—in terms of guilt he might feel?

"Our approach is to provide the kind of setting where the information is available, attitudes can be clarified, implications can be considered, and there is an atmosphere of trust." Ultimately the student is expected to answer his own question responsibly in terms of his own situation.

"A major focus of the curriculum," says Gobin Stair, director of Beacon Press, "is letting the kids in on the fact that there's no one set of values." Essentially, he emphasizes, the course is "a process that a bunch of kids, with adults, go through; we just supply the props."

Beacon's position, says Mr. Stair, is that "this matter of understanding living is a religious question." And although the 166,000-member association of Unitarians is one of the most liberal church groups in the country, Mr. Stair adds, "there's plenty of conservative, tense, emotional reaction" in many places. "But the fact that this course is being used," he adds, "is an illustration of the change that's happening."

The first to see the changes, and to note adult reactions, are the dozens of Unitarian educators around the country who have been introducing the course to teachers and other adults. According

to two teacher trainers in Washington, D. C., there is a faint pattern but no predictability among grown-ups' reactions to the materials.

Cecilia Wood, a teacher at Washington's Sidwell Friends School and a director of religious education at her suburban Maryland Unitarian church, says adults who oppose the course argue that it will "open the floodgates" and that "if they hear about it they're going to try it." Mrs. Wood contends that "children are going to learn anyhow; it's infinitely better that they learn from informed persons."

Enoch Albert, a zoology teacher last year at the University of Maryland who gave workshops with Mrs. Wood in the Washington area, says most adults who voiced doubts about the course were middle-aged parents; most who liked it were young or old. Parents, like their children, "are informed, but they aren't aware of their own attitudes," Mr. Albert says.

Examining the course through a workshop can be "a consciousness-raising experience" for adults, says Mrs. Wood. "One thing that happens," she says, "is surprise at their own rigidity and their preoccupations about what's right." Later on, almost every adult "comes to accept that what he believes is not the only attitude."

☆ ☆ ☆

Primitive Reason

Editor, The National Observer:

How utterly stupid Mr. Hollerroth is!

In answer to the student's question "Is it okay for junior-high kids to have intercourse?" he misses the very primitive reason why it is not okay.

Let me ask one simple question: "Is a junior-high kid capable of paying the cost of an abortion, or is he able to assume the financial responsibility of raising the child he so thoughtlessly begets?"

There is a prime point of morality involved: Somebody else has to take on the task of raising the young bastard, while your eggheads coach the kids from the sideline, "So fornicate, enjoy."

JAMES SENTZ
Ridgewood, N.J.

☆ ☆ ☆

Left, from *The National Observer*, August 23, 1971.

Above, letter to the Editor of *The National Observer* by James Sentz, September 18, 1971.

Medical Chauvinism

By HENRY CHIEFFO, M.D.

Traditionally medicine has been regarded as the combination of an art and a science! In the past century, the science of medicine has made monumental progress from which mankind has benefitted greatly in terms of life expectancy. In this period, the science of medicine has developed highly effective vaccines, principles of sanitation and insect vector control, antibiotics, electrolyte and hormonal balance techniques, cardiac pacemakers, and coronary care units. There can be little or no controversy relative to these medical advances. In other areas, such as organ transplantation, cancer therapy, therapy in psychiatry, and "social" medicine, considerable controversy exists. Some of the issues and practices involved are intimately linked to the specifically moral and personal side of life.

Organized medicine has always jealously guarded her proper domain but has never hesitated to enter the sphere of another discipline. A recent happening will serve to illustrate this point. A resolution proposed to a local medical society in New Jersey wished to regard marijuana usage as a medical problem only and urged repeal of all laws pertaining to users of this drug. A letter opposing this proposal was written by the chairman of a local CUF chapter and sent to the medical society. The letter was indignantly considered, by the president of the medical society, to be an arrogant interference with the private deliberations of the medical society. The letter had noted that even though there were indeed medical aspects of drug abuse, still the motivations of the person contemplating or beginning the use of marijuana involved morality and were, therefore, a matter of grave concern to the members of Catholics United for the Faith. The president of the medical society contemptuously brushed aside the issue of the moral principles involved in the abuse of a mind-altering drug as having no relevancy to the problem. This same type of medical chauvinism is also evident in the matter of abortion and sex education.

On the issue of abortion, medicine has changed its position from one that prohibited interference with pregnancy, except in cases where continuation of pregnancy was a definite threat to the mother's life, to one in which it is now a matter between the mother and her physician wherever abortion is not illegal. This is a radical shift in medical ethics. It contravenes, moreover, the basic medical principle not to destroy human life. Furthermore, it should be clear that abortion is a negative interference with the Natural and Moral Law. When practiced by organized medicine, it represents the invasion and preemption of another domain or discipline. All arguments for the new and erroneous position taken by medicine on abortion are only mere rationalizations! They have nothing to do with strictly medical questions and everything to do with moral and personal questions.

On the issue of sex education in the schools, organized medicine has in one place stated that it is "the primary responsibility of the parents." It has then proceeded to ignore the parents in favor of mandated school programs because "the traditional sources of sex information and guidance for young people are often inadequate." Instead of trying to re-inforce and strengthen the parent's authority and responsibility in this matter, they have encouraged and promoted usurpation of this parental function by public educators. In the forefront of those responsible for this attitude are many psychiatrists and public-health doctors.

These psychiatrists, in the grip of a mental aberration of their own, are among the prime instigators of public sex education. Perhaps they are aware, whether subconsciously or consciously, of their many failures in the treatment of the mentally ill and they need a scapegoat or whipping-boy to explain away these failures. To justify public sex education they theorize that mental illness and abnormal behavior are frequently due to an "unwholesome attitude and a lack of understanding of sex." It never occurs to them that the cause of the trouble is not a matter of information but of formation. They blame moral attitudes on sex for the trouble when precisely the opposite is the cause, namely the lack of morality. Who can doubt that a predominantly moral position on sex will result, for example, in less promiscuity, illegitimacy and venereal disease?

This peculiar aversion for morality in sex appears to be almost an obsession with some psychiatrists. Probably it is because they really do not understand human love and sexuality. They obviously have never read the classical analysis of human love **In Defense Of Purity** by Dr Dietrich von Hildebrand. The general lack of familiarity by psychiatrists with this monumental work may be due to the fact that von Hildebrand is a philosopher and obviously not one of their "scientific" breed. Morality in sex has the same significance as **not starting to use drugs** has relative to drug abuse. A very eminent pharmacologist suggests just this resolve never to start as the best way to control that problem.

The position of many psychiatrists that high moral standards in sexual matters are frequently the basis of abnormal human behavior, is patently false and should be repudiated. Fortunately there are some psychiatrists who do not hold this position, but their voices are muffled by the loud declamations of the protagonists.

Most astonishing and alarming is the position of some public health doctors on this subject of morality in sex. Aside from Dr. Mary Calderone's now infamous "I don't believe in the thou shalt nots anymore," there is the unbelievable statement of Dr. Andrew Rudolph of the U.S. Public Health Center for Disease Control: "If we could get people to stop thinking of venereal disease as a moral issue, half the battle would be won" (**Health News** — "The Silent Epidemic" by E. Lochaya — January, 1971, p. 6). The battle referred to is the effort to control venereal disease which everyone agrees is now of epidemic proportions. The astonishing thing about this statement is its obvious self-contradiction. If moral restraints are removed from sexual activity, we can expect a sharp increase in contacts between infected and non-infected people and thus a sharp rise in the incidence of venereal diseases. This is borne out by the caption alongside a graph in the same article in which the above statement appeared. The graph shows a sharp rise in cases of gonorrhea in the United States from 300,000 to 550,000 cases from 1966 to 1970. The caption states, "The significant rise in gonorrhea may reflect greater promiscuity in our society, use of the pill, and perhaps greater reporting." It is obvious that one of the factors, "greater promiscuity," is the result of either an immoral or amoral attitude toward sexual intercourse. In my opinion, this position of Dr. Rudolph is dangerously erroneous and raises the question of his competence in his chosen field.

And What About Situation Ethics?

We hear so much about population explosion in these days — if there is really such a thing as population explosion. Some reliable authorities doubt it. The proponents of situation ethics now teach that the explosion has to be checked. They too teach that any workable means may be used to check it. The pill does it. Consequently the use of the pill is permissible. But this clearly, is against God's original will and design. He created man, male and female and endowed them with distinct sexual qualities, most evidently to be used in the proper way, in the proper place and for the proper purpose. The proper place or institution as God ordained it is lawful wedlock guaranteeing the care and welfare of the offspring on the part of the responsible parents. Situation ethics would go even further: to control the population explosion even abortion and mercykilling is permissible.

But God says clearly and distinctly: "Thou shalt not kill! "This is an outside norm, eternally established by the Supreme Lawgiver and therefore it must be respected and obeyed. After all God is absolutely and unerringly right. He is the only supreme lawgiver and our conscience must always conform to His laws. Apart from the rhythm method there is only one means of population control, and that is abstinence. But here is the crux. This becomes a matter of self-control, sacrifice and religion. Deeply religious people who really love God above all things will make a sincere effort to comply with God's ruling to the best of their ability, hard as it may be. They may not always succeed in every respect, but they will try time and again. But since the concept of genuine and sincere religion has generally vanished, the spirit of self-control and sacrifice becomes pretty near impossible. The laws of God become a joke! Situation ethics have been made the supreme law and norm of all judgments in order to suit weak human nature.

Left, from *The Wanderer*, September 10, 1970.

On the television here in Philadelphia, there is a commentator who is as filthy as he can be. In discussing sex education, he said he is all for it, that he has no laws, that he has no standards; that he can be with any woman any time who is willing to be with him. He openly says so on the radio, openly talks about it. Ten years ago a fellow like that would have been — well, I don't know what they would have done with him! This whole realm of action which includes sex education is one of the areas where the Communists are really getting through. The humanists, the materialists, those who have no use for God have no understanding of the moral restraints that God has put in this area, and they do not understand that this evil heart of theirs, out of which come these various things, as Jesus said, is the trouble with them and is the trouble with the world itself. Their heart has to be dealt with.

Above, by Carl McIntire; distributed by 20th Century Reformation Hour, Collingswood, N.J.

THE TRUE MORALITY

It becomes more evident every day that the new morality and the sexual revolution, far from being the selfish pursuit of pleasure, will prove to be of immense benefit to society. The old morality, in which sexual intercourse was permitted only in marriage for the sake of raising a family, served a purpose in an expanding industrial civilization. But now we've reached a danger point. If we are to avoid famines, plagues and wars, the population of the earth must stop growing. If future generations are to enjoy the highest possible quality of life, the population must decline.

The principal function of sexuality must now be to provide intensely pleasurable interpersonal communication. This kind of pleasure should be available to everyone. On the other hand, there is no reason everyone should enter into family raising, any more than everyone should study law. A few people are well suited by temperament and talent to the raising of children, and they should be the ones to do it. They would produce enough children to keep the race going. The rest of us should be having sex merely for fun, while making our contributions to society through our work.

So let's see more respect from pulpit and press for our increasing numbers of single swingers. In an age of excessive population growth, they are among the truly moral people.

J. Kelly
New York, New York

Above, letter to "The Playboy Forum," *Playboy Magazine*, November 1970.

Sex: The Radical View of A Catholic Theologian

By Michael F. Valente
Bruce. 158p $2.95 paper

Human sexuality is not exclusively a biological phenomenon but a profoundly personal mode of communication with another person. Its morality is not articulated in a set of *a priori* rules implicit in a static view of nature but discovered in the responsible concrete existential encounter with another person. Responsible sexuality is never isolated from another person, it is always influenced and transformed by a culture, always respects the plasticity of sexual human nature.

Despite its angry rhetoric—there are "revisionists," "orthoxians," "Thomas offers no less than 17 articles on lechery and its parts"—despite some unsophisticated "psyching" done on Augustine and others, this book has value. Valente categorically takes issue with traditional sexual morality and exposes many of its absurdities in the attempts by moralists to codify sexual behavior. My only consistent and gnawing misgiving about the book is that while strongly in opposition to a legalism in sexual ethics, Valente does not recognize the situationalism in his own thinking and does not develop a responsible methodology in the place of what he renounces. To deny intrinsically evil acts in the sexual order is already to make more than a gracious curtsy to situationalism thinking. Valente is just not radical enough.   THOMAS A. WASSMER

Don Mitchell

LETTER FROM A COLD PLACE

Heavy snow and cheerless rhetoric in the mountains of Colorado

PASSING A JOINT among delegates to the White House Conference on Youth, I saw a clean-cut kid crumple a Xeroxed proposal in his hands and ask, "Why don't they *eat* this horseshit?" Uncrumpling the sheet of paper, I read the following resolution offered by Archbishop Philip Hannan of New Orleans:

The Task Force on Values, Ethics and Culture asserts that the development of the individual is derived largely from the family which is the primary unit of society. The individual and the family draw their strength from the mutual love of father, mother and child (or children). The recognition of the family as the primary unit of society is vitally important to healthy social living. Legal approbation of sexual relationships contrary to the present legal and moral position of the family are harmful to the welfare of the family and society.

This resolution was defeated, overwhelmingly, in favor of one which read in part:

Every person has the right to fully express his or her individual sexuality. Furthermore, any sexual behavior between consenting, responsible individuals must be recognized and tolerated by society as an acceptable life-style.

DESTRUCTIVE SEX

I would like to set straight those persons who write to PLAYBOY extolling the virtues of premarital sex: It is *wrong*. First, failure to control one's sexual appetites until marriage is a sign of weakness; it can be likened to the junkie's giving in to his craving for a fix. Second, without the lasting commitment of marriage, genuine love is impossible, and without love, sex is harmful and destructive. In short, the only type of sexual relationship that is not ruinous to one's own character and exploitative of one's partner is one that takes place in the context God established when He sanctioned marriage in order to purify sex.

Jeffrey Arvin Nissen
Yuba City, California

To His Coy Mistress

Had we but world enough, and time,
This coyness lady were no crime.
We would sit down, and think which way
To walk, and pass our long love's day.
Thou by the Indian Ganges' side
Should'st rubies find: I by the tide
Of Humber would complain. I would
Love you ten years before the Flood:
And you should if you please refuse
Till the conversion of the Jews.
My vegetable love should grow
Vaster than empires, and more slow.
An hundred years should go to praise
Thine eyes, and on thy forehead gaze.
Two hundred to adore each breast:
But thirty thousand to the rest.
An age at least to every part,
And the last age should show your heart.
For lady you deserve this state;
Nor would I love at lower rate.

  But at my back I always hear
Time's winged chariot hurrying near.
And yonder all before us lie
Deserts of vast eternity.
Thy beauty shall no more be found;
Nor, in thy marble vault, shall sound
My echoing song: then worms shall try
That long preserv'd virginity:
And your quaint honor turn to dust;
And into ashes all my lust.
The grave's a fine and private place,
But none I think do there embrace.

  Now therefore, while the youthful hue
Sits on thy skin like morning lew,
And while thy willing soul transpires
At every pore with instant fires,
Now let us sport us while we may;
And now, like am'rous birds of prey,
Rather at once our time devour,
Than languish in his slow-chapt pow'r.
Let us roll all our strength, and all
Our sweetness, up into one ball:
And tear our pleasures with rough strife,
Thorough the iron gates of life.
Thus, though we cannot make our sun
Stand still, yet we will make him run.

    Above, a poem by Andrew Marvell (1621-1678).
    Right, from "A Religious Pacifist Looks at Abortion" by Gordon C. Zahn. In *Commonweal*, May 28, 1971.

    Top right, from *The Manchester Guardian Weekly*.

Why Should Men Pay Alimony?

IN THE LIGHT of the recent discussion on divorce reform, I find it nothing less than amazing that men do not rise up in fury and see to it that the divorce laws (whereby a man is impelled to support a woman after divorce whether or not she is quite able to maintain herself) are radically changed to give them fair and equal treatment with the women.

Why should a man be expected to keep in idleness an able-bodied woman for the rest of her life, because he kept her for x years while married to her? Single women work, millions of married women work, but as soon as a woman is divorced she expects to be a pampered parasite.

The time has come for men to free themselves from this iniquitous bondage. This has been done in the three American states of Colorado, Texas, and Pennsylvania, and it is time these feminine gold diggers were made to support themselves like any normal, self-respecting person.

Unless this wrong is put right, and men become more aware of the present unjust divorce laws, the very institution of marriage will be undermined.

—*P. Lewis,*
The Manchester Guardian Weekly.

Even if one were to accept the characterization of a woman's body as "property" (is it not one of the liberationists' complaints that men and man-made laws have reduced her to that status?), the claim to absolute rights of use and disposal of that property could not be taken seriously. The owner of a badly needed residential building is not, or at least *should not be*, free to evict his tenants to suit a selfish whim or to convert his property to some frivolous or non-essential use. In such a case we would insist upon the traditional distinction which describes property as private in ownership but social in use.

To use another example, the moral evil associated with prostitution does not lie solely, perhaps not even primarily, in the illicit sex relationship but, rather, in the degradation of a person to precisely this status of a "property" available for "use" on a rental or purchase basis. It is a tragic irony that the advocates of true and full personhood for women have chosen to provide ideological justification for attitudes which have interfered with recognition of that personhood in the past.

This is not to say, of course, that a woman does not have prior rights over her own body but only that the exercise of those rights must take into account the rights of others. In monogamous marriage this would preclude a wife's "freedom" to commit adultery (a principle, it should be unnecessary to add, which applies to the husband as well).

Birth Control Subverts Morality

By THOMAS A. LANE

CBS Radio was reporting the Irish conflict over birth control. The message alleged that Catholics as well as Protestants were practicing artificial contraception in Northern Ireland and that the legal ban on contraceptives in Eire, adamantly supported by the Catholic Church, was a serious obstacle to reunion. If the Church would stop trying to dictate morality. . . .

The program recalled to mind the 1930 Lambeth Conference at which the Anglican Church abandoned its moral opposition to birth control and embraced the use of contraceptives for family planning. People of sensitive conscience then decided that the breach of the natural law would serve higher ends of conjugal harmony and population control.

We can now regard that decision with forty years of hindsight. A person may in good faith select a new course of action; but he should then be sensitive to the consequences of his decision. Has the Anglican Church realized its hopes of greater conjugal harmony and improved family life within the Church?

Any objective observer of Western Civilization must note the sharp deterioration of individual and family morality since 1930. As the religious rhetoric of peace and charity intensifies, the practice of both decays. Within the family, the true state of affairs is measured in the high divorce rate and the religiously disoriented children. Sexual promiscuity, illegitimacy, abortion and the drug culture illustrate the rejection of Christian moral influence.

There are other subversive influences shaping our society. However, I believe that a serious study of these decades would identify the Christian acceptance of birth control as the breach in the citadel of Christian family life. The Lambeth Conference merely accepted what had been a growing practice in the community; but that church sanction, approving what had theretofore been regarded as sinful, legalized the destruction of the Christian family.

It was a mistake to suppose that contraceptives could be used within the marriage contract without promoting their general use. If marriage was merely an arrangement for sexual gratification, men would try to devise better arrangements for that purpose. If parents could frustrate intercourse to prevent conception, why shouldn't their children do so?

In professing to set a new standard for married love, the Anglican Church set a new standard for all love. It invited the sex-is-fun syndrome of recent decades which hides from youth the truth that illicit sex is tragedy.

Illicit sex is tragedy for married people, too. When persons accept faithfully the duties of the married state, they harvest the rewards of nature fulfilled. When they cheat on nature, they build a burden of guilt. The first lie begets others. The sanctity of the marriage bond is undermined.

And when a church professing to teach the will of God to men sanctions what all men and women know to be wrong, it forsakes its true mission. It becomes merely another human judge of expediency, severed from eternity.

I suggest to the Protestants of Northern Ireland that they should reexamine their beliefs about birth control. They can see in the travail of our society the future of their own, unless they turn back. They **should** return to the pre-Lambeth morality of their church. They should look upon reunion with Eire as an accession of strength in which Protestants and Catholics will work together to preserve the Christian family.

In the world context, these considerations challenge our Anglican brethren to condemn the error of artificial birth control and to restore universal Christian adherence to the natural law. Honesty requires the action. The survival of Western Civilization urges it. This should be a first step of ecumenical reconciliation.

from *The Wanderer*, June 17, 1971.

THE ETHICS OF ADULTERY

In *The Playboy Forum*, a lady from Wichita, Kansas, inquired about PLAYBOY's readers' opinions on mate swapping and asked, "When both partners consent, is adultery immoral?" In the old days, people turned to religious authorities to find out what was moral or immoral. More recently, they have been asking psychiatrists and political theorists. Now, in true democratic fashion, the Wichita housewife wants to poll PLAYBOY's readers. This lady and her husband are already indulging in spouse swapping and are apparently enjoying it, but if the *Forum* published many letters telling her the practice is evil, I wonder, would she stop it?

In my opinion, to ask whether or not a given act, such as mate swapping, is moral is to pose a meaningless question. There are those who still believe that some supernatural monarch has decreed a code of rules by which we must live, but they are on ground only slightly less unsound than those who still reject evolution. Nor can any modern-minded atheist or agnostic prove, philosophically or scientifically, that any set of secular rules or obligations is superior to the individual's own desires. Modern ideologues may tell us we have a duty to humanity, society, reason or revolution till they are blue—or red—in the face, but they are human, like everyone else, and why should one man's code bind another?

People such as your mate-swapping correspondent feel that their personal decisions must be guided by some higher rationale. They need reassurance that there is something more important backing their decisions than their own feelings. But individual feelings are the most important thing there is. Religions, philosophies and ideologies are, in a sense, illusions: They have only such size and power as we assign them.

We must recognize that ethical codes are but convenient (and, too often, inconvenient) fictions. By doing so, we can then make decisions on reasonable, realistic bases, while also giving proper dignity to our genuine feelings. We can end the idolization of abstract principles for which too many people are willing to murder others and be killed themselves ("Better dead than Red" —that sort of thing). To realize that each man is a law unto himself is to arrive at an irreducible basis for libertarian thought—the most valuable and needed viewpoint in avoiding the pitfalls of right- or left-wing totalitarianism.

Therefore, I suggest to the lady from Wichita one rule that eliminates the need for all others: "Think for yourself."

> Dion O'Glass
> New York, New York

Top page, letter to the editor of Playboy Magazine; copyright © 1970, 1971 by Playboy.

Light from the Eternal City

Pope Paul VI . . .

Lust Of The Flesh Leads Man Away From God

Everyone knows what is meant by "flesh" in moral language. It refers to everything connected with undisciplined sensuality; that is, that dangerous interplay of physical sensibility in conflict or in complicity with spiritual sensibility, animal pleasure, voluptuousness, the body in the grip of passion that draws the soul to itself and lowers it to its own instincts, captures it and blinds it, so that, as St. Paul says, "the unspiritual man does not receive the gifts of the Spirit of God" (1 Cor. 2, 14). We do not think there is any need of explanations in this connection. It is so much discussed today, too much, perhaps. It is a rare thing today for the novelist not to pay his sorry tribute, with a few pages at least, to some folly of the senses, or to some Dionysiac rapture, with which the world of literary culture is pervaded, as is that of pleasure-loving dissoluteness, pursued by anguish. Psychoanalytical studies on human instincts, and particularly on neuropathology and sexuality, have given a scientific language to the common empirical experience of erotic passions. They have even been exalted as real new discoveries of man.

SHUN TEMPTATION

And the recommendation follows by itself: we say it to the Father in the usual prayer: "lead us not into temptation"! Let us apply it to ourselves, as if to grant this supreme prayer. We must defend ourselves from the tyrannical temptation of the flesh, if we wish to live the paschal mystery. Inwardly and outwardly; in our hearts, above all, from which come the good and the evil of which we are capable (cfr. Mt. 15, 19; 2 Tim. 2, 22); and in our surroundings. Today men are concerned with ecology, that is purification of the physical environment in which man's life takes place. Why should we not be concerned, too, with a moral ecology in which man lives as a man and as a son of God? This is what we recommend to you, with our Apostolic Blessing.

Above, from The Wanderer, April 15, 1971.

My Answer
Billy Graham

Isn't the real point of living to be free? And isn't Christianity, with its confining moral codes the antithesis of freedom? W.V.

All the talk of freedom by the radicals has no basis in history, in philosophy or in Christianity. True, Christ said, "If the Son therefore shall make you free, ye shall be free indeed." John 8:36. He did not mean that we would be free from God's laws, free from truth and free from service. He did not teach that we are free to sin— but that we can be free not to sin. He also said, "He that is the greatest among you shall be the servant of you all." A physician is not free. He is the servant of the afflicted. A minister is not free. He is the servant of the spiritually oppressed. A teacher is not free. He is a servant of the uneducated. A housewife is not free. She is the servant of her family. A father is not free. He is the servant of his wife and children.

The only free person, in the sense which radicals define freedom is the vagabond, the ne'er do well and some hippies who have an aversion to work. Yet, the above mentioned are less free than most, because they lack a purpose for living. The freest people I know are the people who are free from the bondage and penalty of sin and who render the greatest service to God and mankind. They are free to live beyond the perimeter of self- free to have compassion upon the hungry, the poorly sheltered and the needy. They have broken their prison of selfishness and live in a world of freedom to serve their fellow men. That is the kind of freedom Christ came to bring.

Reprinted by permission of the Chicago Tribune—New York News Syndicate, Inc. Left, reprinted by permission of the Chicago Tribune—New York News Syndicate, Inc.

DEAR ABBY
BY
ABIGAIL VAN BUREN

A friend of mine recently died and left a pretty young widow. The brother of the man who died is married, and he told me himself that he has been doing "double duty" and acting the part of a husband to this widow, if you know what I mean. He says the Bible says it is all right. I can't find anything in my Bible that gives approval to such scandalous goings on. If you can, I wish you would tell me where it is. Thank you.

A FRIEND

DEAR FRIEND: Your friend went back to the Old Testament. In Deuteronomy 25:5. "If a brethren dwell together, and one of them shall die, and have no child, the wife of the dead shall not marry a stranger: her husband's brother shall go unto her and perform the duty of a husband. And the firstborn which she shall beareth shall succeed in the name of his brother which is dead that his name shall not be put out of Israel."

Your friend is using this passage to suit his own purpose. The Deuteronomic Law no longer applies. But the Seventh Commandment does.

DEAR ABBY: It is so difficult to know what is morally right and what is morally wrong these days. What used to be considered wrong 25 years ago is suddenly "right." How is a person supposed to know how to behave?

BIG DILEMMA

DEAR BIG : Let your conscience be your guide. For some strange reason, we now have about 20 million laws trying to enforce the Ten Commandments.

MINISKIRTS

A sermon by
Carl McIntire

It is very significant, I think, that, attending the coming of the miniskirt, those who participated in it, those who promoted it throughout the world, there have appeared most of the other things that have helped degrade and pull down our society.

There is such a thing as modesty. There is such a thing as decency. The person who has become a Christian has a different attitude toward the human body from that of the ungodly person. The person who has become a Christian recognizes that there are certain things in the human body that are not merely degrading, but that lead to all manner of tragedy and disaster and sin.

In our Confession of Faith we are instructed:

"Q. 139. What are the sins forbidden in the seventh commandment?

"A. The sins forbidden in the seventh commandment, besides the neglect of the duties required, are adultery, fornication, rape, incest, sodomy, and all unnatural lusts; all unclean imaginations, thoughts, purposes, and affections; all corrupt or filthy communications, or listening thereunto; wanton looks; impudent or light behaviour; immodest apparel; . . . lascivious songs, books, pictures, dancings, stage plays; and all other provocations to, or acts of uncleanness either in ourselves or others." That is part of the doctrinal standards of our church. See how far away we have gotten from these standards!

Why Speak About Modesty?

Why do we speak of the matter of being immodest? Why do we speak of the matter of women conducting themselves in a decent manner? The answer, so far as the Bible is concerned, is because of the heart of man. We are going to turn now to several passages in the Bible.

First, 1 Peter 1:13-15: ". . . gird up the loins of your mind, be sober, and hope to the end for the grace that is to be brought unto you at the revelation of Jesus Christ; as obedient children, not fashioning yourselves according to the former lusts in your ignorance: but as he which hath called you is holy, so be ye holy in all manner of conversation."

Now look at 1 Peter 4:3 and 4: "For the time past of our life may suffice us to have wrought the will of the Gentiles, when we walked in lasciviousness, lusts, excess of wine, revellings, banquetings, and abominable idolatries: wherein they think it strange that ye run not with them to the same excess of riot, speaking evil of you."

I think the problem with the miniskirt is that our young people are not able to resist the pressures of conformity in the world today. They are not able to resist the pressures that they find about them in their schools and the world about them. They cannot resist these pressures, and consequently they want to put on these very short dresses. They are getting them shorter and shorter.

Some time ago, when I was talking with a man who was interested in coming to Shelton College who was then teaching in a secular school, he said to me, "Dr. McIntire I just cannot take it any more." I said, "What is the trouble?" He said: "I am a decent man, I have a lovely wife and a fine family. But I go to classes where I teach and the kids come in dressed in miniskirts. It is disgraceful. There are girls who sit in the front row, and when they sit down there is not anything covered. And that is not all. These girls will not only sit in their chairs with the boys

around them, but they will throw their legs apart. It is a total disgrace, and I cannot take it. I have got to get out."

Another man I know, a teacher, talked with me some time ago. He has been teaching in a secular institution. He said: "Dr. McIntire, since this miniskirt business has come in, the familiarity and the fondling which take place in the corridors and in the schools you cannot possibly believe. These girls with short skirts are just an invitation to the hands of the boys." He continued: "Not only that, a lovely young girl who came from a Christian background, Presbyterian, one day came to me and said, 'I think maybe you have some good ideas. I would like to talk to you.' I said, 'All right, I will talk to you.' And this was her story — she put on a miniskirt and then became involved in all sorts of things so far as the boys were concerned. Then she listened to all the civil rights talk about equality and she got the idea that, in order to show that she did not believe in any form of discrimination, and that there was absolute equality between the races, she, with other girls, finally made it a practice to go to bed with one of the Negro students — and this was a regular practice which she and other girls carried on."

It was a miniskirt that brought about this! The damage and the harm that is now being done to young Christian girls who adopt this form of dress is absolutely incalculable. This is practiced on campuses where hippies and yippies stir up riots; that is exactly what you have.

How Long?

Young ladies, your dresses ought to be long enough so that the contours of your body and the areas of your body that involve lust and the stimulation of sex will not in any way contribute to such emotions. I say that to you frankly; I say it to you on the authority of the Word of God. It is a terrible disgrace when a woman who is married to one man goes out and entices other men. And it is a terrible disgrace when a young girl in the high school goes to dances, get worked up, goes out with the boys and loses her purity, and her whole set of moral standards are pulled down. Young lady, do not think this is not involving you! It does involve you. It involves everything about you. And, beloved, I do not want it in this church. You young people ought to face the conscience of this church. You ought to be concerned about it. Someone asked me this morning, after I announced I was going to preach this sermon, "What are you going to say about the miniskirt?" I replied, "I am going to say they ought to be lengthened." And they ought to be let down far enough so that there is no possibility of any problems arising. As a matter of fact, every decent woman ought to recoil when some other woman displays herself. And furthermore, any decent man really does not have any respect for the kind of woman who thus displays herself. Am I right? Of course, I am. But what do the ungodly call such principles? Oh, they call it puritanism.

By Carl McIntire; distributed by 20th Century Reformation Hour, Collingswood, N.J.

Pornography–
Sex and / or Violence

A topic of concern in many of the arguments in this section is that of the *definition* of "pornography." This does not, however, reflect a merely semantic or academic interest. Pornography is both a legal and moral issue in our society; traffickers in it are liable to legal prosecution and moral condemnation. It would be unfair to bring a man to trial, punish him, and/or morally condemn him for selling pornographic materials if the concept of pornography were so vague and ambiguous that people could not agree as to what particular things are, in fact, pornographic. Thus the concern with defining "pornography" reflects a legislative, judicial, or moral concern with fairness.

Pornography is most frequently thought of as being associated with various manifestations of sex. As with many moral issues, such as those discussed in the previous section, there are extreme views on the relation between sex and pornography. Some people define "pornography' 'in terms of *any* written, spoken, or pictorial description (including textbooks) of the sex organs or sexual acts; others argue that only certain descriptions in certain contexts should be called "pornographic." Still others claim that no description of anything involving the human body (including the sexual aspects) should be defined as "pornographic."

In part, at least, this disagreement goes much deeper than the apparent dispute over the meaning of a word, for many people might agree as to the meaning of "pornography" yet still strongly disagree about what particular things are pornographic. Thus a number of individuals could agree that "pornographic" *means* "contributing to the moral corruption of anyone exposed to that item," while at the same time disagreeing about whether a particular item in fact contributes to the moral corruption of anyone. (It should be noted that, in this case, something is not morally bad because it is pornographic, but it is pornographic because it is morally bad.)

If one is able to find a generally acceptable definition of "pornography" which is neither vague nor ambiguous, and which does not involve any moral judgments in it, disputes can still arise over nonmoral facts, such as "Does pornography harm anyone?" "Are readers of pornography more likely to commit sex crimes?" and so on. Questions can also be raised concerning the restriction of this concept to matters related to sex. Even if we agree on a definition which restricts the applicability of "pornographic" to sexual material, and if we judge that pornographic material is bad if it causes harm to people or leads to an increase in crime, then (if we are to remain consistent) we must also judge other items with similar effects to be similarly bad. For example, if it is a fact that viewers of violent films are more likely to commit violent acts, then violent films should be judged to be just as bad as pornographic ones, even though one's definition of "pornography" does not include the concept of violence. Additional scientific questions are relevant here also (e.g., does viewing violence in films *cause* people to commit violent acts?), and the reader should be aware that these are as difficult and complex as they are relevant.

Top, © 1971 *The Wanderer*.

Below, from *The National Observer*, April 12, 1971.

The Expanding Arts

If Dirty Art Is Censored, Who Will Do the Censoring?

By Clifford A. Ridley

The gloom-and-doom boys in the artistic spectrum have been warning artists for some time that if they don't use their new freedoms responsibly, they're asking for trouble. The trouble, it appears, is nigh upon us. Many state legislators and other officials, restive in the face of the new morality to begin with, are turning downright surly. And now comes Prof. Irving Kristol, whose liberal *bona fides* are well in order, with a long argument for nothing less than state censorship.

Writing in the New York Times Magazine, Mr. Kristol passes quickly over what many people, including me, consider the real contemporary pornography; the pornography of violence. His concern is chiefly with the pornography of sex, particularly with its power to corrupt and debase. Few would dispute that it has such power—few would dispute that whisky can make you drunk, either—but

Comment

the question is how much and for how many. In the absence of empirical evidence, Mr. Kristol undertakes to prove corruption by logic.

He takes issue, first, with the frequent assertion that nobody was ever corrupted by a book. Well, I think that's a little extreme—a few people *are* corrupted by books—but I don't think Mr. Kristol does his cause any good by suggesting that if no one was ever corrupted by a book, no one was ever improved by one either. Literary self-improvement, after all, is a function of the mind, while literary sexual corruption affects a quite different portion of the anatomy.

Permissible Deaths

It is the corruption of essentially private behavior that particularly bothers Mr. Kristol; as example, he notes that we do not film or televise the gradual extinguishing of humanity—i.e. an actual lingering death. He does not note, however, that we do film and televise the *abrupt* taking of life in our everyday war and crime reportage—with effects that are doubtless both bad and salutary—and we do simulate death of all kinds on stage and screen. If these deaths are permissible but an actual lingering one is not, who is to decide how efficient an actual death must be, how untruthful a simulated one, before it is fit to be shown to us?

It's a moot question, of course. We will never invade the privacy of a slowly dying man simply because no sane person wants to watch such a thing. And although there are a number of reasons why not—fear of mortality, and so on—the prime one is simply that we have an innate delicacy about such occurrences. I honestly believe that most people do respect purely private matters, that they will not willingly debase themselves.

But, you may argue, what about the viewing of stag films and the like? "When sex is public," Mr. Kristol says, "the viewer does not see—cannot see—the sentiments and the ideals. He can only see the animal coupling." And so he can, but isn't that precisely the point?

In other words, the argument goes like this: "The act of love, when made public, is debased because it's not the act of love." But if it's not the act of love, then the act of love is not being debased. The moment two people agree to copulate before a camera, love is no longer part of the action, and nobody should think it is.

Don't misunderstand; I see little point in habitual attendance at stag films; I am arguing only that they really don't debase anybody. Can one, then, condemn pornography on other grounds? Mr. Kristol does. He notes the oft-heard assertion that people eventually grow bored with pornography and insists that they don't, that it in effect becomes a way of life. "Put bluntly," he says, "it is a masturbatory exercise of the imagination. . . . Now, people who masturbate do not get bored with masturbation, just as sadists don't get bored with sadism and voyeurs don't get bored with voyeurism."

Unfair Equation

That is an extraordinary statement. It is unfair, to begin with, to equate sadism and voyeurism, which are illnesses, with masturbation, which is a normal form of sexual release. Beyond that, the suggestion is simply not true; most people grow bored with masturbation as soon as an alternative becomes available to them—just as most viewers of blue movies soon conclude that they prefer the participatory form of this particular drama. (This is as good a time as any to note that

here, as elsewhere, I am talking about adults; children are another matter.)

But Mr. Kristol insists on his view of pornography as autoerotic infantilism; it is the cornerstone of why he thinks it does no less than endanger civilization as we know it. "Those who are for pornography and obscenity, on radical grounds," he says, "take it very seriously indeed," and he suggests that once campus radicals have been appeased on the issue of public four-letter words, they have "won the day." Thus missing the point entirely, for the reason the campus radicals set such store by public obscenity is precisely because they know many *other* people take it seriously and are bugged by it.

Perhaps, on grounds of prevailing community standards and with great attention to what community you're talking about, public obscenity may be forbidden, but in aim it is no more than a harassing device, a diversionary tactic, a razzberry, a put-on. It's not designed to accomplish anything; it's designed to annoy people, as are verbal assaults on patriotism and the church. To be sure, the kids don't like their elders' uptight view of verbal communication, but they don't expect to change it by a few posters.

Proceeding on the dubious grounds that pornography corrupts, Mr. Kristol goes on to argue for censorship within the pre-Twentieth Century view of democracy—which, he says, addressed itself to the quality of its citizens' collective lives as well as to the mechanics of the means by which they lived together. Implicit in this argument is the notion that free people will inevitably corrupt themselves; and since I neither buy that gloomy prognosis nor agree with Mr. Kristol's view of corruption, I won't rise to the bait.

I think it worth mentioning, however, that the arts available for censorship today and those similarly available 70-plus years ago are quite different things. In the old days, the censor scanning his day's work knew pretty much what to expect. There were few surprises; changes in attitude and technique arrived with assimilable slowness. Today, however, in an age when one often must meet with a book or movie two or three times simply to determine what the creator is up to, plucking the weeds of salaciousness from the garden of metaphor can be a backbreaking task.

What About 'Blow-Up'?

Putting it another way, not long ago censoring sex meant censoring sex—period. Today, however, censoring sex can mean censoring the whole point of a piece of art, for the sex often exists in some kind of interrelation with something larger than itself. Would Mr. Kristol shunt *Blow-Up* to the back room because of its celebrated nude romp in the photographer's studio, a first-rate stand-in for the aimlessness of the fellow's existence?

I use "back room" advisedly, for Mr. Kristol apparently would not ban things;

he would "restrict" them to "serious" viewers or readers. As an example, he cites the British "club" system of presenting allegedly erotic plays—although the British have discarded it as unworkable. He acknowledges that his proposal would create an elitist pornography; and although he finds this irrelevant, I do not.

In one sense, pornography is elitist already; studies indicate that our most strait-laced citizens are in the lower socio-economic brackets. The danger is that in institutionalizing this elitism, the permissible stuff will not be that which might serve some artistic purpose by talking to people's experience—the commonly bawdy, or the eroticism peculiar to a particular subculture—but the "sophisticated" pornography of the elite. You have only to recall that Jack Valenti thought *Myra Breckinridge* a fun spoof to determine what kind of shaky standards might obtain if we left censorship to our leaders.

Mr. Kristol thinks the dangers of censorship are minimal. He notes that we have been visited by few suppressed old masterpieces since the gates were opened, and so we have. But—noting only in passing that the suppression of even one masterpiece is a crime—what does that prove? We also have been visited by few masterpieces on potato farming, or in which the hero is lefthanded. Masterpieces are few by nature, and no subject or technique is going to produce very many of them.

Theater Isn't Dirty

As for the present, Mr. Kristol grouses that "the cultural market in the United States today is being pre-empted by dirty books, dirty movies, dirty theater." In theater, at least, that's simply not true; and if it *is* true in books and movies, which is debatable, it's true only if one assigns the broadest kind of interpretation to the word "dirty." Which gets me at long last to the inevitable nub of this censorship business: What are you going to throw out, and who's doing the throwing?

It would appear, for instance, that the prevailing literary mood thus far in 1971 is black sexual farce—witness *The Bushwhacked Piano*, *Lion Country*, and *Wake Up, We're Almost There*, all treated in these pages (the last of them this week), with at least a couple more around the bend. Each of these books has been reviewed here in terms ranging from approving to ecstatic. Are these the books Mr. Kristol has in mind to censor?

Or does he have Harold Robbins in mind? Few people would argue that Harold Robbins is good—but then that's not why people read him. I know a nice lady who has read practically the entire *oeuvre* of Harold Robbins because she says he takes her mind off being scared in airplanes, and to my knowledge she hasn't gone out and assaulted anybody yet. Since I think it implicit in Mr. Kristol's argument that censorship is a perfectly simple matter because he knows precisely what ought to be censored, I think I ought to warn him: He's going to have to deal with my mother.

151

A Disservice to Our Democracy

By WILLIAM RANDOLPH HEARST JR.

Editor-in-Chief, The Hearst Newspapers

* * *

Before getting further into this terribly complex subject—a matter which should command the attention of every American concerned with the quality of our national existence—it is necessary to come to grips with the fundamental question of censorship.

In my role as an editor and publisher of newspapers, naturally, I find the mere idea of any form of government censorship to be repugnant. Such control, furthermore and in a general way, is forbidden by the constitutional guarantee of a free press.

So how can an American publisher possibly deny the right of any other to print and sell whatever may be profitable? I'll tell you how and why.

I don't believe for one instant that the authors of our Constitution ever intended for its guaranteed freedoms to be synonymous with license. Freedom of speech, as an eminent jurist once noted, does not mean the right to shout fire in a theater without cause. Freedom of action does not mean the right to drive wrongly on a one-way street, or to attack policemen.

And freedom of the press does not mean the right to print and circulate material which clearly is offensive to the vast majority of our citizens, or contrary to the prevailing moral standards of that majority.

The exercise of any constitutional freedom must necessarily be limited by the well-being of the majority.

Responsible publishers recognize this and impose self-censorship in accordance with prevailing public morals and good taste.

The purveyors of pornography do not—and thereby compel the controls which society must have to protect itself from their corrupting influence.

Anti-pornography laws, in other words, are not automatically an abridgement of freedom. They are and continue to be an expression of the majority will, no matter how widely they are being violated.

* * *

A basic question is to what extent society may define and maintain certain moral standards. In our permissive generation, and with our admittedly declining morals, this is a tough question.

Just the same there is a workable answer. It lies in generally following the moral attitudes of the majority of our citizens—those largely-unspoken attitudes which are being assaulted by the flood of pornographic books, pictures and plays now spilling through the loopholes of law.

According to the majority report of the commission, "no more than 35 per cent of our people favor adult controls in the field of obscenity." Father Hill calls this an "astounding" and wholly indefensible conclusion—and so do I, with proof to the contrary.

In the summer of 1969 a nation-wide Gallup Poll showed that 85 out of every 100 American adults questioned said they favored stricter anti-pornographic laws.

Thus, contrary to the commission's own slanted survey, and contrary to the seeming acceptance of so much filth in our midst, the Puritan ethic under which this country grew and prospered is still very much alive—and should be heeded.

The commission's other major finding—that all anti-pornographic laws involving adults could be repealed without damage—is equally suspect and open to challenge.

There is not space here to go into Father Hill's voluminous proof that the commission report deliberately suppressed and twisted evidence, or that it represented the preconceived views of leading members who belong to the notorious American Civil Liberties Union.

Denmark notwithstanding, our history books are loaded with detailed proof that powerful nations have rotted and crumbled when moral discipline declined.

And certainly no person has ever been ennobled by the textual or pictorial representation of man's creative instinct being reduced to the animal level.

In spurning the commission report, President Nixon said:

"American morality is not to be trifled with. As long as I am in the White House there will be no relaxation of the government effort to control and eliminate smut from our national life."

Most Americans, I am sure, agree with that statement and sincerely hope it will be translated into more effective action—the sooner the better.

Meanwhile it also is to be hoped that our Supreme Court, before which a number of landmark pornography cases are pending, will take time out to read Father Hill's scholarly and devastating indictment of a report he properly calls "A Magna Carta for the Pornographer."

The commission's report was, indeed, a disservice to our democracy.

Censorship of Pornography?
YES

by REO M. CHRISTENSON

Unhappily, all of the major premises on which our society rests derive from the realm of intuition—the viscera. Can anyone *prove* that the family is a desirable institution? That higher education promotes human welfare? That technology makes men happier? That love is better than hate? That democracy is superior to dictatorship? None of these is provable. But this does not stop us from acting on our best judgment, knowing that all human judgment is fallible. If, then, the regulation of pornography comes down to a matter of visceral hunches, why should not the majority of viscera prevail?

Is "pornography" such an imprecise term that it lacks sufficient clarity to meet the "due process" test?

Current state laws could be updated and made more explicit if they were refined to forbid actual or simulated exhibitions of sexual intercourse or sexual perversion on stage or screen—or pictorial representations thereof in other media—when such exhibitions or pictorial representations are primarily intended for commercial entertainment rather than for education.

Censorship of Pornography?
NO

by A. S. ENGEL

Finally, I cannot seriously believe that Christenson can really be comfortable as the champion of visceral supremacy or of majorities armed with more feelings than facts. I need hardly remind him that those are the very conditions under which many a community has attempted to legislate its prejudices concerning race, or political belief, or religious favoritism. Simply because we cannot prove scientifically that atheists are headed for hell, although the majority has pretty strong feelings on the subject, does not entitle the majority to legislate its prejudices. Why we should now depart from that rule, which insists that majoritarianism be tempered by minority rights, is not made clear to me.

The Supreme Court on obscenity

The recent decision by the Arizona Supreme Court upholding the state's obscenity statute represents a necessary attempt to come to terms with reality.

The Court declared that there is indeed such a thing as hard-core pornography and that "we find it objectionable and illogical to hold . . . that hard-core pornography can be made publishable by interspacing it with items of alleged redeeming social value."

The unanimous opinion, written by Justice James Cameron, agreed with a Maricopa County Superior Court ruling that "I Am Curious (Yellow)" is obscene.

The thicket of legal and moral questions surrounding the subject of obscenity is formidable and complex. However, this is no excuse to regard the subject as incapable of definition.

Doubtless, some people would advocate a stamp of pornography being placed on practically any artistic work.

But these censorious sorts are far fewer today than the muddled but vocal legalists who claim there is no possible way to define hard-core pornography.

The Arizona Supreme Court, agreeing with a definition formulated by the New York Supreme Court, held that hard-core pornography "focuses predominantly upon what is sexually morbid, grossly perverse, and bizarre, without any artistic or scientific purpose or justification.

" . . . It is to be differentiated from the bawdy and the ribald . . . depicting dirt for dirt's sake . . . the blow to sense, not merely to sensibility," in the words of the New York Court.

This trenchant insight, we believe, should be of considerable assistance to prosecutors who have contended that obscenity guidelines have been unsatisfactory.

While pornography may be difficult to define, the State Supreme Court, in dealing with the issue, has not allowed itself to be paralyzed with the indecisiveness that argues there are no parameters to the obscene.

Top page, from *The Progressive*, September 1970.
Above, from *The Arizona Republic*, October 24, 1971.

Ruling On Obscene Film Refreshing

By WALTER TROHAN

WASHINGTON, September 15th — Crime is increasing and morality is decreasing. In part, crime is increasing because of a false compassion and unjustifiable obsession with the rights of criminals. Morality is decreasing, in part, because respect for the law and the maintenance of order are being discouraged by some courts, particularly courts of appellate jurisdiction.

It is therefore, refreshing to find a jurist concerned about the rights of society as a whole and one who does not believe that justice is a matter of expediency, but in the general conscience. I cite Chief Judge Harry I. Hannah of the 5th Judicial Circuit of the Illinois Circuit Court of Appeals and his ruling in an obscenity case.

The case involved an "X" rated motion picture, so rated by the industry as unfit for the young, which depicted eight scenes of sexual intercourse — two of husband and wife, two with the husband's friend, another of the wife with a policeman, one of the wife with her brother, two between women, and an attempted rape by a Negro egged on by the woman's brother.

If you and I are shocked, so was the jury of three women and nine men, ranging in age from 23 to 51 and in education from grade school to college. They found the defendants guilty of obscenity in showing the movie. The defendants appealed.

Chief Judge Hannah said, in part in his memorandum opinion: "Much emphasis is placed upon the constitutional guarantee of the right of free speech and expression. However, it has been repeatedly held that this provision does not fold its protective arms about obscenity. We are beginning to wonder if the courts are not becoming unmindful of the fact that the protective arms of the Constitution were intended to protect ALL segments of society with the ultimate purpose of preserving a sound, stable and moral society, according an equal freedom to all, limited, however, to the extent that it not destroy itself.

"Expressed in another manner, are the courts going overboard in their efforts to make sure no one individual is denied what has almost reached an unrestricted right of expression to the exclusion of the right of another segment of the public to insist that the moral standards necessary to the preservation of a stable society be not endangered?

"What was the purpose of the framers of the Constitution — the unrestricted right of expression to the individual or a limited reservation that would preserve the essential moral standards? And who is a better judge of what are contemporary standards in a community than a cross section of the community in the form of a jury selected and chosen by a fair and impartial formula by the parties themselves?"

* * *

The Judge continued: "Many civilizations have preceded ours, civilizations whose skills and education in many aspects excelled the modern civilization. History tells us they have fallen, because, basically, of moral decay. We use the word moral in a broad sense.

"Unrestricted moral decline and decay go to the core of society. A stalwart society can only fruit from a sound core of moral standard. To whom, in the final analysis, do the people look for the preservation of their rights as established by the Constitution and the statutes? "The prime responsibility rests with the judiciary, of which our jury system is an integral part."

Chief Judge Hannah upheld the jury, finding that their verdict was fully supported by the evidence, by the intent of the statute against obscenity and by the light of constitutional provisions. It will be interesting to see whether his view will prevail.

— **Reprinted from the "Chicago Tribune," Wednesday, Sept. 16, 1970**

Right, W. Kaufman in *The New Republic*, October 17, 1970.

Left, reprinted courtesy of the *Chicago Tribune*, September 19, 1971.

Pornographic action that is filmed or staged or posed for still photographs – pornography *done* by people, not invented by writers or draftsmen – runs right into the matters of social change mentioned above. Performed pornography is an exercise in the humiliation of women. (It can be argued that porno fiction humiliates them, too, in value, but at least they don't physically participate.) The men who are involved in porno performance, though not precisely ennobled, are not being so humiliated. They are treated as masters, usually, and the performances are done for their satisfaction. Those male performers are vicars for the almost entirely male audience. Performed porno is a species of male revenge on our social systems of courtship and monogamy, courtship in which a man has to woo a woman to get her to bed or wed him or both, monogamy in which he has nominally to forego the favors of other women all his life in order to get hers. Performed porno makes every man a sultan.

But it is time out from civilization. Vindictiveness is mean, essentially, and money-coercion is brutal – whether the coercion is on Madison Avenue, in Detroit, or in a sex-flick studio; and it's especially brutal when it produces, not just profit but pleasure.

Ask Them Yourself

Want to ask a famous person a question? Send the question on a postcard, to "Ask," Family Weekly, 641 Lexington Ave., New York, N.Y. 10022. We'll pay $5 for published questions. Sorry, we can't answer others.

FOR GLORIA STEINEM,
journalist, women's activist

How do you feel about pornography? Don't you feel the smut peddlers degrade women by using them to make money?—Mary R. Burns, Fort Worth, Texas

● Yes, most pornography does degrade women because most of it is written from the traditional male viewpoint that women are objects to be used, and therefore humiliated, by men.

But I don't object to pornography as it is usually defined. There is nothing wrong with writing about sexual pleasure.

The problem is that very little sexual writing depicts women as autonomous human beings, with dignity and sexual rights of their own.

Perhaps, what I think of as "pornography" extends beyond glorifying sado-masochism in sex. It is *any kind of propaganda that urges finding personal pleasure in the physical pain or humiliation of another. That kind of "pornography" includes the glorification of war or any other violence against individuals.*

To me, for instance, both Joseph Alsop and the Marquis de Sade are pornographic writers. It's just that the Marquis had more imagination.

Says Pornography Incites To Sexual Crimes

In a recent article in The Los Angeles Times, Judge Macklin Fleming, California Court of Appeal, says it is the experience of most judges, chiefs of police and prosecutors that sexual crimes triggered by pornography are not rare.

Judge Fleming gave as an example a case where a man, excited by pornographic material, sought out a sexual victim and committed murder. In sustaining the murder conviction, the California Supreme Court said he had clearly set out to commit rape and that "he admitted that he became sexually aroused after viewing photographs of nude women in a magazine. . . ."

Judge Fleming wrote, "In the experience of must judges, prosecutors, and chiefs of police, such crimes are by no means rare, and at any given time society contains some sexually unstable persons who may be triggered to violence by exposure to sexually suggestive materials.

"I think any discussion of obscenity and pornography which ignores this connection is bound to be unpersuasive to the general public."

He went on to say, "The advertising effect of obscenity and pornography, that is, the power of explicit sexual materials to suggest and influence the conduct of stable persons, is more difficult to evaluate than the influence of such materials on unstable personalities, but if we start from the premise that society wishes to discourage and inhibit certain types of conduct (forcible rape, child molestation, incest, sodomy, bestiality, etc.), then a strong case can be made for the discouragement of materials which explicitly depict such acts or suggest the desirability of their performance."

Top, courtesy of *Family Weekly*, September 19, 1971.
Above, from *The Wanderer*, February 18, 1971.

155

Whose morality?

The backlash, as we all know, is against sexual permissiveness. But a backlash implies a return to a different norm. What are we proposing to return to? This is the first question to examine if we are to make sense of a moral controversy that has already been rumbling on for years and looks like keeping its point for a good many years to come. Is there some more healthy, stable, and satisfying morality to which we can return? To the morality of the interwar years? To the Edwardians or the Victorians? Hardly anyone is seriously proposing that, partly because even a strict theologian nowadays allows that there is no unchangeable moral code that can be summarised in a decalogue, and partly because we know that Victorian morality was a fraud, sweeping prostitution and pornography into dark corners.

Indeed what we are still experiencing now is an overdue backlash against Victorianism and its hangover into the twentieth century. The reaction against permissiveness today is more accurately described as a counter-backlash.

That sex should be exciting so much argument is not surprising, for we find ourselves in a situation without precedent. The old taboos were securely based as a defence against the risk of pregnancy. The development of effective contraception has altered the context and consequences of extra-marital sexual relations and has made loving and responsible sexual relationships possible outside marriage. For those who do not acknowledge the religious prohibitions it seems arbitrary and unnecessary to deny the place of sex in extra-marital love. With the disappearance of the old taboos it has also become natural to talk openly of sex and sexuality and for the writer and artist to depict the sexual aspect of relationships explicitly. All this offends deep-seated convictions or prejudices in some people, but others ask what is the harm if this greater openness makes for greater fulfilment and personal happiness? Is it not a positive advance in the human condition?

We cannot be too sure, because this is virtually unexplored territory, and one where the experts — psychologists, sociologists, and educationists — disagree among themselves. It is good to take the sense of guilt out of sex. On the other hand every intimate personal relationship carries with it the risk of neurotic hang-ups. To recommend promiscuity as a form of self-education (to take an issue raging furiously at the moment) would seem to invite the misery of rejection, and emotional insecurity.

As for pornography, we cannot be too sure of that either. Probably it can deprave and corrupt. On the other hand, the bawdy and the erotic have a place in literature and the arts.

If we look for the enrichment of the individual personality most people would say that a more relaxed and knowledgeable enjoyment of sexual relationships is a plus point on that test. This is no Sodom and Gomorrah we live in even though there may be fringe extravagances. There is some virtue in having a rather more easy-going, openminded, and plain-speaking society than we have had in the past.

Above, from *The Guardian*, London, May 15, 1971.

Vonnegut's Otherworldly Laughter

by BENJAMIN DeMOTT

● Youthcult holds that the attempt of the elders to hide the prevalence of brutality from the young (and from themselves) is both criminally evasive and doomed to failure. Vonnegut says the same. At the end of *Mother Night* Howard Campbell, on trial for genocide, receives some junk mail from Creative Playthings pitching for toys that prepare kids for life and help them to "work off aggression." Campbell answers:

I doubt that any playthings could prepare a child for one millionth of what is going to hit him in the teeth, ready or not. My own feeling is . . . [against] bland, pleasing, smooth, easily manipulated playthings like those in your brochure, friends! Let there be nothing harmonious about our children's playthings, lest they grow up expecting peace and order, and be eaten alive. As for children's working off aggressions, I'm against it. They are going to need all the aggressions they can contain for ultimate release in the adult world . . . . Let me tell you that the children in my charge. . . . are spying on real grownups all the time, learning what they fight about, what they're greedy for, how they satisfy their greed, why and how they lie, what makes them go crazy, the different ways they go crazy and so on . . . .

From *Saturday Review*, May 1, 1971.

156

Boxing Poses a Challenge to Religion

The Moral Conflict Spotlighted by Case of Muhammed Ali

By The REV. LESTER KINSOLVING

Despite more than 400 deaths in the boxing ring since 1900—plus the unnumbered army of brain damaged ("punch drunk") ex-boxers—the expressed concern of organized religion about boxing has been minimal and isolated.

Nearly two decades ago, Jesuit Father Alfredo Boschi wrote that "Boxing cannot be justified from a moral viewpoint, but must be condemned as something gravely illicit in itself. It not only produces, but aims to produce serious injuries which can become permanent and lead to death . . . It makes a beast of a man . . . adoration of brute strength, of the fist which can pulverize the brain."

(Replied the Vatican's L'Osservatore Romano: "Rocky Marciano is a fervent, practicing Catholic . . . Many boxers, both in Italy and the U. S., cross themselves before entering the ring, which would be sacrilegious if boxing were essentially immoral.")

In 1963, the Rt. Rev. Nelson Burroughs, Episcopal bishop of Ohio, noted that "Five men have been killed in the boxing ring since the first of January." Bishop Burroughs, now retired, went on to assert: "To encourage their potential violation of the Sixth Commandment and to pit man against man under the guise of American entertainment is in my judgment a denial of Our Lord's emphasis on the sacredness and value of human personality."

YET SUCH ECCLESIASTICAL concern has been rare—despite organized religion's historic (if initially unpopular) opposition to a considerable number of bloody "sports" from gladiatorial games to bear-baiting.

Currently the strongest opposition to boxing comes not from the clergy but from many of those most closely acquainted, such as sportswriter Jim Murray. Recently this widely syndicated columnist drew a beat upon a TV announcer who enthusiastically shouted the gory details of the physical dismemberment of a boxer named Quarry.

"Quarry is bleeding from the nose!" screamed this announcer. "He can't see out of his eye! . . . His lip is split!. . . . He's a punching bag!"

Commented Murray, in italics: "What if he were blind altogether? Champagne all around? . . . Can you get me four tickets to a train wreck? . . . How would you like a nice set of recordings made at midnight at Gestapo headquarters?"

"If there is a nobility in prize fighting, it lies not with the crowd, which is a collection of 16,000 sick jokes," concluded Murray. "Boxing today is about as scientific as an avalanche. You fight with your face. It's for people who would cackle at watching a sledgehammer on the Venus de Milo."

CURRENTLY RELIGION is a point at issue in boxing regarding America's most celebrated pugilist—and ham actor. Muhammed Ali contends that he should be exempt for military service because he is a Black Muslim minister.

Just how "pacifistic" is this theologically fantastic hate group is well documented in the autobiography of the late Malcolm X, who expressed little doubt as to the identity of those seeking after his life for his having dared to object to the unofficial harem of Black Muslim leader Elijah Muhammed.

The entire concept of clergy draft exemption has been substantially challenged by Father Peter Riga of California's St. Mary's College. But for the Rev. Mr. Ali to demand that he be exempted from military service so that he may make several fortunes by brain-bashing is as grotesque as the military chaplain who recently prayed for a large body count of the enemy in Vietnam.

THAT THE Rev. Mr. Ali's present occupation is in fact lethal is apparent in the research conducted by Prof. Robert Francis of the University of Wisconsin. He found that a 145-pound amateur (lightweight) could exert 600 pounds of pressure in just one punch. When such force is exerted against the brain, (average weight: three pounds), which is not anchored but rather encased in fluid, Dr. Ward Halstead of the University of Chicago notes: "Even a light blow causes the brain to bounce—it is appalling the ruin boxing causes the brain."

Hence the Rev. Mr. Ali is particularly skilled in what should rightfully be known as "the manly art of murder—or, death in small doses."

Perhaps the ultimate irony in this case is in the thousands of his fellow blacks who have either been without the funds to prolong draft resistance in the courts—or who have died, often very bravely, such as the black medic who saved the lives of his comrades by falling on a live grenade.

And if the parents, wives or children of such men have ever expressed any outrage at this irony, it has scarcely been heard.

Overemphasis of sex and violence on television will be a deterrent to your child. Why? In the formative years, what he sees now, later on he will do. He will ape the actions of the actor.

Good logic. Correct. If so, your kid is better off watching a stag movie than *King of Kings*. Mine, anyway. Because I just don't want my kid to kill Christ when he comes back. And that's what's in *King of Kings*—but tell me about a stag movie where someone got killed in the end, or slapped in the mouth, or heard any Communist propaganda. So the sense of values would be, the morals:

"Well, for kids to watch killing—Yes; but *schtupping*—No! Cause if they watch *schtup* pictures, they may do it some day."

Above, from *The Essential Lenny Bruce.* Copyright 1967 Ballantine Books/A Product of Douglas Book Corporation.

Left, permission of National Newspaper Syndicate.

157

The Unnecessary Deaths

By KENNETH A. GIBSON

NEWARK, N. J. — The bloodshed that occurred in Attica, N. Y., disturbs me more deeply than any event in recent memory.

The use of coordinated organized violence in overcoming the inmates at Attica state prison stands as one of the most callous and blatantly repressive acts ever carried out by a supposedly civilized society on its own people. All of us who oppose violence must deplore this use of force by so-called responsible authorities. Further, we must attempt to understand this event fully.

The demands of the inmates at Attica were basically reasonable and human. They asked for more relevant vocational shops, true religious freedom, a chance to work at renovating the facilities, and other things which we recognize as necessary for a man to function as an alert, healthy being. The fact that they had to take over the prison only suggests the extent of their frustration and the lack of other channels to express totally legitimate grievances.

We understand why these demands had to be made.

But we must understand more than this. We must recognize the political awareness present in the inmates' actions. And we must see in this awareness an awakened desire of people actively and constructively to change and improve their condition.

Across the country young men and women in prisons are becoming aware of the forces which have controlled their lives. Many of these people have previously been uninvolved, alienated, without direction. They now attempt to learn how to deal with these forces and institutions so that they might be able to shape their own destiny and that of their children.

We applaud this as a vital and human development, recognizing that it is good for people to become involved in the process of changing their lot.

And we say that if this practice involves challenges to existing institutions then those institutions must be open to the challenge for it is made out of genuine legitimate concerns. Yet, we must recognize that those in positions of power who feel threatened by this political awareness react in a most violent and repressive manner. We condemn this repression, because awareness and involvement of people in controlling their own future is something to be encouraged.

And there is still more to understand. When we look at pictures from Attica or the Tombs or San Quentin, we see black and Spanish faces. In some prisons inmate population is 80 per cent or more black and Spanish. Those people who have been victimized by the society on the streets are now victimized in prison. When we look at prison conditions and the brutal use of force at Attica we see the same force of racism which caused and then put down with force civil disturbances in this country's ghettos. This racism cannot be tolerated.

The inmates of Attica were victims of a systematic violence which pervades not only our prisons but the streets and towns of this society. We must admit as a nation that the deaths at Attica should never have occurred and we must act to erase the possibility of their recurrence.

Mayor Kenneth A. Gibson of Newark wrote this statement on Monday, Sept. 13, immediately after hearing of the Attica catastrophe.

From *The Rat/Underground Press Syndicate.*

Beast-of-Belsen Type or Relieving Tension?

Why Does He Laugh at Movie Violence?

By DAVID ELLIOTT
Chicago Daily News Service

Michael Caine shoved a knife into the gangster's lung, the victim crumpled to the ground, and the man sitting behind me at the theater laughed, loudly. In fact, every time Caine killed somebody, which in "Get Carter" means every few minutes, my neighbor was thrown into a fit of raucous good humor.

Maybe this was what they mean by the evil of movie violence, but for me the man's behavior was more baffling than obnoxious. Despite considerable past experience with the type, I had to ask again the old question: Why is that man laughing?

Was he, burdened by too active an imagination, simply relieving his tension? Was he a devotee of technique, enjoying the cool dispatch of Caine's style? Or was he a real Beast of Belsen type, perhaps even the son of the man who in 1953 guffawed when Lee Marvin threw that pot of scalding coffee in Gloria Grahame's face in "The Big Heat?"

THE FRANK TRUTH is that many American filmgoers, especially men, seem to enjoy nothing more than virile, vicious, bone-crashing violence. There is even a kind of comradeship in the taste. While scenes of intimate sex will usually throw a pall of tense embarrassment over an audience, "good" violence will often bring out the collective animal spirits. Sex tends to isolate each viewer alone in his seat, while violence pulls the crowd together.

Yet, despite this apparent democratic virtue, and even a small clique of critical support (the "tough guy" critics led by Manny Farber), violence by and large has had a very bad press.

Sex is today a matter of bored approval, at least among many sophisticated viewers, but frequently we hear complaints of too much killing from critics, and even more ritually we hear producers and directors huff and puff about the unfairness of the rating system, which winks at slaughter while slapping Xs and Rs on sexually "adult" films.

"Get Carter," a functional little murder machine, provided a nice litmus test on the issue. In the film Caine plays a hood who murders six or seven people, all disgusting types, to avenge the death of his brother. The killing is fast, brutal and dominant—except for Caine's gritty performance, the film has little else to recommend it.

In an interesting nonreview in Life magazine, Richard Schickel told us that "Get Carter" was an obsessional, sadomasochistic movie, a disturbing specimen of what he feels is a new, amoral toying with deaths in films today.

As opposed to that, he praised the more discreet and supposedly more moral murdering of the 1930s, in which, said Schickel, "Violence was a kind of punctuation mark . . . designed to emphasize some larger point of the director's about the nature of society or, perhaps, the workings of human nature."

One can quarrel with this in several ways. First, it's doubtful that 30s violence, which had to be more restrained (i.e., less plentiful) due to the production code then in effect, influenced audiences any differently than does today's mayhem. We now have more of it, more frankly elaborated, but there's little doubt that in the '30s it was that frequently brutal, enormously entertaining violence that brought the audiences back for more. (Plus, of course, such engaging killers as Cagney, Bogart and Muni.)

In fact, the killers of that day were often lit up in a nimbus of romantic buccaneering whose appeal to the audience might have been even more morally questionable than Caine's Carter, whom we never doubt is a professional bastard at heart.

It can also be shown that "Get Carter," without ever being pretentious about it, does make a point about the "nature" of a special society: A smut-ridden gangster subculture given to functional, dispassionate, almost priestly murder. And beyond that, there are intimations in the film of a wider society for whom violence is a daily diet.

★ ★ ★

STILL, SCHICKEL is on to a worthy issue. "Get Carter" was heavily advertised as a violent movie. It drew many people who therefore apparently wanted violence and, by reduction, enjoyed it. So we have a right to ask whether this is moral or not, whether it should be condoned or condemned.

We first have to disabuse ourselves of the notion that violence today is in a class by itself. In the movies it is simply the oldest, most obvious, if least honored form of physical entertainment. Slapstick comedy thrived on it, as did the first westerns. The ganster era gave it a shot of "gats and guts" adrenalin, World War 2 another (under the protective mantle of patriotism), and the new realism after the war added a further edge of visceral effectiveness greatly assisted by rough language and a mood of weary cynicism.

Some highlights (or low)lights of the past: The epic brawls in each successive version of "The Spoilers" (and almost every John Wayne film), Humphrey Bogart being kicked in the head by Elisha Cook Jr. in "The Maltese Falcon," the giggling of killer Richard Widmark in "Kiss of Death," the pathological cruelty of James Cagney in "White Heat," the gruesome shot of Jack Palance being mashed by the treads of a tank in "Attack," Marlon Brando trashing Vivien Leigh's sanity in "A Streetcar Named Desire," the sardonic carnage of director Stanley Kubrick's "Paths of Glory."

But, unquestionably, there is a new tone, a new streak of license in contemporary violence. The Clint Eastwood spaghetti westerns showed that an audience will, at least for a time, go for wholesale bulk killing, and the Bond films demonstrated a taste for elaborately contrived torture.

Yet before we leap into a state of Calvinistic anxiety about this, we should pay careful attention to specifics and details. Sure sex is creative, therefore a natural good, and violence is destructive, therefore a natural evil, but in the movies such terms are almost meaningless.

Violence is really moral or immoral only in a world of absolutes. For better or worse, that is not the world of commercial films. Most films are melodrama—westerns, crime, and horror, psycho-terror, spectacle, spies and suspense pictures—in which absolutes are notoriously bullied by the imperatives of plot. Plot usually boils down to action, and violence is action maximized.

Sam Peckinpah's 1969 western "The Wild Bunch," though in some respects an admirable film, failed as art on the issue of gore. The long massacre at the end of the movie, with bodies piling up like a stockyard inventory, tried to give gore both a moral and an esthetic bite. However, those aims undermined each other.

The killing was physically graceful, which robbed it of moral impact—we finally became not indignant but sort of charmed by the pretty patterns of the blood spurting and the bodies tumbling. At the same time, the beauty was undermined by our nagging doubt that death had a right to be lyrical, to be made a director's conceit.

Aside from artistic pretensions I suspect that another reason for our greater queasiness about violence today is that it is often combined with sex. There has always been an erotic overtone to violence, but when the two elements are as frankly mingled, as in "Get Carter," we are put on edge.

Is there really such a thing as "good" film violence? In a real moral sense, probably not. But within the confines of film drama, certainly. As critic John Simon has pointed out: "The truth about violence is that it is most effective—and most meaningful—when used sparingly but magisterially." Good film violence is tough, credible and wrenching, and it needs good actors and a skillful director to come alive.

★ ★ ★

AND SO: Why was that man laughing? We'll never know for sure, but I suspect that his motives were probably much more complex, and more morally ambivalent, than we first assumed. Fans of violence are ultimately not that much different from any other specialized group of film buffs.

The major point is to recognize that when talking about film violence the emphasis must be upon the word film, a context which is neither quite real nor ideal, one in which violence carries neither the sting of real brutality or the purgation of ideal suffering.

That is why a moralist is the worst critic, the worst defender and simply the worst audience any movie can have

SECTION XVI

Science, Technology, and Ethics

We are closing this collection of arguments with some selections which provide a glimpse into the immediate future and the kinds of moral problems with which we will have to deal. Unlike the other sections of this volume, these arguments do not focus on any single normative problem. Rather, the unifying element in this section is the *source* of the moral problems represented, that source being recent developments in the areas of science and engineering. It would not have been unreasonable for someone to have believed as recently as a century ago that the problems of morality were part of the human condition, and that as the human condition is unchanging, so also one should not expect to come across new moral problems. However, with the development of the concept of progress in the intellectual and political realms, and of the concept of evolution in biology, the human condition no longer appears to be static. Therefore, we should not be surprised to find ourselves confronted with new moral problems which could not have been anticipated even a few years ago.

Advances in science and technology involve much more than an increase in knowledge; an equally important (or perhaps even more important) result of such advances is the increasing rate of change in the human condition. Science and scientists are playing an ever growing role in modern society as science becomes increasingly a religion in itself (the scientists serving as priests). Not only are new moral problems being created, but, as several of the following selections demonstrate, attempts are being made to change the traditional meanings of basic ethical terms. Whether these new definitions are justifiable or perhaps unavoidable is at least as much a problem in normative judgment and meta-ethics as it is a scientific question. It is in dealing with such questions that man must use his intellectual powers of abstraction to the fullest to attempt to probe beyond the simple characterizations both of science as a purely objective study of neutral facts and ethics as a subjective expression of personal values.

There are at least two basic kinds of moral problems generated by scientific activities. One is the general problem faced by mankind as a whole when presented with a new body of knowledge or a new invention, a situation in which the burden of decision rests on the society as a whole or on delegated members to determine how that knowledge or invention shall be used. An example of this kind of problem is provided by Einstein's theory of relativity, which was used to produce the atomic bomb (among other uses), the ultimate use of which we all know only too well. This kind of problem may be viewed as essentially a special case of the problem of making public policy.

The second kind of problem generated by science and technology is that which confronts only the individual scientist or engineer, and with which he often must deal alone. Simply stated, it is a problem of whether an individual scientist should work on a project which is directed toward a goal he believes to be immoral, or, in a slightly different situation, whether he should make public the results of his work if he believes that it *could* be put to an immoral use. A concrete example of this is the question of whether a scientist ought to knowingly work on a project to develop new weapons for war, even if the rest of the society condones it and the government supports it financially. This is a special case of the general problem of individual versus group morality, and is part of what is frequently called "professional ethics."

The comments thus far have been concerned with science and engineering in general. But there is a particular branch of these enterprises which has a special relevance to ethics—the disciplines usually grouped as the social and behavioral sciences, whose primary object of study is man. Many people feel that these are not really sciences at all; others are anxious that they will ultimately obviate ethics. While there is a certain basis for such fears, there is a more basic moral problem underlying the work of psychologists, sociologists, anthropologists, and so on—the problem of the control, manipulation, and invasion of the privacy of individual human beings by other human beings. The fundamental question is not that of whether or not one person or group *can* control or manipulate another individual or group, but rather whether one *ought* even to try to do this. The stumbling block for the proponents of such a view is the deceptively simple question "Who has the right to control other humans, and what is the source of his special authority?"

Man's study of man and of the rest of nature can be viewed pessimistically as a serious threat to all that man values and has struggled to create. However, there is an alternative to this view, which holds out much more hope for man and his future. It *is* possible for men to study other men with the goal of ultimately controlling them, and undoubtedly some men will try. But there are other uses to which the study of man can be put, one of which is the deepening of each individual's understanding of himself. As long as the knowledge acquired by man's study of man is made available to *all* men, it is to be hoped that no one will be able to use it for ends other than controlling himself.

As science and technology advance, and as our knowledge and understanding of ourselves and our environment increases, we will find open to us choices for action which are now inconceivable. Not only will this fact *not* obviate the need for ethics and individual competency in ethical deliberation, but it will also *increase* our need. For, whatever else it may be, ethics is primarily concerned with providing a sound basis for rational decision among alternative courses of action in particular situations. The greater the number of choices we have open to us, the greater is our need for ethics.

...science and
technology
fathers men
of hope

"A considerable part of the success of the scientific community in advancing knowledge must be attributed to its value system in which an impersonal devotion to truth is regarded as the highest value to which both personal and national pride must be subordinated."   Kenneth E. Boulding

An impersonal devotion to truth can father faith, if only because in its integrity it chooses the right road even though it proves most frustratingly difficult. Science and technology, can inspire man to a devotion to truth, even when the sounds of violence are all about him. It is at times like these that man needs a faith in this higher value system.

EMBOSOGRAPH DISPLAY MFG. CO. CHICAGO, ILLINOIS 60614

Courtesy of Embosograph Display Mfg. Co.

Meanwhile we find ourselves confronted by a most disturbing moral problem. We know that the pursuit of good ends does not justify the employment of bad means. But what about those situations, now of such frequent occurrence, in which good means have end results which turn out to be bad?

For example, we go to a tropical island and with the aid of DDT we stamp out malaria and, in two or three years, save hundreds of thousands of lives. This is obviously good. But the hundreds of thousands of human beings thus saved, and the millions whom they beget and bring to birth, cannot be adequately clothed, housed, educated or even fed out of the island's available resources. Quick death by malaria has been abolished; but life made miserable by undernourishment and over-crowding is now the rule, and slow death by outright starvation threatens ever greater numbers.

And what about the congenitally insufficient organisms, whom our medicine and our social services now preserve so that they may propagate their kind? To help the unfortunate is obviously good. But the wholesale transmission to our descendants of the results of unfavorable mutations, and the progressive contamination of the genetic pool from which the members of our species will have to draw, are no less obviously bad. We are on the horns of an ethical dilemma, and to find the middle way will require all our intelligence and all our good will.

Above, from *Brave New World Revisited*, © 1958 by Aldous Huxley.

Detrick Birthday: Dispute Flares over Biological Warfare Center

A scientific symposium honoring the 25th anniversary of Fort Detrick, the Army's biological warfare research center in Frederick, Maryland, provoked sharp opposition in the biological community and suffered a boycott that is believed to be unparalleled in the recent stormy history of relationships between the military and the scientific community. At least 16 scientists refused to give papers at a Detrick-sponsored symposium on nucleic acids as part of a half-spontaneous, half-organized protest against the use of science for destructive military purposes. Some scientists rejected Detrick's invitation to speak shortly after it was received; others accepted the invitation, but then, after receiving letters and calls from their colleagues, decided to withdraw. Four scientists even withdrew after the final program had been printed, thus forcing Detrick to rearrange the program at the last minute.

The scientists who attended the Detrick conference, and the AIBS officials who supported the conference, cited a variety of reasons for their action, including the following:

▶ The symposiums were unclassified and relatively open. As AIBS president McElroy expressed it: "Open scientific meetings should be endorsed whether they be held in Cuba, Russia, Spain, China, or Johns Hopkins University."

▶ Participation does not imply endorsement of biological warfare.

▶ The work was basic, not applied,

and would have been available to Detrick scientists through the open literature anyway. Moreover, the basic researcher can't control the applications others make of his work and can't be certain whether his work will relate to weapons development. "Can we place the blame for Hiroshima on Einstein?" asks McElroy.

▶ A boycott of the symposiums harms the very people at Detrick who are most deserving of support—namely, the civilian scientists who are engaged in basic research. If these people are undermined, Detrick will become even more secret and defensive.

▶ Outside scientists should maintain contact with Detrick in accord with the principle of civilian control over the military.

▶ Detrick has done work that most scientists would agree is "worthwhile," such as work on the detection of infectious diseases before the onset of clinical symptoms.

▶ Biological weapons are a necessary part of the nation's arsenal in today's world and someone has to work on them, so it's not fair to ostracize Detrick.

▶ Where do you draw the line in boycotting? If you boycott Detrick, why not boycott other defense agencies, universities, and institutions that perform defense work, scientists who hold defense grants, and so on?

On the other side, the boycotters

also cited a variety of arguments, including the following:

▶ Biological weapons are immoral and destructive of life and should be opposed by life scientists.

▶ Even if scientists accept the need for biological weapons, they should not celebrate the anniversary of an institution devoted to destructive purposes.

▶ Participation in Detrick activities by outside scientists provides an aura of respectability for work on biological weapons.

▶ Participants who discuss their work at a Detrick conference may directly contribute to development of biological weapons. Detrick scientists profit more from a meeting, where they can question scientists and learn of work in progress, than they would by waiting for results to be published.

The boycott was surprising to almost everyone involved. The Army and the AIBS had not anticipated such sharp opposition to the program. And most of the protesters had not anticipated that such a sizable number of their colleagues would refuse to speak. The episode probably reflects the mood of a nation that is tired of warfare in Vietnam and in the cities. But whatever the underlying cause of the protest, it provides an intriguing glimpse into the dynamics of a moral crusade, and into the ways in which moral feelings are awakened—or bent into shape, as the case may be.—PHILIP M. BOFFEY

Above, P. M. Boffey in *Science*, *160*, pp. 285-288, April 1968.

Deterrent Value of CB Research

In their letter (21 June), Allen, Emerson, Grant, Schneiderman, and Siekevitz roundly condemn the majority resolution of the American Institute of Biological Sciences for jointly sponsoring two symposia with Fort Detrick. The authors proclaim that the issue is a moral one, and take the position that since, by their lights, chemical and biological warfare, and research activities pertaining to it, are immoral, no life scientist, let alone members of the AIBS, should take part in any symposium, however worthwhile it might be, which could be construed as honoring Fort Detrick.

Morality is a sometime thing. It changes, for example, attitudes towards sex, and to take a moral stance is perhaps the last refuge of the scoundrel. It is also a pretty weak one. We know that the Russians, and no doubt the Chinese, are engaged in research in this area, and if we are to insure that Chinese and Russian weapons of a chemical or biological character are not some day used on us, it is elemental wisdom to have our own ready to reply. At least, deterrence has shown that it works.

Perhaps the strongest argument for research in this area is not the obvious one of offense, but of defense. For if we do not know the potential of a given biological or chemical weapon, we cannot protect our country or its population against it. I do not wish to ascend to clouds of morality, as the authors do, to justify my position. I just look at the world as it is, and although I wish it were not so, I feel it is necessary that the United States carry out a vigorous research program on chemical and biological weapons. If called upon, I shall contribute what I can to the program.

Finally, scientific symposia, irrespective of the sponsor, do have value. Even the authors might have learned something from the one they proposed to block.

DONALD P. WALLACH
9679 Sterling Road,
Richland, Michigan 49083

Left, letter to the editor of *Science* by Donald P. Wallach, August 26, 1968.

Below and right, From "The Prolongation of Vigorous Life" by Alex Comfort in *Impact of Science on Society,* © UNESCO 1970.

The philosophical implications of increased longevity are outside my field, but there are certain points about a systems breakthrough here which are of direct practical relevance to medicine. It would represent the first instance of which I am aware in which science can be said to produce an artificial betterment of biological function, as against the best observed natural performance.

More important, perhaps, is the possibility of anguished and unproductive argument between a naturalist view (that turnover is a good in itself, which should not be 'resisted' by the individual out of a selfish desire to survive) and the general humanist position, that the quintessence of respect for people is to preserve them as individuals as long as possible. This argument has been obscured in the past by the imperfect character of the attainable preservation. Fortunately for the humanist view (which I, for unconscious as well as conscious reasons, hold to be the right one), the Rubicon of an initial systems breakthrough is highly likely to be passed before the argument becomes general. Thus, as in the case of birth control, Hudibrastic arguments will come too late, long after general-public acceptance.

By far the most likely moral effect of greater longevity now, with the prospect of further longevity later, could be a large enhancement of respect for life, based on respect for our own skin, and comparable to but larger than the enhanced respect for death—our own and other people's—which is attributable to the decline in the conviction of spiritual immortality.

I mention these general considerations, not to resolve them, but because it would be culpable to devote oneself to gerontological research without bearing them in mind. They also influence the likelihood of research support, application of results, and society's choice of priorities.

Even more important, perhaps, in all projections of the future and uses of such research is the present condition of the old in developed countries. This condition has its unconscious origins in the attitudes I have defined, and leads to the conclusion that for most consumers, the total abolition of 'old age', though biomedically far more remote, would have an even higher priority than longer life followed by a normally patterned old age.

THE STATUS OF THE OLD IN DEVELOPED SOCIETIES

To a humane person who has had the opportunity to observe it extensively, rather than merely in selected vigorous individuals, the existence of old age—the progressive extinction of strength, skills, well-being and the sense of futurity—is not tolerable. The biological losses are undergone by the old in all cultures, but many of the simpler societies provide compensations, such as status, respect, authority, magical attributes and guiltless dependence. These compensations are wholly denied to the old in privileged cultures, of which the United Kingdom and the United States are models.

To the biological losses are added, in our society, loss of role, of activity, of self-esteem, and of social worth. The dependence which, in age-reverencing cultures, is gladly accepted as a right is a source of consuming guilt and fruitless effort among the technopolitan old, as well as of isolation (it is a violation of the independence value-system to live with children or grandchildren). The anthropology of this added group of deprivations has been brilliantly set forth in a recent study by Kalish *et al.* Virtually all modern Anglo-American values militate against any kind of social compensation for the already onerous biological deficits of being old.

Old age having been seen to be intolerable, our culture is obliged to see if it is also preventable, and this view, which has been brashly but sensibly described by Harrington, is likely to be determinative for future societies, even if we were to learn to treat the old in a civilized way. Accordingly we need to look at the realities of future research beyond the immediate prospect (postponement of the senile decline).

165

At the other end of the life spectrum, genetic control and new techniques for manipulating prenativity may lead to asexual reproduction by *in vitro* (in glass) fertilization and gestation, or by parthogenesis (fertilization of the ovum with the nucleus of a cell from the body of the female who produced the egg). A woman who wishes to avoid a genetic accident will take an injection to induce superovulation, be artificially inseminated, conceive a number of new human lives, abort them, keep the one she wants (to be grown *in vitro*) and throw the rest away. Or she may shop for a fertilized egg in the freezer of a state-controlled store and, if she so elects, the embryo of her choice will be implanted in her uterus. Ridiculous? Hyperovulation, artificial insemination, removal, transportation and implantation of cattle ova is a perfected and practiced procedure.

If someday we are able to control the beginning and ending of life, won't we also have mastered the power of controlling what happens in between? "Mind and matter, brain and behavior are one," asserts Rosenfeld (*sans* citation to Thomistic hylomorphism). If we can control the brain, we can control behavior. It is already possible, by way of electronic stimulation of the brain, to alter the motor activity, moods, attitudes and basic character of animals. Mind altering drugs like LSD are all too familiar. As we achieve a better understanding of the function of the nucleic acids within the brain, we shall discover the means to computerize human behavior—perhaps by respecification of the genes in the embryo or by transplants of memory-storing RNA from one individual to another; which is to say, a complex electro-chemical system will program an individual's behavior while, all unaware, he stays in a state of euphoria induced by electrodes in the pleasure centers of the brain. Meanwhile, over and above all sits an unprogramed Big Brother. All this, Rosenfeld predicts, will be within the reach of science. Man may end up manipulating man from the womb (or the test tube) to the grave. (In New York, of course, intrauterine homicide is already routine.)

Do we really want these things to happen? The question has profound moral overtones touching the value we put on human life and human freedom. Rosenfeld does not ignore the moral dimension. When he can refer to the Declaration of Helsinki on the ethics of human experimentation, or to a medical-moral expert like Dr. Frank Ayd on the artificial prolongation of life, he is on firm ground. Beyond that, however, he is adrift in a sea of secularism. In fact, his book is most valuable as an unintended revelation of the anomie—the lawlessness—afflicting the technologically secularized mind searching for a relevant moral norm.

Rosenfeld's instincts are good, and he begins promisingly enough by telling us that what we believe about man will profoundly affect what happens to man in the new "genesis." He recognizes too that fascination with technological phenomena rather than with people results in a Nazi-type dehumanization. Yet almost immediately, he switches gears—apparently without even realizing it. "What is man" becomes on the very next page, "What are people for?" Obviously, he is not asking what they are for teleologically, but what they are for technologically: how should they function as a mechanism. He becomes fascinated with the manipulative technology of life control as a phenomenon. For example, in a revealing footnote, he sees a mutilating "sex change" operation as a genuine change of identity. Ultimately, he can do no better than embrace the new morality, and settle for the theology of the technocracy expounded in the situation ethics of Joseph Fletcher and the scientific humanism of Julian Huxley. Even then, he is never really comfortable. Thus, he is sympathetic to the objection that "a disregard for the human body can easily lead to a similar disregard for human life in general."

Man's capacity to abuse and mutilate the processes of human life is as old as Onan and as perverse as Sodom. Yet man now stands on the threshold of startling breakthroughs in the life sciences. Either he will cheapen life (discardable frozen embryos), destroy his family (asexual reproduction) and mutilate his body, or he will realize, as Archbishop Iakovos has put it, that "if it is true that man cannot live by bread alone, it is equally true that man cannot live by science and technology alone."

Which way man goes is a challenge to the moral leadership of the Church. For it is the Church's responsibility, as Cardinal Villot reminded us, to be "witness to that which is transcendental and that which is absolute." To put it another way, the Church, at all times in the coming technological revolution, must expound both the infinite dignity of every human-in-being as an image and likeness of God, the Creator, and the absolute inviolability of the procreative act.

But the American Church stands in seeming disarray: a dedicated hierarchy (by and large) crying out in a wilderness of old-line apathy (interested only in preserving the comfortable status quo), egomoralistic rebellion (looking to pull off a Church power coup), and secularized, intellectual irrelevance (contemplating how non-Catholic one must become in order to be both Catholic and catholic, while all the time "rethinking" Catholicism). The Church had better put it all together soon, or else it may awaken one day to find its once lovely flock turned into an ugly pack of technologically mutilated, "transhuman" mutants.

The Rosenfelds of the world rightfully demand a relevant moral system to humanize and direct the new technology. Catholic morality is eternally relevant, which presents the Church with a glorious opportunity and responsibility that should not be lost. Will it meet the challenge? ◼

From a review of *The Second Genesis* by Robert Byrn in *Triumph*, April 1971.

AN IMMENSE PROPOSAL
a leading psychologist urges medication
"to contain human cruelty and destructiveness."

By Kenneth Clark   From American Psychologist

Given these contemporary facts, it would seem logical that a requirement imposed upon all power-controlling leaders and those who aspire to such leadership would be that they accept and use the earliest perfected form of psychotechnological, biochemical intervention which would assure their positive use of power and reduce or block the possibility of their using power destructively. This form of psychotechnological medication would be a type of internally imposed disarmament. It would assure that there would be no absurd or barbaric use of power. It would provide the masses of human beings with the security that their leaders would not or could not sacrifice them on the altars of their personal ego pathos, vulnerability and instability.

It is possible to object to the era of psychotechnology on "moral" grounds and to assert that these suggestions are repugnant because they are manipulative and will take away from man his natural right to make errors — even those errors which perpetrate cruelties and destruction upon other human beings. In the light of the realities and possible consequences of nuclear weaponry, these allegedly moral arguments seem mockingly, pathetically immoral. It would seem that man could afford to indulge in this type of abstract, prescientific moralizing in the past when his most destructive weapons were clubs, bows and arrows, or even gunpowder. To continue this type of thinking in an age when nuclear weapons are capable of destroying millions of human beings in a single irrational man-made event would seem to be a form of self-defeating and immoral rigidity.

There could be the further objection that biochemical intervention into the inner psychological recesses of motivation, temperament and behavior of human beings is an unacceptable, intolerable tampering with the natural or God-given characteristics of man. The negative connotations presently associated with discussions of drugs and the drug culture, particularly among young people, could be invoked to support this objection. One could also object on the ground that, in effect, what is here being suggested under the guide of an imperative psychotechnology is just another form of Utopian mechanization of human beings through drugging the masses and their leaders.

These objections seem to be based upon semantic grounds rather than upon essential substance. In medicine, physical diseases are controlled through medication. Medicines are prescribed by doctors to help the body overcome the detrimental effects of bacteria or viruses — or to help the organism restore that balance of internal biochemical environment necessary for health and effectiveness. Medicines are not only used to treat the diseases of individuals, but are also used preventively in the form of vaccines. All medicines are drugs — and all drugs used therapeutically are forms of intervention to influence and control the natural processes of disease. Selective and appropriate medication to assure psychological health and moral integrity is now imperative for the survival of human society.

From Dr. Kenneth Clark's presidential address given to the American Psychological Association on September 1971. Reprinted from *American Psychologist* in *Intellectual Digest*. Copyright 1971 by the American Psychological Association, and reproduced by permission.

Manipulating
Men's Minds

✦ TODAY'S drug culture led the way, but its adherents didn't have the right drugs. Or so it would seem. What is needed to solve the world's ills, suggests psychologist Kenneth B. Clark, is a drug to be administered to successful politicians to prevent abuse of power in public office; at a later stage such a drug might be useful for all mankind "to contain human cruelty and destructiveness." And this mind-controlling drug may already be in the offing; in a September 4 address to the American Psychological Association, of which he is president, Dr. Clark said: "Upon the basis of the presently available evidence, it is reasonable to believe that . . . a . . . type of precise, psychotechnological intervention, geared toward strengthening man's positive human characteristics, could be obtained and implemented within a few years." Admittedly, the possibility of a pharmacological substitute for virtue intrigues us — especially in view of the failure of the church and other supposedly humane institutions to make much headway toward curbing man's baser instincts. Seriously, though our respect for Kenneth Clark is considerable and though we are confident that his motives are honorable, we suspect that his cure-all might turn out to be something of a witches' brew. Certainly the prospect of compulsory mind-controlling medication raises all manner of questions — including the philosophical and theological issue of free choice. But let us put the latter aside and ask a very practical question: Who would determine dosage and administer the drug? Would not those in charge of administering it be susceptible to the very "abuse of power" that Clark wants to eliminate — unless they themselves had been properly drugged? And who would drug *them*? And so on, ad infinitum. The risks of misuse of such medication would seem to be limitless. Clark calls for international agreements to assure that use of the drug would be inaugurated in all countries. But what if one country held out — might not other countries then be at its mercy? Universal agreement on mind control is no doubt even less likely than on disarmament. Clark's Brave New Worldish prescription indeed raises more questions than it answers, and at least until he furnishes further details we are counterprescribing a healthy dose of skepticism.

Good things are positive reinforcers. Things that look good reinforce us when we look at them. When we say that we "go for" such things, we identify a kind of behavior that they frequently reinforce. (The things we call bad are negative reinforcers and we are reinforced when we escape from or avoid them.)

When we say that a value judgment is a matter not of fact but of how someone feels about a fact, we are simply distinguishing between a thing and its reinforcing effect. Physics and biology study things themselves, usually without reference to their value, but the reinforcing effects of things are the province of behavioral science which, to the extent that it concerns itself with operant reinforcement, is a science of values.

Things are good (positively reinforcing) or bad (negatively reinforcing) presumably because of the contingencies of survival under which the species evolved.

The concept of responsibility is particularly weak when we trace behavior to genetic determiners. Individuals presumably differ, as species differ, in the extent to which they engage in sexual behavior or are affected by sexual reinforcement. Are they, therefore, equally responsible for controlling their sexual behavior and is it fair to punish them to the same extent? If we do not punish a person for a clubfoot, should we punish him for being highly susceptible to sexual reinforcement? We cannot change genetic defects by punishment. What we must change is not the responsibility of autonomous man but the conditions, environmental or genetic, of which a person's behavior is a function.

Out. Although people object when a scientific analysis traces their behavior to external conditions and thus deprives them of credit and the chance to be admired, they seldom object when the same analysis absolves them of blame. The alcoholic is the first to claim that he is ill; if he is not responsible, he cannot be justly punished.

Top left, from *Beyond Freedom and Dignity* by B. F. Skinner.

Right, from "Brain Researcher Jose Delgado Asks: What Kind of Human Would We like to Construct?" by Maggie Scarf. *New York Times Magazine*, November 15, 1970.

Sometimes it may happen that the voluntary impulse of an animal opposes an electrically evoked movement such as raising of a foreleg; in that case, the movement might not occur. "But," Delgado says, "by increasing the intensity of stimulation it is always possible to get the animal to respond as 'directed.'"

Similarly, human beings are unable to resist motor responses elicited by E.S.B.: Delgado describes a patient under treatment for psychomotor epilepsy who slowly clenched his hand into a fist each time he was stimulated through an electrode in the left parietal cortex. When asked to try to keep his fingers extended through the next stimulation, the man simply could not do it. "I guess, doctor," he commented ruefully, "that your electricity is stronger than my will."

Survival? Yes.
But in What Form?

GERALD FEINBERG

In particular, what the human race must do for itself is to establish ethical principles to guide the implementation of the spectacular technological developments that may come from scientific advances. These ethical principles, it seems to me, should, to a large extent, be based on what humanity sees as desirable long-range goals for itself. If we are to consider possible changes in society as fundamental as those I have alluded to, which could influence our future in such a comprehensive way, then our decisions should not be based on what we want to happen tomorrow, or next year. Rather, we should base them on what we wish to happen over 20 years, 50 years, and into the indefinite future.

It has been argued that it is the job of scientists to make decisions on matters like this. For example, if a group of scientists develop techniques for extending the human life span, then some people say that those scientists should take it upon themselves to decide what is to be done with their work. I think that this would be a very unwise principle to follow.

This argument involves a substantial misunderstanding of the nature of ethical principles. There is no good reason for this misunderstanding because it has been recognized by sensible philosophers since the time of David Hume what ethical statements are and what they are not. Ethical statements are not statements of objective fact, as are the statements of science, nor are they derivable from such statements of fact. Neither are ethical statements analytically true, as are the statements of mathematical theorems. Rather, ethical statements are expressions of people's individual feelings. This being the case, it is quite arbitrary to say that scientists should make the decisions about what is to be done with

their discoveries. Of course, a scientist has every right to choose whether to tell people of a discovery he has made. But if he chooses to do so, he retains no proprietary interest in the discovery which entitles him to decide how others should use it. Scientists are no more "expert" in matters of ethics than anyone else, and to leave decisions on what are essentially matters of feeling to them, or to any other special group, is to give up the responsibility that really belongs to all members of society.

Also, it should be said that if decisions on what kind of world we want are made the exclusive concern of any elite group, then the special interests of that group are likely to play an important role in coloring the decisions that are made. For example, scientists as a group feel very strongly that the growth of human knowledge is a very important thing. If decisions are left to scientists, then the particular criterion of advancing human knowledge is sure to play an essential part in these decisions. Being a scientist, I believe that it is good to advance human knowledge. But I realize that others who are not scientists may have other principles which they feel should be more central in decisionmaking than the growth of knowledge. For that reason, I do not think that we can expect generally acceptable decisions to come from any special group. And in a situation where the future of mankind is being shaped, it is essential that decisions be generally accepted.

Consensus on Goals

How then can we set up ethical principles for decisions? My contention is that we should try to find a consensus among the people of the world as to what kind of long-range goals we want. Why do I think

that any such consensus is possible, since nothing of this kind has been achieved up until now? Here I would argue that human beings are all biologically quite similar to one another. Furthermore, substantial aspects of our upbringing are also similar. For example, we each go through a period of early dependency when we cannot fend for ourselves, and must rely on adults for our sustenance. Both common heredity and common upbringing suggest that there should be goals that human beings can agree would be good for all of us. Of course, it is highly unlikely we can agree on everything, but it seems plausible that if we make the effort to find common principles to agree on, that we will indeed find such principles.

It also seems to me that it would be worth making the effort because of the possible benefits of reaching such agreement. One such benefit is that if there were some agreement among the people of the world as to what we want some aspects of our common future to be, then this might go a long way to mitigate the remaining disagreements among the people of the world, which now loom so large. In other words, it would help to make us recognize that human life is not a zero sum game, which is unfortunately the model that is often taken. By recognizing specific areas of agreement, we would abandon the notion that any development that is good for one group of people is necessarily bad for some other group at war (hot or cold) with the first group. The recognition of cases where something would be good for everyone could have the substantial psychological effect of making the areas of disagreement seem less important than they appear now. In this way, agreement on long-range goals could play a critical role in insuring the physical

From *Bulletin of the Atomic Scientists,* May 1971.

survival of the human race, which is a sine qua non for us if we are to have any kind of future.

If we can reach agreement on long-range goals, and if we develop intellectual tools for accurately calculating the results of our actions, then there are few limits to what we as a species can accomplish. There is nothing either in the laws of nature or in the incidentals of our environment that will prevent us from achieving our mutual heart's desire. This, again, is an outlook not lately in vogue. Popular accounts of the views of some of those involved in the environmental movement paint a much more restricted picture of what the human race can and cannot accomplish. I think that these views are based on a severely limited knowledge and imagination relative to the possibilities available to us. My own view is that what we now are and now have is only a very pale shadow of what we could be and could have if we set our minds to it. We have only to find out what we want, and then work together towards making it real. Let us not delay too long in doing so.

A New Ethic for Medicine And Society

THE TRADITIONAL WESTERN ETHIC has always placed great emphasis on the intrinsic worth and equal value of every human life regardless of its stage or condition. This ethic has had the blessing of the Judeo-Christian heritage and has been the basis for most of our laws and much of our social policy. The reverence for each and every human life has also been a keystone of Western medicine and is the ethic which has caused physicians to try to preserve, protect, repair, prolong and enhance every human life which comes under their surveillance. This traditional ethic is still clearly dominant, but there is much to suggest that it is being eroded at its core and may eventually even be abandoned. This of course will produce profound changes in Western medicine and in Western society.

There are certain new facts and social realities which are becoming recognized, are widely discussed in Western society and seem certain to undermine and transform this traditional ethic. They have come into being and into focus as the social by-products of unprecedented technologic progress and achievement. Of particular importance are, first, the demographic data of human population expansion which tends to proceed uncontrolled and at a geometric rate of progression; second, an ever growing ecological disparity between the numbers of people and the resources available to support these numbers in the manner to which they are or would like to become accustomed; and third, and perhaps most important, a quite new social emphasis on something which is beginning to be called the quality of life, a something which becomes possible for the first time in human history because of scientific and technologic development. These are now being seen by a growing segment of the public as realities which are within the power of humans to control and there is quite evidently an increasing determination to do this.

What is not yet so clearly perceived is that in order to bring this about hard choices will have to be made with respect to what is to be preserved and strengthened and what is not, and that this will of necessity violate and ultimately destroy the traditional Western ethic with all that this portends. It will become necessary and acceptable to place relative rather than absolute values on such things as human lives, the use of scarce resources and the various elements which are to make up the quality of life or of living which is to be sought. This is quite distinctly at variance with the Judeo-Christian ethic and carries serious philosophical, social, economic and political implications for Western society and perhaps for world society.

The process of eroding the old ethic and substituting the new has already begun. It may be seen most clearly in changing attitudes toward human abortion. In defiance of the long held Western ethic of intrinsic and equal value for every human life regardless of its stage, condition or status, abortion is becoming accepted by society as moral, right and even necessary. It is worth noting that this shift in public attitude has affected the churches, the laws and public policy rather than the reverse. Since the old ethic has not yet been fully displaced it has been necessary to separate the idea of abortion from the idea of killing, which continues to be socially abhorrent. The result has been a curious avoidance of the scientific fact, which everyone really knows, that human life begins at conception and is continuous whether intra- or extra-uterine until death. The very considerable semantic gymnastics which are required to rationalize abortion as anything but taking a human life would be ludicrous if they were not often put forth under socially impeccable auspices. It is suggested that this schizophrenic sort of subterfuge is necessary because while a new ethic is being accepted the old one has not yet been rejected.

It seems safe to predict that the new demographic, ecological and social realities and aspirations are so powerful that the new ethic of relative rather than of absolute and equal values will ultimately prevail as man exercises ever more certain and effective control over his numbers, and uses his always comparatively scarce resources to provide the nutrition, housing, economic support, education and health care in such ways as to achieve his desired quality of life and living. The criteria upon which these relative values are to be based will depend considerably upon whatever concept of the quality of life or living is developed. This may be expected to reflect the extent that quality of life is considered to be a function of personal fulfillment; of individual responsibility for the common welfare, the preservation of the environment, the betterment of the species; and of whether or not, or to what extent, these responsibilities are to be exercised on a compulsory or voluntary basis.

The part which medicine will play as all this develops is not yet entirely clear. That it will be deeply involved is certain. Medicine's role with respect to changing attitudes toward abortion may well be a prototype of what is to occur. Another precedent may be found in the part physicians have played in evaluating who is and who is not to be given costly long-term renal dialysis. Certainly this has required placing relative values on human lives and the impact of the physician to this decision process has been considerable. One may anticipate further development of these roles as the problems of birth control and birth selection are extended inevitably to death selection and death control whether by the individual or by society, and further public and professional determinations of when and when not to use scarce resources.

Since the problems which the new demographic, ecologic and social realities pose are fundamentally biological and ecological in nature and pertain to the survival and well-being of human beings, the participation of physicians and of the medical profession will be essential in planning and decision-making at many levels. No other discipline has the knowledge of human nature, human behavior, health and disease, and of what is involved in physical and mental well-being which will be needed. It is not too early for our profession to examine this new ethic, recognize it for what it is and will mean for human society, and prepare to apply it in a rational development for the fulfillment and betterment of mankind in what is almost certain to be a biologically oriented world society.

From *California Medicine*, September 1970.

The "New Ethic"

By FRANK MORRISS

An editorial in last September's issue of **California Medicine** has one virtue — extreme candor. This "Official Journal of the California Medical Association" suggests we have done with the hypocrisy of suggesting that life in the womb isn't human, which it says is contrary to medical fact. Instead, we should simply become adjusted to taking human life as the changing public attitude demands.

It seems, according to this editorial, that our distaste for taking human life is tied to our Judeo-Christian heritage, "which has been the basis for most of our laws and much of our social policy." But as everyone knows this "traditional ethic," though still dominant, "is being eroded at its core and may eventually even be abandoned."

As this process progresses, the editorial says, "it will become necessary and acceptable to place relative rather than absolute values on such things as human lives. . . ." Apparently determining these relative values will be the pressure of population, depletion of resources, a "quality of life" linked to "personal fulfillment," preservation of the environment, and most ominous of all, "betterment of the species."

Then comes the call for doctors to get ready to fulfill their duty to the "new ethic." Just as it has responded to the call for abortion (even though bothered by that hypocritical debate over what is being aborted, when every scientist knows it is a human), medical science must be ready to respond when the day dawns for "death selection and death control."

California Medicine is worried that doctors won't be asked to bring their expertise to bear in the determination of these policies, and it insists that "the participation of physicians and of the medical profession will be essential in planning and decision-making at many levels." To guarantee all this, doctors are told that "it is not too early for our profession to examine this new ethic, recognize it for what it is and will mean for human society, and prepare to apply it . . . in what is almost certain to be a biologically oriented world society." There is the distinct impression that **California Medicine** can hardly wait until doctors cannot only serve humanity without reproach by killing admitted humans in the womb, but can extend that service to cover old persons or anyone else standing in the way of that "quality of life" which a biologically oriented world society will make the norm.

All in all, this editorial is one of the most chilling bits of horror writing I have ever come across, perhaps because of its extreme honesty. It is a little as if we should dig up in the ruins of some Berlin building an exhortation to German doctors to get ready to serve Hitler's Reich by exterminating all of the enemies of the "good Nazi life." Here we have the medical profession being told by one of its official agencies to prepare to wipe out all who are enemies of the "good American life," and not be worried about the silly question of whether innocent humans should be killed — for of course they should be if society demands it.

I have called the extreme candor of this editorial a virtue. It is, and it may serve a good purpose if it will only awake our Jewish and Protestant brethren who have been hitherto apathetic to warnings about the implication of abortion. Some of these friends have tried to insist that abortion is well within the Christian and Jewish ethic. I respect the **California Medicine's** view on that issue more than the ignorance of those who don't see what the true issue is.

The Judeo-Christian ethic is being discarded, and what that means is that human life will become valueless as such, and will be protected only in its ramifications for society. No true Christian or Jew can ever allow such a situation to come about without fighting it even to the point of martyrdom. **California Medicine's** appeal for legalization and acceptance of murder must be matched by the religion's determination it shall not happen

(I am indebted to L.I.F.E., 615 W. Civic Center Drive, Santa Ana, Calif., 92701, for a copy of the editorial discussed above.)

From *The Wanderer*, Copyright 1971.

Hit and miss opposition may achieve short range goals, but it is impotent in the long run. As far back as the 15th Century, Da Vinci refused to publish plans for a submarine because he anticipated that it would be used as a weapon. In the 17th Century, for similar reasons, Boyle kept secret a poison he developed. Such individual actions,however, are eventually outflanked by the work and cooperation of other researchers. Now especially, scientific knowledge is accumulating so rapidly that opposition to any specific project is often obsolete before the struggle against it has run its course. Questioning the "humanity" of individual scientific projects is not enough. Scientific workers themselves are seriously wrong in assuming that personal prostitution to the rich and powerful can be avoided simply by refusing to participate in only that work which is narrowly useful to those in power, such as weapons, counterinsurgency, or technological research. For these reasons we need an analysis of the role of science in our society which will enable us to act collectively against socially destructive uses of science.

It is not surprising to find the ruling class funding applied research which is narrowly beneficial to them. Because their goal is to increase their own power (and/or wealth), this work is counter to the real interests of those upon whom that power is exercised, that is, the majority of the people. We are all aware of examples of this type of research: developing guidance systems for inter-continental ballistics missles, inventing weapons like chemical Mace, designing new techniques of drilling for oil, etc. Applied research of this kind which is clearly malevolent and exploitive requires no further discussion.

An analysis of scientific research merely begins with a description of how it is misapplied and maldistributed. The next step must be an unequivocal state-ment that scientific activity in a technological society is not, and cannot be, politically neutral or value-free. Some people, after Hiroshima and Nurenberg, have accpeted this. Others still argue that science should be an unbridled search for truth not subject to a political or a moral critique. J. Robert Oppenheimer, the man in charge of the Los Alamos project which built and tested the first atomic bombs, said in 1967 that "our work has changed the conditions in which men live, but the use made of these changes is the problem of governments, not of scientists." A pathetic comment from a man so alienated from his best creative efforts that he felt no responsibility for the uses to which they are put. But also a ridiculous comment, like a claim of innocence and disinterest from someone who has just left a loaded gun on a table between two others he found locked in a passionate and irrational argument.

Oppenheimer's attitude, justified by the slogan of truth for truth's sake, is fostered in our society and has prevailed. It was first advanced centuries ago by people who assumed that an increase in available knowledge would automatically lead to a better world. This was a time when the results of scientific research would not easily be anticipated. Today, in a modern technological society, this analysis is a rationalization for socially destructive behavior, put forth by people who at best are motivated by a desire for the intelligent pleasure of research, and often are merely after money, status, and soft jobs. It would be lame indeed to continue to argue tha t the possible unforeseen benefits which may arise from scientific research in a capitalist society will inevitably outweigh the clearly foreseeable harm. The slogan of truth for truth's sake is defunct, simply because science is no longer, and can never again be, the private affair of scientists.

No particularly nasty trick of scientific application was visited uponthe nuclear physicists who did the research which resulted in the bomb. They simply assumed a somewhat notorious vanguard role. We don't have two governments, one which beneficently funds research and another which malevolently kills in the ghetto, in Latin America, and in Southeast Asia. Nor do we have two corporate structures manipulating for profit on the one hand while desiring social equity and justice on the other. Rather, there is a single government-corporate axis which supports research with the intention of acquiring powerful tools, of both the hard and software varieties, for the pursuit of exploitive and imperial goals.

A handout at the Chicago meeting of the American Association for the Advancement of Science in December, 1970, by the Peo-ple's Science Collective, New University Conference.

People's Science Collective
New University Conference